MW00529637

The
Rent Collectors

ALSO BY JESSE KATZ

The Opposite Field

The
Rent Collectors

Exploitation, Murder,
and Redemption in Immigrant LA

Jesse Katz

ASTRA HOUSE
NEW YORK

Permissions Acknowledgments: Part 1 Image: Forest Casey, Part 2 Image: Guillermo Buelna,
Part 3 Image: Miguel Rodriguez, Part 4 Image: Stephen Tourlentes
For information about permission to reproduce selections from this book,
please contact permissions@astrahouse.com.

Astra House
A Division of Astra Publishing House
astrahouse.com

Printed in the United States of America

Library of Congress Cataloging-in-Publication Data

Names: Katz, Jesse, author.
Title: The rent collectors : exploitation, murder, and redemption in immigrant LA / Jesse Katz.
Description: First edition. | New York : Astra House, [2024] | Summary:
"The gripping true story about a botched gang murder set in the
invisible economy of LA's immigrant street vendors"— Provided by publisher.
Identifiers: LCCN 2024000138 (print) | LCCN 2024000139 (ebook) |
ISBN 9781662601736 (hardcover) | ISBN 9781662601743 (epub)
Subjects: LCSH: Gangs—California—Los Angeles—Case studies. | Immigrants—California—
Los Angeles—Case studies. | Latin Americans—California—Los Angeles—Case studies.
Classification: LCC HV6439.U7 L73326 (print) | LCC HV6439.U7 (ebook) |
DDC 364.152/30979494—dc23/eng/20240203
LC record available at https://lccn.loc.gov/2024000138
LC ebook record available at https://lccn.loc.gov/2024000139

First edition
10 9 8 7 6 5 4 3 2 1

Design by Alissa Theodor
The text is set in WarnockPro-Light.
The titles are set in KCTallboy-Inked.

Table of Contents

Columbia Lil Cycos
Organization Chart

GODFATHER

Puppet
(Francisco Martinez)

LAWYER

Coach
(Isaac Guillen)

SHOTCALLERS

Tricky
(Sergio Pantoja)

Morena
(Ingrid Tercero Flores)

LIEUTENANTS

Face
(Juan Pablo Murillo)

Oso
(Eduardo Hernandez)

Baby
(Edgar Hernandez)

SOLDIERS

Big Guy
(Yovanni Velasquez)

Silly
(Ralph Santiago)

Lil Primo
(David Gonzalez)

Clever
(Luis Silva)

Rusty
(Giovanni Macedo)

Ranger
(Javier Perez)

Midget
(Flor Aquino)

Grumpy
(Cipriano Estrada)

Raven
(Stefani Brizuela)

Barrios
(Guadalupe
Torres Rangel)

Atlas
(Juvenal
Cardenas Mejia)

SOUTH-CENTRAL SQUAD

WITNESS INTIMIDATORS

RENT COLLECTORS

Part One

1980–2007

Photo by Forest Casey

1

A Forgotten Planet

When at last he opened his eyes, it was because he was falling. That meant he wasn't dead, not yet. The earth below Giovanni was like cinder, slick from an overnight mist and steep as a windswept dune. With each flinch of his body the slope loosed beneath him—a hiss of shale, a rush of gravel—propelling him downward.

A ribbon of lavender broke the darkness, revealing the day's first glimpse of La Rumorosa, the coil of borderland highway that writhes around the Sierra de Juárez, halfway between Tijuana and Mexicali. The gusts that moan through the rusted canyons and granite crags have given La Rumorosa its name: the Whispering Woman. In the span of fourteen miles, Carretera 2D twists more than seventy times, corkscrewing as it plunges four thousand feet from shrouded mountaintop to swirling sands. La Rumorosa is a gash in the Baja desert, a white-knuckle trek and a dumping ground. Mythologized in ghost stories and second-guessed by safety engineers, the passage stirs primordial awe—a "forgotten planet," the Mexican poet Adolfo Sagastume calls La Rumorosa, a "silent uterus." A city boy, Los Angeles born, Giovanni had never heard of the place. Now it was swallowing him.

Flailing his arms, pawing at dust, Giovanni felt the scrape of chaparral. He wrapped a hand around a gnarled root. It broke his slide. For a moment he was suspended, the cliff still once more. Blinking away the fog, Giovanni tried to make out the road above him; too high to see. Below, the gorge looked bottomless. He realized then that his shoes were gone, the black-suede Jordans he'd bought with the check from his first honest job. Only socks covered his feet. He stared at his shirt, a white tee with the curly Sean John logo, now stained with vomit. Blood, too, had soiled the cotton. His neck throbbed, so much he could barely turn his head. The skin burned. He thought maybe he'd been shot, until he touched a finger to his throat. A collar of torn flesh, pulpy and raw, branded his windpipe. That was where the rope had seared him, where his killers, before tossing him over the edge, had cinched it tight, yanking like some soul-snatching repo men.

Now he remembered.

Giovanni rolled onto his elbows. His chest heaved. Tears stung his eyes. He tried to replay the previous night, to piece together the whole disastrous week. He was barely eighteen, but in just a few days of 2007, he'd lived a lifetime, from duress to euphoria to revulsion to catharsis, and finally betrayal. He'd been given a jale, a real heavy job. A test of his callousness and credulity. If he had the stomach for it—for dirtying himself in the name of an enterprise that flouted all checks on its power—he might at last earn the one thing he craved: respect. It was an easier word to say than love. If he backed out, he'd confirm every doubt and suspicion. Giovanni didn't stop to question why he'd been selected, what made him the right candidate for such a foul mission. The minute they'd put the .22 in his hand on a crowded LA sidewalk, he had no choice but to step up—to prove himself worthy. And then he'd gone and botched it.

News crews were now doing live shots from that same stretch of blood-splattered pavement. Pastors were leading vigils. The Los Angeles Police Department's elite Robbery-Homicide Division was combing the neighborhood. The most nefarious prison mafia in America was demanding a scapegoat. The city was dangling a $75,000 reward for information leading to the capture of the suspect—"a threat to everyone," the mayor declared, "everywhere."

Hiding out in Mexico hadn't been Giovanni's idea, but he'd embraced the melodrama of a run for the border. He was a desperado blending into the jangle of Avenida Revolución, losing himself in a TJ blur of clubs, strippers, booze. In a few months, the heat off him, his penance complete, Giovanni expected to make his return: back to the girl from Subway with the irresistible dimples, whose name he'd inked that summer across his right hand; back to his mom, a janitor at the mall, whose despondence he'd both fueled and fled; and back, if all went well, to his tribe of bald-headed soldiers and slangers, the outlaw capitalists of MacArthur Park, who offered an identity more consequential, more urgent, than the routines of a neighborhood whose sweat kept the city scrubbed and fed and prosperous.

Don't die, he told himself. *Don't die like this.*

Giovanni had a baby face, even with a pencil's width of fuzz clinging to his upper lip. His grin began sly but soon grew plentiful, and his eyebrows formed twin arches that seemed to scout for approval. Built like a flyweight, all clavicles and ribs, he'd been fidgety for as long as anyone could remember, a rat-a-tat of bouncing knees and rubbing hands. His first-grade teacher noted that Giovanni "needs to learn to stay on task and work cooperatively." His third-grade teacher predicted that Giovanni "could be outstanding if he were more serious and less distractable." His fifth-grade teacher found Giovanni "so restless he seldom finishes an assignment."

Giovanni's first great passion was *Street Fighter*, the arcade game, which he played at a mini-mall donut shop with quarters filched from his mom's change jar. He favored the role of Akuma—orange hair tied in a topknot, sculpted arms bursting from shredded sleeves—whose signature move resembles an act of frustration. Rearing back, the fighter slams his fist down to the earth, a godlike blow that unleashes a lethal shock wave.

In middle school, Giovanni signed up for a different kind of martial experience, a National Guard youth contingent called the California Cadet Corps. He'd started seventh grade the week before 9/11, and with Americans rushing to enlist, he sensed a shared purpose in the program's starch and creases, a narrative that offered strength and stability. He learned to polish his shoes and center his garrison cap. He marched, heel-first, in formation, pivoting to the column and flank commands, and saluted his major with sharp karate chops to the brow. He wished he'd volunteered for the rifle drills, to learn to port and present arms with one of those triggerless wooden parade models, but he'd been too nervous—afraid of an embarrassing bobble or a breach of some protocol he'd failed to consider. If he'd been asked then what he planned to do with his life, Giovanni wouldn't have hesitated: join the army. He wanted to belong to something that mattered.

Giovanni's dad, a sad-faced man from Guatemala, seesawed between sentimentality and affliction. Juan washed dishes and buffed floors and knocked down walls for a demolition crew. Despite five DUIs, he also valeted cars at a Hollywood club; he carried a picture of himself with Jean-Claude Van Damme from the time the action hero handed him the keys. Before his borracheras blew up the family, before Giovanni's mom reached for a kitchen knife to silence his rants, Juan had done what he could to guide Giovanni and channel his excitability. He gave his son a pit bull they called Rocky, and together they built a doghouse in their backyard. He strung a sand-filled punching bag from a tree out there too, encouraging Giovanni to pummel it until his arms grew limp. To bulk him up on the cheap, Juan fed Giovanni 99-cent Whoppers, MacGyvering the burgers by slipping a fried egg between the buns.

As the eldest of three kids—he had a brother a year younger and a sister born six years after that—Giovanni took the brunt of Juan's disappointments, reminding his jefito of his own interrupted dreams. In those moments of shame and frustration, Juan resorted to the old-country discipline he'd been raised on in the mining province of Chiquimula. He'd dump uncooked rice on the kitchen floor and force Giovanni to kneel, bare-legged, until it felt like fire ants were burrowing into his skin.

It was only by accident that Giovanni learned his dad was his stepdad. Not even the difference in their last names had tipped him off. His mom's last name didn't match his or Juan's; Giovanni assumed everyone could just choose their own. He was thirteen when it happened: rooting in a bedroom closet for Juan's trove of VHS porn, Giovanni stumbled on a family photo album. For the first time he saw pictures of another man, a proud father showing off a newborn, and felt a pang of recognition. Mystery dad looked like a swashbuckler—Ray-Bans, acid-washed jeans, '77 Olds—and in his taut gaze Giovanni glimpsed a stolen past, a stunted future.

The discovery confused and then enraged Giovanni, leaving him with the sense he'd ingested a toxin: *What other lies had he been fed?* His mom, Reyna, begged him to understand. She had been so young—a runaway—pregnant at seventeen, and again at eighteen with his brother. She had meant to tell him once he was old enough, but she'd never found the right time or words. It was a story she wanted to forget, anyway, to bury along with the man in the picture. The explanation she offered her son—that his biological father had fallen ill when Giovanni was barely a year old, that the doctors had given him just months to live, that he had left her and the boys in LA so he could return to Mexico to die—was only partially true.

With adolescence came the freedom of skating: a license to turn obstacles into exploits. Giovanni pored over the California Cheap Skates catalog, a universe of coastal-cool regalia that promised style and status, even if Reyna's paycheck couldn't possibly stretch that far. His first board, a Darkstar, came to him hot. A dude rolled by in a van, asked Giovanni if he liked to skate, and fobbed it off on him for $20. What Giovanni coveted most were Chad Muska shoes. The San Diego freestyler had a scraggy, fearless aesthetic, blond mane flopping as he nose-slid down handrails cradling a boom box. The sneakers featured a Velcro compartment—a stash built into the tongue. By the time his mom scraped together the cash to award him a pair, Giovanni had caught on to the design. He ollied through the hood in pegleg jeans, hair gelled and spiked, Chili Peppers and Metallica on his headphones, and yerba squirreled away under his laces.

Smoking weed made Giovanni's heart race and his throat tighten. He was fourteen the first time he panicked. His mom took him to Children's Hospital in East Hollywood, but the EKGs and X-rays showed nothing. Three weeks later he was back in the ER complaining of dizziness and chest pain—and then four more times over the next two months. His mom feared something catastrophic. The doctors diagnosed anxiety and depression, instructing Giovanni to "take deep slow breaths and think of pleasant thoughts."

As a child, Reyna had been cast north by El Salvador's civil war and secreted across the border in the trunk of a sedan. It was an uprooting she never quite recovered from, a tale of movement and survival that instead of offering hope left her feeling out of step. She wore her hair in bangs and applied her eyeliner in feline swoops. She'd worked as a housekeeper and a hotel maid and a server at a late-night pretzel stand. Her Spanish was snappy and insistent, but when she switched to English, her voice grew softer and warier, as if every word were a question. Unlike most of the men in her life, Reyna was not a drinker; she preferred McDonald's coffee, cut with four sugars and four creamers. There were sorrows she didn't know how to drown.

One morning in 2004, not long after Giovanni started high school, he poked his head into his mom's bedroom. In his younger years, he'd creep and then pounce, waking Reyna with a belly flop; she'd muss his hair and call him mono. Her little monkey. This time he found her under the covers, trembling, a bundle of whimpers and wails. "What the—," he blurted. Then he saw the mess of pills. He knew he hadn't done much to make her life easier, but Giovanni couldn't imagine that his own mom would no longer have it in her to raise her children, to muster worries, to dispense reprimands. He dialed 911. The operator told him to keep her awake until paramedics arrived. Giovanni shook his mom. He begged her to open her eyes, demanded she not leave him. Reyna arrived at Good Samaritan sobbing. She confessed that she'd been popping ibuprofens for the past day and a half—an overdose of Motrin—maybe sixty-five in all. "I don't want to be in this world anymore," she told the doctors. On her chart, they wrote: "family problems." Giovanni would always remember how he felt at that moment, as if the earth were spinning too fast to hold him in place. He had saved his mom. He was losing his way. It was Giovanni's fifteenth birthday.

As the sun inched higher, rousing the lizards from their blanched hideouts and stirring the quail that grub seeds in La Rumorosa's brush, Giovanni saw that he was alone. Nobody was watching to make sure he'd died. Nobody was around to offer help. If he couldn't scratch his way up, nobody would ever spot him hugging the cliff, not until it was too late. Giovanni dug his feet into the sediment. He lunged and clawed. His neck screamed. The cliff held. Giovanni did it again, squirming faster, reaching higher. He'd been disposed of, and now he'd awoken. Carretera Federal 2D was just above him. He didn't know where he was going or how to get there or what he would do if he made it. He just knew he had to pull himself out, to rise from this woeful tomb.

The Shadows of Life

Giovanni Macedo, the son of Roberto Macedo and Reyna Flores, was conceived in 1988, in a studio apartment on the top floor of a four-story brick building in MacArthur Park. When it opened on Union Avenue in the 1920s, the Hotel Strand advertised the "finest furnished" rooms and a "luxurious social hall," where the Pastel Concert Trio performed operatic selections and the California Veterans' Political Club held its weekly luncheons. Half a century later, it was a flophouse in the most turbulent quarter of Los Angeles. Rooms went for $10 a day, $60 a week.

So much of the neighborhood was like that: faded glamour, precarious dreams, repurposed space. MacArthur Park revolved around a thirty-two-acre village green that sloped inward like an amphitheater before spilling into a turbid, mushroom-shaped lagoon, a body of water that shimmered from afar and, closer, simmered with foamy debris. Known as Westlake since the nineteenth century and rechristened MacArthur Park during World War Two, the park became a synonym for the community that grew around it. The name referred to both; the geography of one shaped the culture of the other.

Just four blocks from the place of Giovanni's creation, the park grounds sustained an urban wonderland of flora and fauna—forty-two varieties of trees, from black walnut and wild plum to Australian tea and African sausage, plus nine species of birds and at least five kinds of fish—alongside a carnival of squatters and grifters and junkies. MacArthur Park in the 1980s was the seedbed of LA's crack epidemic, a marriage of pain and profit. Something like a thousand smokers and suppliers congregated there every day, their deals and tricks befouling the ryegrass, yet even then the grand old park managed to accommodate soccer tourneys and soup kitchens, union rallies and master-level chess matches.

Evangelists bellowed into battery-powered megaphones about el infierno. Gamblers rolled dice on the concrete pathways. Photographers lugging accordion-lens Polaroids created instant souvenirs at the lake's rim, and anglers—they called themselves ghetto carpers—probed the murky depths for fish that could top thirty pounds. Four street gangs vied for a cut of MacArthur Park's commerce, including two that would swell into international federations: Mara Salvatrucha (the park's west side) and 18th Street (the park's east side). So many squad cars plowed across the grass in those days, gardeners were forever repairing crushed sprinkler heads. To deter crime and improve sight lines, the city yanked out benches, chopped down bushes. It even removed the barbecue grills, to discourage the down-and-out from dining on the lake's waterfowl.

The city had engineered the park a hundred years earlier, flooding an alkaline swamp with millions of gallons from the municipal water supply. Westlake instantly became one of LA's most fashionable destinations, an open-air resort scarcely a mile from the hubbub of downtown. Elegant hotels and smart boutiques ringed the park, its waters the embodiment of "Nature's face, as 'twere some open book that God had writ," as the poet and philanthropist Eliza Otis put it. She was married to General Harrison Gray Otis, the *Los Angeles Times*'s founder, and at the dawn of the twentieth century they lived on a prime corner of the park, in a mansion called the Bivouac. The lake beckoned in postcards. It hosted floating trees at Christmastime and mock warship battles during the Fourth of July, light shows, logrolling contests, pet seals, and generations of rowboats, canoes, and gondolas. Charlie Chaplin filmed at the water's edge. In 1907 a manacled Harry Houdini plunged into the lake from the roof of a boathouse.

Even then, in that golden age, the lake proved a mirage, a stage for the aggrieved and dejected. By the time Houdini defied death there, at least nine people had chosen the waters for their final exit—causing one long-gone newspaper to lament that Westlake "will soon become a reminder of the shadows of life instead of a diversion." The unfortunate included a pastor's wife suffering from "melancholia," an insurance man burdened by gambling debts, a hotel chambermaid spurned by her philandering husband, the water-fearing sister of the British vice-consul, and a bartender at a German saloon, who had fastened a rock to a shoestring and roped it around his neck. More attempted to drown themselves, only to be rescued, and more threatened it, only to be exposed as hoaxers. For a time, whenever anyone went missing in Los Angeles, the first impulse was to check the lake.

A city high on land speculation eventually outgrew Westlake. Encapsulated in cars and propelled by freeways, Angelenos sought out more room, greater privacy. It was a pattern that would repeat and accelerate: the affluent gravitated west, toward the ocean, or north, up into the canyons and foothills; the middle class branched out to the valleys and then the desert, distancing themselves from whatever they deemed worn and unruly. As the hotels sagged and their neon dimmed, MacArthur Park began to fray. It became a pensioner's haunt, a panhandler's haven. Still the lake exerted a strange allure. There were reckless boaters and overconfident swimmers and rescuers who became mired in the muck. A sailor's wife. An Englishman with an umbrella. Max, the pinochle player. In 1951, police detained a man in the park on a morals charge, code for the official entrapment of cruisers. He broke loose and flung himself in the lake, preferring to die in the water than face public scorn.

MacArthur Park evolved into a bohemian refuge, a counterculture lab. The songwriter Jimmy Webb used to meet his lover, an office worker at the adjacent American Cement Building, for lakefront picnics. When the romance ended, he channeled his longing into a celebrated and maligned anthem about a "cake out in the rain" (recorded by everyone from Richard Harris and Waylon Jennings to the Four Tops and Donna Summer) that immortalized MacArthur Park in the pop canon. When engineers drained the lake in the 1970s to install an aeration system and pave its fourteen-foot-deep floor, a retired aerospace worker went foraging in the sludge. He assembled his finds into baroque sculptures, folk art monuments that featured brass knuckles, false teeth, rusty bullets, and more than a hundred guns.

By the 1980s, MacArthur Park had become an immigrant crossroads: America's new Ellis Island. Tens of thousands of Salvadorans and Guatemalans, displaced by oppressive US-backed regimes and their paramilitary forces, poured into the neighborhood. Thousands more Mexicans, fleeing economic collapse, and Cubans, thrust onto hasty boatlifts, added to MacArthur Park's transformation. They found a toehold in the shabby tenements, freedom in the trodden parkland. Largely ignored by a suburbanizing city, the newcomers rummaged and salvaged, remaking MacArthur Park in their own image. The Westlake Theatre, a Churrigueresque movie palace, became an indoor swap meet. California Bank was reborn El Piojito, a discount store, and Miss Clayes, an importer of chinoiserie, would become Pollo Campero, the Central American fried-chicken king.

The sudden concentration of so many dreamers—refugees and exiles, former soldiers and onetime insurgents, wanderers, castaways, pilgrims, Spanish speakers, K'iche' speakers, Zapotec speakers, and other Indigenous peoples escaping pogroms across the Americas—made MacArthur Park feel both futuristic and primal. No other place in Los Angeles thrummed with its subversive energy or labored under the weight of so much trauma. It was the kaleidoscope that rendered every superficial trope about the city unrecognizable, the crystal ball that anticipated the fractures that would jag through every facet of American life: politics, immigration, housing, crime, education, the economics of staying afloat. MacArthur Park became the epicenter of the fake ID trade. It birthed the worst police scandal in LA history. Its fire station was the busiest in the country. With some one hundred thousand people squeezed into roughly two and a half square miles, many of them sleeping head to toe in the warren of rooming houses that had fallen into the hands of the city's most notorious slumlords, the neighborhood at its densest was nearly fifty times more crowded than the rest of LA; it was more tightly packed even than Manhattan.

MacArthur Park helped cement Los Angeles's renown as the nation's undocumented immigrant capital. It was the most visible expression of a megalopolis that was home to a million of the country's eleven million people without papers and to another three-quarter million US citizen or legal resident Angelenos living with an undocumented family member. To speak of an immigration system, as if there were a legal option for the vast majority of foreign-born people desperate to enter the country, was to deny reality. LA was proof that the border, no matter how militarized and menacing, could be beat. Immigration agents caught a million-plus crossers every year. Hundreds more succumbed to heat or drowning or suffocation. Still that could not stem a diaspora hastened by the US government's geopolitical meddling and the American people's appetite for cheap and tenacious labor. And then once those who had risked everything to cross were already here, that same government, our same nation of employers and consumers, couldn't agree on what to do with them.

It was a cold bargain: toil at the margins, stay out of trouble, swallow your humiliations, forgo the ability to vote or serve on a jury or collect unemployment or ever feel secure in your skin, and if you're lucky, America might just leave you in limbo. Ten years, twenty, a generation. MacArthur Park strained under the exigencies of that shadow population, a virtually permanent subclass left to invent its own opportunities, to improvise its own survival.

Reyna's path to MacArthur Park began when she was nine, in 1980, and living in a cinderblock-and-rebar shanty that doubled as a dressmaking shop in San Salvador's Barrio Santa Anita. Three generations of her family, including the doting matriarch, Mama Nelly, rented two dirt-floor rooms in the back; the seamstress lived in the front with her three children. Reyna didn't yet grasp that Mama Nelly was not her mother but her grandmother, or that her four older cousins all seemed to be lacking mothers too. The poverty and persecution that were beginning to jolt El Salvador in the 1970s were also fracturing her family. Both of Reyna's aunts, and then her mother, had already stolen away from the house on Quince Avenida Sur, embarking on dangerous, degrading journeys north.

By leaving their children behind, the women volunteered to shoulder all the risks of the crossing, to establish themselves first in the US and then send for their kids. It was a familiar gambit, repeated by many thousands of Central American parents—the least bad option for a people whose countries had been commandeered as Cold War battlefields. "It's a mistake, and it's a necessity," says Reyna's Tía Dina, her mom's older sister, who left two children with Mama Nelly. Even when the initial risk paid off, when parents later procured visas and plane tickets to reunite with their daughters and sons, the years apart were often hard to recover, the trust slow to mend. "And it's a stroke of luck," says Tía Dina, "when a child arrives and can comprehend it."

Reyna's mom made her way north in 1973. As the youngest of three siblings, she'd lived the longest under the heavy hand of the man in Mama Nelly's life, an algebra teacher with a volcanic temper. "When he drank, he was another man, very, very offensive," Tía Dina says. "He'd tell us we were nothing. He'd say, 'And you, what are you going to do with your life—become a prostitute?' I'd tell my mom, 'Look, I'm not going to let this old man insult me.' And she'd say, 'You know what, mija? You have to learn to shut your mouth.'" Reyna's mother was twenty when she left Reyna; so was Reyna's father, who lived across the street. Reyna was not yet two.

The family of seamstresses had one son, Mauricio, who studied economics at the University of Central America, a Jesuit school. Although he was a dozen years older than Reyna, "Mauricio used to play with her and call her nicknames, friendly nicknames, and she would, you know, have a very nice relationship with this guy," says one of Reyna's cousins, the second of Tía Dina's children. On March 22, 1980, shortly after the military seized control of the Salvadoran government, the Policía Nacional stormed the campus, spraying bullets and spreading terror. Among their atrocities, they gunned down Mauricio.

"MAURICIO'S ONLY SIN: BEING YOUNG AND A STUDENT," screamed the headline in the university newspaper, which published a picture of his bullet-riddled body.

The priests scooped him up before the security forces could. They did their best to stanch the blood, to swab his face. Then they drove Mauricio to Quince Avenida Sur and presented him to his mother. Between sobs, she and her daughters pushed aside the sewing machines, transforming the front of the little house into a mortuary. All night the two families sat with the body, crying, reciting rosaries, worrying that the police might catch on and disappear Mauricio's corpse before he could be buried. "As kids, we saw the whole process—bringing the dead body to the house, seeing that young man, that young university student dead," says Reyna's cousin. "It was then that we understood that things were going wrong, very wrong. And it was very scary for all of us. Very, very scary." The cousin, a translator and computer instructor, is unsure what Reyna witnessed: he remembers her being at the wake; the dates tell him she'd already left for the US. But Reyna has no trouble recalling the dread. "At night, if I went to the bathroom, I was afraid that I'd see Mauricio," she says, "that his ghost would be out there."

Mauricio's murder came just a month after the Archbishop of San Salvador, Óscar Romero, made an open plea to President Jimmy Carter, warning that continued military aid to El Salvador's new dictatorship would only fuel injustice and repression. And it came just two days before a death squad ambushed Archbishop Romero as he celebrated Mass in a hospital chapel. One of the most heinous acts of political violence in El Salvador's tragic history, the assassination plunged the country into a decade of civil war, ultimately claiming more than seventy-five thousand lives. If Reyna's parents hadn't already sent for her, they surely knew that now was the time to get their daughter out.

Their years of working nights, cleaning office buildings in Los Angeles, had earned them a corner of a 1920s-era triplex on the southeastern lip of

Hollywood, not far from Paramount Studios. But unlike Reyna's aunts, who'd succeeded in securing papers for their children, Reyna's parents still bore the weight of their illegal entry—employed as custodians, categorized as intruders. If they ever wanted to reassemble the pieces of their family, they would have to subject Reyna to the same smuggling network that had brought them to the US. So much sacrifice, such dogged faith, and still they were powerless to spare her that peril.

A woman showed up on Quince Avenida Sur. She taught Reyna to recite a fake American name and a fake American birth date. Guided by the coyote, Reyna rode buses out of El Salvador, through Guatemala, and across the long expanse of Mexico, crying for the mother—the second mother—she'd been separated from. During that week or two on the road, Reyna was inconsolable, unable to eat or even find comfort in the reconciliation that awaited; any memory of her parents had been lost.

In Tijuana, they were met by another smuggler, a man in a car who instructed Reyna and a small boy, possibly a cousin, to crawl into the trunk. Nothing about the space had been altered for safety or comfort—no fresh air, no reassuring light, only the grim rumble of a sedan lurching and then braking, over and again, as it inched to the border checkpoint. Time stopped in that dark coop. Reyna can't even guess how long she was left in there, holding still and keeping quiet, unable to protest or panic. She felt vacant when the latch opened and the brilliant San Diego sun streamed in.

Reyna's parents had married during their first years in LA, exchanging vows at a Catholic church near the ocean. When Reyna was at last reunited with them, she not only had to accept that these two adults she didn't remember were responsible for ripping her away from Mama Nelly, but that in her absence they'd added a competitor: Reyna now had a US-born baby brother, the English-speaking prince of the family.

From the beginning, it was all out of whack, the mix of personalities, cultures, and expectations, a reconfiguration that offered little joy or relief. Like many children of displaced families, Reyna resented her parents for leaving her behind as a toddler, and she resented them even more for insisting on her obedience years later. On the cusp of adolescence, Reyna felt both rejected and besieged, a salvadoreña Cinderella, saddled with endless chores and babysitting duties. Her parents' severity may have been born of worry, to prepare her for the demands and temptations of an American life, or of necessity, to give them the extra set of hands their nocturnal schedules needed. In either case, Reyna had little chance to make friends; her parents were wary of unfamiliar, loosely supervised conventions such as playdates and sleepovers. "I felt like I was in jail," Reyna says. She shared her despair with a teacher. A social worker visited, cautioning Reyna's mother that she couldn't force her daughter to do all the housework. By middle school, Reyna had begun looking for a way out: skipping class, accepting rides from strangers.

When Reyna's parents discovered she'd begun talking to boys, her father—a drinker in those days—whipped her with a belt. After she started wearing makeup, he smashed her head into the refrigerator. During Reyna's freshman year, an administrator at Fairfax High School recommended birth control. Reyna's mother objected; it went against the family's beliefs. Reyna began running away. Her parents called the police each time, until finally, when she was sixteen, officers told them to just let her go.

Reyna had lived half her life in El Salvador and the other half at the edge of Hollywood, and instead of making her whole, the two pieces exposed a cleft she didn't know how to mend. Empty-handed, at once frantic and energized, she made her way to a corner of town so clamorous and transitory, so packed with hustlers and vagabonds, that a sad teenage girl from Central America could lose herself in the bustle. Reyna headed straight to the lake, to the center of MacArthur Park.

La Vida Loca

G iovanni stood before the bathroom mirror with a $2 razor. It was 2004, the autumn after his mom's hospitalization. Reyna and the three kids had broken free of Juan two years earlier, leaving the rental they shared in South-Central Los Angeles for a new boyfriend's apartment in Long Beach, and then when that relationship combusted, returning to the only part of LA that had ever reminded Reyna of home. They found a courtyard apartment on Burlington Avenue, $600 for a putty-colored bungalow with a clay-tile roof about five blocks from the no loitering, no alcohol, no littering, no camping, no swimming, and no open fires signs at MacArthur Park's northeast entrance. In Giovanni's fifteen years, it was his tenth address.

He lathered his head. The blade carved through the suds. Each stroke released a layer of conformity, revealed a hardness he wanted the world to know about. Giovanni had a dad-shaped hole in his soul—big enough to account for two missing men—and a mom so starved for cariño that it stunted her capacity to care for her children the way she wanted, the way they needed. The wreckage left Giovanni feeling devalued, unable to conjure an image of his future self that didn't appear disfigured. The razor accelerated the inevitable. His scalp gleamed: incongruous, menacing.

"It's just like a switch flipped," says his closest childhood friend, Dennis Molina, who had lived alongside Giovanni in a spearmint-green fourplex near Historic Filipinotown for a few years during elementary school. Until the razor cut through, Dennis says, Giovanni had been a "dirty punk rock skater type of kid"—scruffy, nomadic—and a dud with girls. They went out that night to test Giovanni's new look at CityWalk, the LED-lit shopping and entertainment promenade at Universal Studios, where Giovanni's mom had begun working the late shift at Wetzel's Pretzels. In simpler times, maybe five years earlier, Reyna and Juan had treated the kids to a day at the theme park, only to lose sight of Giovanni after the Terminator 3D show—his young brain overloaded by the strobes and thunderbolts and simulated gunfire. With little faith that anyone would mount a search, Giovanni headed for the exits and plotted a way home. He wandered a mile or more, across the Hollywood Freeway, to a car dealership; his parents found him there, finally, clutching a lollipop.

For his makeover, Giovanni went all in: creased denim, white tee, Nike Cortezes. "He was like Mister Hot Shit walking around," says Dennis, "and all the girls were coming up to him—super inviting, you know, they found him very attractive. I don't think I could fully grasp the ramifications of what was going to happen."

Giovanni wasn't in a gang, but he was trying on the uniform, doing his best to announce that he was someone who counts. All around MacArthur Park he saw them, the baldies, lost boys with shaved heads who wore the armor of dominance and excess. "There was times that I was, like: Fuck, am I doing the right thing?" Giovanni says. "I think at that point I was, like, having an identity crisis."

He still liked to skate, kickflipping off the loading docks behind the Food 4 Less on Sixth Street or tictacking past the Metro station on Alvarado Street, just across from Langer's, the venerable deli that had been clinging to the park's southeastern corner since the Truman administration. Giovanni was still just a kid in other ways: no driver's license, no bank account, no email address, no cellphone in what was the Razr and BlackBerry era. He had a round rug, stitched like a soccer ball, next to his bed. Inspired by the *Jackass* series on MTV, Giovanni devoted himself to playing the goofus; he bought a goldfish at the neighborhood pet store and, like Steve-O, swallowed it live. Now he was making bolder moves, sending riskier signals. Without calculating the costs, he'd begun mortgaging adulthood for the near-term gain of acceptance from the homies. "Eventually, they started seeing me," he says, "you know, 'Who's this guy right here?'"

Giovanni's patch of MacArthur Park was ruled by the Columbia Lil Cycos, a subset of the sprawling 18th Street alliance. With as many as twenty thousand members in Southern California—and thousands more spread across at least a hundred and twenty US cities and half a dozen Latin American countries—18th Street was likely the largest gang in the United States, if not beyond. It grew by breaking the mold of traditional, multigenerational Mexican American gangs, which tended to adhere to a strict racial caste system and century-old turf lines. It was the first Latino gang to embrace new immigrants, to capitalize on the Central American exodus, the first even to accept non-Latinos into its ranks. As demographic patterns altered the face of the city, 18th Street was also the savviest about replicating itself on new terrain—a mobile, adaptable, twenty-first-century gang. "Kind of like a big franchise," says Edgar Hernandez, a Los Angeles Police Department gang officer who began spotting Giovanni on MacArthur Park's streets. "Like McDonald's or Starbucks."

Eighteenth Street itself barely registers on the LA map, existing only as a broken line paralleling the Santa Monica Freeway, a mile south of MacArthur Park. But after founding the gang in the 1960s, 18th Street's mythmakers spun a narrative that emphasized geographic supremacy and economic clout. They invested the *1* and the *8* and its many iterations—*XV3, X8, 666, BEST* (Barrio Eighteenth Street)—with a mystique that transcended boundaries. They cloned themselves into dozens of semiautonomous cliques spread across the full constellation of LA neighborhoods and municipalities, from Long Beach to North Hollywood, Inglewood to Cudahy, Downtown to Rancho Park—so broadly dispersed that they grouped themselves into geographic quadrants. To be "from" 18th Street had nothing to do with a physical address; it was a social cooperation network, an organizing principle.

The Columbia Lil Cycos, a set of some three hundred 18th Streeters packed into a half-square-mile hive, couldn't even claim Columbia Avenue. A little-traveled side street, it ran a few blocks east of their hood, on rival terri-tory. But the Columbia Lil Cycos had something better than a namesake. They had density and desperation: an overcrowded, under-resourced postage stamp of turf that offered a captive consumer base for whatever they wanted to sell and a largely undocumented labor force for whichever activities they chose to extort. By the time Giovanni came along, the gang had operated as MacArthur Park's taxation authority for more than a decade, charging "rent" to anyone dealing drugs or working outside the formal economy.

Crack was the commodity that built the Columbia Lil Cycos' empire. They referred to fat wedges as "hamburgers" and thin slices as "taquitos." To transform powder cocaine into smokable rocks was to "cook the meat." The gang supplied and patrolled about a dozen sales hubs, among them Sixth and Alvarado, Sixth and Bonnie Brae, Fifth and Westlake, and the two that sandwiched Giovanni's home, Fifth and Burlington and Third and Burlington: twenty-four-hour drive-thru exchanges that sustained not only neighborhood addicts but also outsiders feeding on the neighborhood's distress. Some members of the gang slanged dope themselves, but that was risky and dan-gerous work; standing on a street corner with a mouthful of plastic-wrapped rocks exposed them to theft, loss, arrest, or worse. The Columbia Lil Cycos' particular innovation was to employ a platoon of mercenaries, usually recent arrivals without papers or prospects, and set them up with product. It was an arrangement built on class and culture: the homies, all shorn and inked, tended to be more Americanized, proficient in English or at least Spanglish, and proud of their outcast insignias; they lorded their status—their fixation on "representing"—over the scruffier and more diffident newcomers, whose usefulness hinged mainly on their ability to blend in.

The dealers were called traqueteros, an onomatopoeia derived from the Spanish word for rattle: the sound of a trafficker on the move. The Columbia Lil Cycos charged each traquetero a tax of $100 to $175 a day to work a desig-nated street, usually in a twelve-hour shift. If a traq was late with the rent, a $50 fine was added to his tab, and if he abandoned his post in search of a livelier street, he was likely to suffer a beatdown. The gang also managed the other end of the supply chain, selecting exclusive wholesalers—mayoristas— and charging them a tax as high as $15,000 a week for the opportunity to replenish the retailers.

The Columbia Lil Cycos dispensed MacArthur Park's drug corners to their own like fiefdoms, rewarding their designees with a passive income stream worth thousands of dollars a week. Dealers paid the street captains because they had to but also because they benefitted from the gang's capacity for violence. In exchange for rent, the traqueteros and mayoristas practiced their trade under a mini monopoly: fixed prices, steady supplies, predictable hours, and a round-the-clock security force to scare off competition.

The Columbia Lil Cycos didn't stop there. They taxed the chiveros who gathered each day to roll dice in the park, the sex workers who turned tricks at the Barbizon (a hotel that in its heyday, belonged to heavyweight champ Jack Dempsey), the cellphone pirates who offered long-distance calls on hijacked numbers, and the miqueros who steered laborers and fugitives and underage students to clandestine ID mills. The whole system of fees and tariffs had turned the Columbia Lil Cycos into 18th Street's most profitable hood, maybe the most prosperous crime turf by square footage in all of Los Angeles. From a thicket of just twenty-eight blocks, the Columbia Lil Cycos were strong-arming the community for a good $25,000 to $50,000 a week— and, in the best of times, $85,000—which is to say millions every year in rent.

The gang burrowed into everything. There were 18s painted on brick and on asphalt, carved into trees, scratched onto pay phones, plastered across security shutters and trash bins and moving vans. In MacArthur Park, the doo-wop tune "Eighteen with a Bullet" had special meaning. So did Indianapolis Colts quarterback Peyton Manning; the Columbia Lil Cycos draped themselves in his number eighteen jersey as if it were a vestment. On the side of USA Donuts, a mural announced the gang's sensibilities: Bare-chested veterano. Snake-wrapped woman. Blazing submachine gun. Radiant Virgen de Guadalupe. Statue of Liberty dissolving into a prison cell. And across the top, a roll call of

18th Street monikers. Titled "La Vida Loca," the mural spanned two walls, facing east and north, a supernova of indigo and saffron and lime that stamped the Columbia Lil Cycos' brand on the neighborhood. By defining social interactions and regulating economic opportunities, the gang ensured that almost everyone outside Giovanni's door labored and played, hungered and schemed, dreamed and prayed, in a world propped up by an outlaw enterprise.

Burlington Avenue, in particular, loomed large in Columbia Lil Cycos folklore. In the 1990s, the street had been their crown jewel, what prosecutors have described as the retail drug capital of the city. A block north of Giovanni's future address, the gang installed itself in a three-story, sixty-seven-unit stucco apartment building, using it as the distribution center for the thriving crack trade outside. When a manager complained to police, the Columbia Lil Cycos decided to "do a little fire," as one member would later testify, to shut the busybody up. They doused a mattress with lighter fluid, then set it ablaze outside the manager's second-floor apartment. The flames didn't travel far, but the smoke did—it billowed down hallways, choking off escape routes and turning the afternoon black. Panicked residents, almost all of them immigrants from Central America, collapsed as they groped for the stairs. Others hurled themselves from balconies. Police called it the most horrendous case of arson in LA history. The toll: ten dead, most of them kids.

Two years after the Burlington fire, the Columbia Lil Cycos faced another disruption to their business model. A jealous 18th Streeter from a different hood dared to muscle in with a mayorista of his own, declaring himself both supplier and collector. The disrespect, and from a presumptive comrade, set the Columbia Lil Cycos off. The next time the interloper came by, accompanied by the middle-aged woman who served as his wholesaler, they sprayed his Suburban with a pair of AK-47s—more than thirty rounds. That bloodbath went down on the block Giovanni would later call home.

Even if Giovanni didn't know much about Burlington Avenue's history, he couldn't miss how the gang consecrated its combatants. If you looked carefully at the monikers spray-painted on the USA Donuts mural, you could still see the names of the killers who presided over each Burlington Avenue attack.

The gang's audacity stemmed partly from the Los Angeles Police Department's shortcomings. The LAPD already had a long history of mistreating poor brown and Black communities; its excesses provoked the uprising of 1992, an explosion of rage that left the city scarred and shaken. Amid political pressure to restore order and contain violence, the department allowed a "culture of war" to fester in the years that followed. The Rampart Division, which encompasses the MacArthur Park neighborhood, embodied the bunker mentality: officers called the station Fort Apache. Taking aim at 18th Street, a cabal of rogue Rampart cops brutalized suspects, fabricated evidence, intimidated witnesses, and lied with impunity. For a logo, they adopted a skull in a cowboy hat flanked by the so-called dead man's hand— aces and eights—which looked a lot like the number eighteen.

What became known as the Rampart scandal plunged LA into one of the worst law-enforcement disgraces in American history. The FBI's public corruption unit swooped in—federal agents investigating local cops—putting new strains on what had long been a testy relationship. The US Department of Justice threatened to sue the LAPD for "a pattern or practice" of civil rights abuses, resulting in a consent decree that placed the police under federal oversight. In the end, two dozen officers were suspended, fired, or forced into retirement. More than a hundred criminal convictions were overturned. And to settle the wave of lawsuits, the city paid out more than $125 million.

The largest check, for $15 million, went to an 18th Streeter from Honduras known as Sniper. When he was nineteen, two Rampart gang cops shot him, unarmed, in an abandoned apartment, leaving him paralyzed from the waist down; they planted a Tec-22, its serial number buffed out, next to his body and arrested him for assault on a police officer. He served two and a half years of a twenty-three-year prison sentence before the miscarriage was exposed.

A Columbia Lil Cyco known as Oso, who'd dogged the Rampart Division with complaints of mistreatment, was hauled into the station house and slammed into a wall. The city council awarded him $169,000. Another Columbia Lil Cyco known as Baby scored a settlement in the neighborhood of $475,000 after he was framed by Rampart officers on a drug charge and sent off to a juvenile prison. Not long after Baby's windfall, a *Los Angeles Times* reporter chronicling the lives of MacArthur Park's nouveau riche gangsters encountered him in a glossy BMW. "See that?" said Baby, opening his wallet and waving several hundred-dollar bills toward downtown's lustrous skyline. "That's what the LAPD gave me right there."

Compared to the Crips and the Bloods, or even MS-13, the infamy of 18th Street never quite penetrated popular culture, perhaps because the name sounded unromantic—mathematical. But to those in the know, the Columbia Lil Cycos had an insolence that set them apart from the endless patchwork of LA gangs, an unapologetic frankness that captivated Hollywood filmmakers. For his 2005 shoot-'em-up, *Domino,* Tony Scott wanted authentic gangsters to populate the cast. He turned to an acclaimed street photographer, a chronicler of LA barrio culture who'd helped orchestrate a scene on 18th Street turf the previous year for Michael Mann's *Collateral.* Those connections led to Oso, who, emboldened by his Rampart payday, accepted an invitation to pretty much play himself.

When the star, Keira Knightley, bursts into a roomful of gun-toting gang members—another half dozen Columbia Lil Cycos—she wriggles out of the jam by offering Oso a lap dance. "C'mon, girl, let's go," says Oso, who flashes the *E* of 18th Street with his thumbs and forefingers while gloating over her gyrations.

Unlike most street gangs, whose activities lean toward disorganized crime, the Columbia Lil Cycos had a well-defined internal structure: a clear division of labor and a strict pecking order. At the highest levels there was someone in charge of muscle—a sergeant at arms, if you will—who regulated conduct and curbed dissent. That was Oso. He was forever exhorting young members to patrol the streets with greater vigor, to be "more on the hood." There was also someone in charge of the gang's financial affairs, a shotcaller, who was said to have the "keys" to the neighborhood "car." In 2005, Tricky ascended to that role.

Sergio "Tricky" Pantoja was pushing thirty, bald and puffy-faced, with a faint mustache and colossal ears that provoked snickers behind his back. He had *XVIII* tattooed in thick Old English script across his chest and *EST* on his loose belly. A plumed serpent curled from his right shoulder to the bottom of his throat. Tricky was heavy into coco puffs—cigarettes sprinkled with crack—and a regular at Sam's Hofbrau, a topless club on the industrial fringes of downtown where the dancers looked like real homegirls, not centerfolds.

Tricky was also an artist and, to a degree, a lawful merchant. After apprenticing under another 18th Street shotcaller, he opened Unico's Tattoos and Airbrush in the International Mall, a three-story showroom on Sixth Street next to the donut shop mural. The building had once housed the Legal Aid Foundation; now it was a labyrinth of immigrant stalls—apparel, beauty, transport—and at the back, in suite nine, Tricky's studio. It had a swinging saloon door for an entrance and walls covered with laminated images of his handiwork, most of it steeped in Aztec symbolism, even though Tricky's family was from El Salvador, not Mexico. If a visitor wasn't looking for a tattoo, there was also a glass display with sex toys and cannabis paraphernalia.

With the help of his Guatemalan-born wife, who went by Morena, Tricky used the shop to run the Columbia Lil Cycos' business and monitor the commerce raging outside his doors. He collected ten grand a week on crack sales around the corner on Burlington, right where Giovanni was broadcasting his availability. He also sold crack over the counter to midmarket dealers: eight hundred here, twelve hundred there. While Tricky was the titular head, everyone said that Morena, three years older, was the one who made the wheels turn. She had a cascade of dark-brown hair, parted down the middle Farrah Fawcett–style, big eyes, and a tight, pursed mouth. Quick with numbers, she took charge of inventory, placing orders and negotiating prices with the neighborhood's wholesaler, who always addressed her, respectfully, as señora. They had three kids and did their best to put up a front, bringing Tricky's mom to live in a granny flat behind their house, a simple A-frame guarded by wrought-iron spikes, steps from the Los Angeles Memorial Coliseum. "Family and my gang life is two totally different things," Tricky would say. And Morena: "We tried never to bring that into the house, what was happening, to not harm the children."

Turnover at Tricky's level was constant. Without an external system for resolving personal grievances and adjudicating business disputes, the top job demanded a zeal for vigilance and an appetite for confrontation. It could be exhausting even for a committed gangster. The Columbia Lil Cycos burned through a shotcaller almost every year, enduring a seemingly endless series of mutinies, purges, and realignments. Greedy became an informant. Termite went rogue and took a bullet. Santos succumbed to gambling debts. Shaggie squandered a hundred and seventy grand on a failed brothel in Guadalajara. Husky simply threw in the towel, too stressed by the responsibility. That wasn't Tricky—he wanted this. He lobbied to preserve his hold on MacArthur Park, to cement and expand his status.

Tricky wasn't a fatalist either, resigned to an early grave or a prison cell. He believed he was different—too smart to falter. "You just had to be bright," he says. "Sharp. Think quick. Do things now and ask questions later." It was Tricky's way: a prescription for disaster.

4
Social Citizenship

Everyone in MacArthur Park hustled. To retreat was to starve. Even with the Columbia Lil Cycos looming over the neighborhood, the sons and daughters of Usulután and Sacatepéquez and Tlacolula devised their own street-level economy, bringing the hand-to-hand commerce of their homelands to MacArthur Park's thoroughfares. Morning to night, rain or shine, the vendedores ambulantes took to the sidewalks by the hundreds, selling whatever they could make or recycle or procure at a discount.

Just a dozen blocks west of the polished-granite and smoked-glass towers of the LA skyline, MacArthur Park pulsed with gumption: a bucket of boiled peanuts perched in a baby stroller, flank steak sizzling over a shopping cart lined with foil and packed with mesquite, a rainbow of knockoff perfume bottles balanced atop an overturned milk crate, rows of bootleg DVDs, from animated classics to anatomically specialized porn, laid out on a fleece blanket like a game of solitaire. Most days there was somebody juicing oranges with a manual press and somebody searing pupusas on a butane-powered griddle. There was a tostada lady and a corn-on-the-cob guy, a diaper gal and a battery dude. A mango carved into a rosette fetched a dollar. So did a couple of loose cigarillos. After a spate of arson fires gutted the Hotel Californian on Sixth Street, the fence around the razed lot served as a display case—coat hangers, draped with secondhand clothes, clung to every inch of the chainlink. Across the street, aloha shirts hung from a parking sign. At the corner of Alvarado, sweatshirts dangled from a giant sago palm.

Giovanni's mom relished the cash-only mercado, the effusiveness and tenacity of the vendors. Their greetings and invitations, to come see for herself how rico the tacos were, how fresca the fruit, helped alleviate Reyna's gloom.

She still ached for the world she'd been snatched from, the familiar faces and landmarks and rhythms of her Salvadoran youth; MacArthur Park oozed with flavor, the opposite of America's cold efficiencies. Giovanni cared little about the echoes of a homeland he'd never known; a combo plate at the China Bowl Express on Sixth and Burlington more than satisfied his needs. But MacArthur Park's vendors still had something for a disaffected teenager—Giovanni could buy a cigarette out there without anyone asking for ID.

Some of the merchandise was junk, stuff that middle-class folks would have donated to Goodwill or tossed but that in MacArthur Park could be monetized. An enterprising grandpa on Sixth Street rode the bus to yard sales in Santa Monica or Beverly Hills every weekend, returning with a haul of barely used name-brand clothing to cash in. "I only went to elementary school," he says, "but in business I think maybe I'm very advanced." Others took advantage of bargain stores, buying in bulk and selling piecemeal. The sock queen of Alvarado, La Tía, got her start after El Piojito advertised baby socks for 30¢ a pair. Laid off from a garment factory job, she scraped together $10 and invested in 33 pairs, which she then sold door-to-door for $1.50 each. Flush with nearly $50, she kept buying more, growing her inventory, until she had a shopping cart of hosiery to roll down the street. "You have to lose your embarrassment," she says. "With embarrassment, you're not going to eat."

Across LA some fifty thousand vendors, most undocumented, were performing a version of the same venture, generating a half-billion dollars in annual street sales. For a population lured by the promise of work yet barred from the formal workforce, these impromptu bazaars represented an entry-level marketplace with almost no barrier to participation. Vending rewarded self-sufficiency and reimagined public space, turning pavement into employment. It also catered to the appetites and budgets of a consumer base that by necessity, eats and shops on foot—nannies, busboys, dishwashers, gardeners—folks without cars or kitchens or enough room at home to ever truly relax. While some vendors enlisted out of utter destitution, most of MacArthur Park's stalwarts saw themselves as scrappy capitalists. They were their own bosses. They set their own hours and implemented their own business strategies. Given the many less socially beneficial alternatives that a frustrated labor pool could pursue, to vend was to create and contribute: to earn what academics call "social citizenship," where legal recognition is denied.

The vending economy, in other words, made perfect cultural and commercial sense, which is why most world capitals celebrate their street food and accommodate their flea markets. Even cities that regulate vending, that cap the number of permits or restrict where vendors can sell, recognize sidewalk commerce as an urban amenity. Just not LA. Despite its reputation as a liberal city and a street food incubator—a sanctuary for immigrants, the birthplace of the taco truck—Los Angeles has long viewed peddling as a nuisance. Code for foreignness and civic disorder. The antithesis of the modern, clean, ahistorical city that the business and political class has been seeking to build ever since California ceased belonging to Mexico.

As far back as the 1890s, the police looked for ways to curb the proliferation of tamale wagons, those "unsightly movable dyspepsia emporiums," as a turn-of-the-century newspaperman put it. A 1906 roundup of vendors filled an LA courtroom with a "motley array of representatives of at least a half-score of nations," and the arrests a few years later of eighteen Chinese fruit and vegetable peddlers sought to break up their "disease-breeding traffic." In the years after the Depression, a downtown merchants association demanded that the city do something about the hucksters, beggars, moochers, fakirs, and buskers invading the central city, proof that "the Los Angeles sidewalks are the most misused . . . of any in the United States." The 1950s brought a campaign against newspaper hawkers; the 1970s took aim at flower stands. By 1980, the city council just threw up its hands and banned the curbside sale of *anything*—the only way, in the words of the ordinance's author, to "give our sidewalks back to the people."

The prohibition was codified in a municipal ordinance, 42.00(b), which dictated that "no person . . . shall on any sidewalk or street offer for sale . . . any goods, wares or merchandise." Soon the LAPD was issuing close to a thousand vending citations a year. Some years, the number topped two thousand. Although the maximum penalty (six months in jail and a $1,000 fine) was rarely imposed, enforcement still criminalized what was for the most part honest work. A ticket forced the vendors to finance their own exclusion from the workforce, to hand over money they earned on the streets to a government that denied them legal opportunities. For people with little access to credit, even a modest fine could amount to a financial emergency, dragging a vendor into a cycle of warrants and collections, not to mention all the inconvenience and indignity and potential immigration consequences of navigating the American courts.

Defenders of the ban spoke most often of protecting their communities: from unaccountable competition, from impassable sidewalks, from noise and trash, from food-borne illness. But protection was also a euphemism for exclusion—for refusing to share public space with the poor, for hording economic opportunity. As vending proliferated, homeowners and shopkeepers and civic leaders complained about people from "who-knows-where" selling goods on their street, intruding on their "quality of life," turning their neighborhood into a "Third World" city. Or as the city clerk's tax and permit division put it in the 1980s, indiscriminate selling promotes "a poor image of the City of Los Angeles."

It fell to the police to quell an entrepreneurial phenomenon. Few cops considered the vending ban a priority, especially in a place like MacArthur Park, which had actual criminal industries to contend with. The immigration laws weren't their concern either. Despite a vexed history with communities of color, the LAPD realized early on that public safety would suffer if undocumented populations feared the police; since 1979, the department has barred officers from even inquiring about a person's immigration status. Still, like any police force, the LAPD responded to political pressure. Officers cruised the perimeter of the park, up and down Alvarado Street, east and west on Sixth Street, barking "no más" from squad car windows. That was usually enough to halt business for the day. Most vendors scooped up their wares in a blanket or tablecloth, loaded their dollies and wagons and rolling suitcases, and scuttled off. Some dawdled, though, making a show of packing up. Some left, only to circle back within minutes. No cop was going to lose a battle of wills. Faced with defiance, the police played the heavies: not just writing tickets but also confiscating merchandise, tossing food and trashing grills, even slapping handcuffs on a vendor who tried to make a run for it.

None of it worked. Crackdowns begat protests, then reprieves and compromises and finally cave-ins, until the sidewalks churned with even more commerce than before. Without the political will to either legalize vending or consistently suppress it, Angelenos reaped the worst of both worlds: a law so erratically and arbitrarily enforced that all sides recognized it as an exercise in hypocrisy.

Only once did the city entertain a solution. In 1989, the year of Giovanni's birth, a group of MacArthur Park activists appealed to a first-term council member, an urban planner by trade, who couldn't understand why LA had "the most restrictive street vending ordinances of any major city in the country, maybe even the world." He formed a task force, which proposed the creation of special vending districts, where licensed peddlers could operate with the consent of neighborhood merchants. It took a decade to get off the ground, but in 1999, MacArthur Park welcomed the city's only legal vending district—a corner of the park grounds at Seventh and Alvarado.

To administer the program, the city retained a nonprofit cochaired by a fair-housing advocate from Pasadena named Sandra Romero. Although new to MacArthur Park—and initially taken aback by the "no-man's-land" assigned to her—she proved to be a force of nature: nurturing and optimistic, with purple ribbons braided through her hair and a warm, gap-toothed smile that exploded into generous dimples. Soon everyone knew Sandi Romero as Mama.

In Mama's vision, the vending district would be not just a marketplace but an incubator, a stepping stone to leadership skills and microloans that would help catapult sidewalk peddlers into full-fledged business owners. "It was

God's work," she says. Then the bureaucrats took over. Rather than allow vendors to make their own judgments about what to sell, the city wanted to showcase folkloric crafts, as if MacArthur Park were a version of touristy Olvera Street and not a community locked in a daily fight for survival. Officials also required that the items be sold from ornamental pushcarts with colorful canopies and spoked wheels—at $6,000 to $9,000 a pop—an extravagance aimed at beautification, not the optimization of sidewalk economics.

Of the fourteen vendors who'd agreed to go through the inaugural training and permitting process, most wanted to accommodate MacArthur Park's appetite for budget-friendly food. Public health authorities nixed all outdoor cooking and homemade fare. Searching for middle ground, Mama proposed one of the beloved prepackaged staples of the Americas: tamales. Wrapped in corn husks or banana leaves, they could be prepared in a commissary and kept warm in mobile steam trays. So was born Mama's Hot Tamales, a storefront restaurant, kitchen, and classroom on Seventh Street that became a community anchor when the first vendors rolled into the park. Thanks to a combination of city funds, philanthropic grants, and private donations, Mama charged each vendor just a dollar to participate.

Although Mama's tamaladas spread hope and deterred crime in her corner of the park, red tape continued to hobble the experiment. Her apprentices were allocated spots, largely by lottery, and forbidden to wander with their carts even within the vending zone. They could post no signage. They had to stop selling at sunset. And, of course, they were all selling essentially the same product, even if they tried to distinguish themselves by highlighting regional variations. "The MacArthur Park legal vending district had the feel of a moribund petting zoo," a law professor who visited in the early 2000s would write. Meanwhile, directly across Alvarado Street, the lawless sidewalk trade chugged along at all hours, an in-your-face reminder that working within the system meant missing out. No matter how many times the police ran them off, the "illegal vendors would re-emerge like flowers after the spring thaw."

After burning through $1 million in rent and equipment, the city's lone experiment in legal sidewalk sales ended with a whimper in 2005. "I really felt abandoned," Mama says.

As it turned out, 2005 was also the year of Baby's epiphany: MacArthur Park's street vendors were easy marks for the Columbia Lil Cycos. The gang was already extorting just about everyone else in the neighborhood's illicit economy. Without legal protection for their trade, the street vendors would be in no position to protest or run to the police if the Columbia Lil Cycos added them to the tax rolls. "I saw an opportunity to make money," Baby says, "without working all that hard."

Baby was twenty-three, just five foot four but well past two hundred pounds—a heavyweight in the hood. He managed crack and heroin sales on a stretch of Burlington Avenue, across from Giovanni's apartment, and projected a swagger that had only swelled since he'd pocketed his six-figure Rampart settlement. If he hadn't thought before to exploit the street vendors' vulnerability, it was because Baby had love for them, at least the ones who provided nourishment. He considered MacArthur Park's peddlers a neighborhood asset—the taquera on Fifth, the frutero on Bonnie Brae—self-starters whose presence added life to a community short on investment. The vendors had seen him grow up, the eighth of thirteen children born to a single mom from the Mexican state of Durango, and had looked out for him, even slipping him a tortilla or a mango back when he was small and hungry. What struck him in 2005 was an imbalance between the regulars and a new wave: poachers who used MacArthur Park as a distribution base and offered nothing in return.

Baby noticed a vibrant trade in tools. "Good-quality stuff, you know, Craftsman, Milwaukee, all kinds of good tools, and brand new," he says. "So I started doing my research." He discovered that a cargo theft ring had been jacking freight trains, then unloading their loot on Columbia Lil Cycos turf. It was a common practice: steal merchandise from wealthier quarters and fob it off on a population less likely to quibble about its provenance. "They were making a killing, man," Baby says. He thought it only fair that the bandits should break off a piece for the hood.

Baby then turned his attention to the DVD trade, another less-than-sympathetic vendor class. It had evolved from the days of shaky cameras and fuzzy duplicates to first-rate facsimiles ripped directly from Hollywood screeners. You could buy the latest releases—often before they were released—for as little as $5. The movie studios, which unleashed their own squad of investigators on MacArthur Park, claimed annual losses in the billions. "So I did my little research again," says Baby, who concluded that with the right equipment he could fabricate a copy for less than 75¢. He invested in a couple of burners and set them up in a nearby public-storage facility, then started cranking out the hits. "The screeners used to come from, I guess, Hollywood, the Hollywood industry," Baby says. "The guy I used to work with, he had the connections. He'd say, 'Hey, this is going to be a good movie, we need to get this master,' and sure enough, boom, everybody was asking for it."

As a manufacturer, Baby consistently doubled his money, wholesaling each pirated disc for $1.50. But on the retail end, in a community priced out of Best Buy and Sam Goody, business was even better. He fronted a box of 150 DVDs to a woman he knew; she'd lost her job and needed help getting back on her feet. "In two hours," Baby says, "she had paid me what that box is worth." It was another opportunity to tilt the scales in the gang's favor, to add a tax to the cost of doing business on MacArthur Park's sidewalks.

Although his reputation placed him in the gang's upper echelon, Baby thought it prudent to run his scheme past the big homies before he started levying fees. He was tinkering not only with the Columbia Lil Cycos' revenue streams but also leveraging the organization's consumer data and market penetration, like a ride-hailing platform expanding into the food-delivery business. "I wasn't risking it," says Baby, who by then had moved to the Latino suburbs of the San Gabriel Valley and was working, at least on paper, for a sheet-metal shop. "I didn't want to mess up, do something before I had, like, an approval from other people."

He started with Oso, fresh off his Hollywood cameo. Then he went to the shotcaller, Tricky. Nobody objected. Baby was pleased with himself. By just paying attention and applying some basic economic principles, he'd broadened the gang's reach, putting the squeeze on a dubious breed of vendor. The concept may have been predatory, but the calculus was rational. "It was a good idea," Baby says. "I didn't know it was going to escalate."

It killed Reyna to feel so helpless, so inadequate as a parent, so alone.
She'd lost Giovanni's father too soon, and then she'd tried to make it work
with her smagicand and then it had been one questionable boyfriend after

5

Marked for Life

I n 2005, just about the time Baby was hatching the vendor tax, he spotted
Giovanni flaunting his bald head out on Burlington Avenue. Baby didn't
know what Giovanni was up to, why a kid who'd bounced around LA for so
many years—spending more of his youth outside the MacArthur Park neighborhood than in it—would want to sign away his life to the Columbia Lil
Cycos. The gang was a parasitic business entity. It would never love Giovanni
back. "This is not for you," Baby warned him. Another time, after overhearing
Giovanni smart off to his mom, Baby socked him in the chest. "This is not a
good life," he insisted. "Stay away from this."

Giovanni persisted. He volunteered to sell crack. He drank Mickeys till he
blacked out. He lit an M-80 firecracker and tossed it through the door at
McDonald's, the one on Wilshire Boulevard where his mom bought her coffee, just to prove no prank was too ill-advised for his adolescent imagination.
It wasn't exactly gangbanging; Giovanni hadn't yet learned to project his
despair onto the young men of other neighborhoods—boys indistinguishable
from him—and brand them his mortal enemy. But as he approached sixteen,
Giovanni was beginning to believe the worst about himself and his place in
the world, that he'd been let down, shortchanged, and that the Columbia Lil
Cycos were the antidote to poverty and belittlement. The word "gang" comes
from the Old Norse gangr, a "going" or "course," and the Gothic gagg, an "act of
going," terms that a thousand years ago referred to a journey or passage; that's
why the ramp to a ship is a gangway, why gangplanks became a fixture of pirate
tales. The gang was Giovanni's crossing, his ticket to no-fucks-given land.

"I was hurting," he says, "and I wanted for other people to hurt as well."

It killed Reyna to feel so helpless, so inadequate as a parent. So alone. She'd lost Giovanni's father too soon, and then she'd tried to make it work with his stepdad, and then it had been one questionable boyfriend after another—none was a match for the tribal energy of the Columbia Lil Cycos. Reyna was still estranged from her parents, most of all her mother, who'd remained icy with her into adulthood. They lived nearby, in a North Hollywood condo, but had little contact with Giovanni or his quieter, more risk-averse brother, Israel. Reyna had also had a child with Juan, a girl, which gave her a princess to fuss over, to dress in pink and adorn with bows, as her eldest grew more defiant and farther from reach. It made Giovanni even angrier to think he was the product of a lie while his baby sister got to be the consentida, the spoiled one.

Reyna didn't know where to turn, what she could do to protect Giovanni. He'd saved her by calling 911; who could she call to save him? In a bleak moment, she contacted the county, asking if she could relinquish Giovanni to a foster home. When she was told that she couldn't pick and choose—she'd have to surrender all her kids if she was unfit to handle one—Reyna dropped the idea, and later regretted having considered it. "I didn't think I was a bad mom," she says. "I wanted something good in his life."

A counselor at Belmont High School noticed that Giovanni was little more than a phantom. He paid Reyna a house call. "I picked up a sense of guilt, of her not really knowing how to deal with the situation," says Eric Hernandez, the pupil services and attendance counselor, who'd also come to the US from El Salvador as an undocumented child. "She would get very emotional at some of our meetings, saying, 'If I could just get out of here and start somewhere else.' That sense of powerlessness was very devastating." He referred Giovanni to an LAPD boot camp for wayward kids. The police gave Giovanni a T-shirt with his name stenciled on the chest. They ran him through fitness drills and brought him to a shelter in Skid Row to serve coffee and donuts. But the military-style rigidity that Giovanni had welcomed as a junior high cadet now suffocated him. "I'm like, damn, what do I have to do this for?" he says. He dropped out after a few weeks.

The LAPD started paying closer attention to Giovanni. The cops recognized all the warning signs: unstable home, struggles at school, no supervision. "I actually felt bad, really bad for him," says Rampart gang officer Edgar Hernandez, who plucked Giovanni off the streets on several occasions, delivering him to the apartment on Burlington. In those days, Reyna was gone almost every evening, rarely returning from her pretzel job before 2 A.M. "She was nice, you know, trying to do the best she could," Hernandez says. "But the thing is, the mom, she has to work. That's what people don't understand. They'll be like, 'Why can't the parents take care of these kids?' Because, you know what? The mom has to work just to survive."

Giovanni tuned out all the advice, rejected every effort to preempt his initiation. Baby might have thought him naive and clownish, but the Columbia Lil Cycos needed constant replenishment at the lower rungs—and Giovanni's willingness to put others in harm's way, to expose himself to harm, made him a candidate. That same year, 2005, he earned an invitation to the 500 Building, an 18th Street redoubt at 500 Westlake Avenue. A city slumlord task force had sued a prior owner, an orthopedic surgeon, for allowing the ninety-year-old brick tenement to fall into disrepair: leaky plumbing, moldy walls, exposed wires, vermin droppings. The latest owner was facing the same complaints—neglect that the Columbia Lil Cycos wielded to their advantage. Tricky held court there, taunting his minions at rooftop meetings. Oso remodeled, busting down a wall on the third floor to turn a single unit into a double, and then installed a stripper pole. The gang filmed themselves in the 500—rap videos, would-be documentaries—and posted the footage on YouTube; mugging for the camera, the Columbia Lil Cycos boasted of the "stronghold" they governed and proclaimed themselves "deep as fuck."

"It was the mecca," says the LAPD's Edgar Hernandez. "Five hundred South Westlake. Even the manager was Eighteenth."

There in the 500 Building's back alley, amid the trashed sofas and spray-painted scrawls, the Columbia Lil Cycos gave Giovanni the baptism he desired. Traditional cultures have done it forever. So have drill instructors. They separate the recruit from the larger society, tear him down, challenge his resolve, and rebuild him in their ideal of an adult or a man or a warrior—a symbolic death and rebirth. The Columbia Lil Cycos counted to eighteen as Giovanni absorbed their blows, barred by protocol from fighting back. They whipped him good. It felt to Giovanni like care. When it was over, he chose his new identity: Listo. It meant ready, as in "ready to go whenever the homies told me to," he says. But the Columbia Lil Cycos had already allocated that name. They determined he should be Rusty. It sounded like the opposite of readiness. Giovanni never asked for an explanation.

Reyna tried again to intervene. She turned to the LAPD, just showed up at the Rampart station one day that summer and let it all spill out: how her son had joined a gang, how she suspected him of selling drugs, how she needed the cops to set him straight. It was an incautious plea. Reyna didn't pause to consider the consequences of accelerating Giovanni's entry into the criminal justice system. Nor did she calculate how the gang might respond if it learned she'd reported one of their own. As a mom, she just knew she had to do something. "I thought he was going to learn a lesson," Reyna says.

The cops swung open Giovanni's bedroom door at 5 A.M. It was August 24, a Wednesday, the early days of what would have been his junior year. "Get up," they ordered. "Get dressed." Giovanni was confused. What was la jura doing in his house? He just wanted to sleep. The officers pointed at his shoes. "And take your laces out."

With a huff Giovanni pushed aside the covers. He still wasn't much of a gangster, the most serious offense on his record a truancy violation. Now the LAPD was pawing over his stuff, pulling a few plastic-wrapped nuggets of cocaine from a pair of balled-up boxers. Giovanni knew there was only one explanation for the intrusion, only one person who would have dared to sabotage his entry into the Columbia Lil Cycos. He clenched his fists and seethed.

"I know he hated me that day," Reyna says. "I couldn't even look at him."

The LAPD transported Giovanni to Central Juvenile Hall. His arrival created confusion. Prosecutors rejected the case. But Reyna refused to pick him up—she preferred that Giovanni stay in custody. "He didn't understand what I was going through," she says. "He was just living his crazy life." Unable to release a minor onto the streets, a probation worker took Giovanni to a Transitional Independent Living Plan facility on the south side of Los Angeles, a halfway house for kids caught between homelessness and foster care. He ate hot dogs for dinner. When it was time for bed, Giovanni tested the burglar bars on the window, then spotted the emergency release. He shimmied out, bummed some change for the bus, and was back in his own bed less than twenty-four hours after his rude awakening. He felt unstoppable. "Just the thought of doing wrong and getting away," Giovanni says, "pumped me with adrenaline."

The system soon caught up. The case was refiled, and by that October, Giovanni was at Boys Republic, a private, nonprofit school and farm for troubled teens about thirty-five miles to the east, across the San Bernardino County line. Its most famous alum, the action star Steve McQueen, landed there in 1946 after a hubcap-stealing spree; he credited Boys Republic with saving his life. Giovanni lasted two months. In the middle of the night, a few days before Christmas, he hoisted himself over a chain-link fence, followed a concrete-lined culvert under the Chino Valley Freeway, and ended up on a ranch. He found a truck with the keys still in the ignition and was about to reach in when the owner spotted him. "He was like, 'Hey, what the fuck!'" Giovanni says. "And I'm like, 'Look, man, I'm just trying to get home, you know, make it home for Christmas.'" The owner introduced Giovanni to the two women he'd been partying with—the escapee had stumbled into some kind of teenage male fantasy. They offered him drugs. Giovanni declined but cajoled the ladies into giving him a ride. They took him as far as West Covina.

He slept in a park. In the morning, he called his mom and told her where he was, but only after making her promise not to turn him in again.

Going AWOL a second time raised Giovanni's profile with the Columbia Lil Cycos. It also earned him a hood present: an invitation to Unico's Tattoos. Giovanni walked down Burlington, through the gauntlet of vendors on Sixth, and into the International Mall. This was the real initiation—visceral, permanent—and Tricky himself, the gang's shotcaller, was there to do the honors. Giovanni had never merited an audience with the big homie before, much less up-close, hands-on attention. He arrived sober; this wasn't the time or place to act a fool. Tricky pointed Giovanni to an adjustable tattoo chair. Giovanni sunk in chest first and extended his arms backward, locking his elbows. Working a pedal-powered machine, Tricky sketched a foot-long *1* down Giovanni's left forearm and a matching *8* down his right. The outlines burned, the shading a little less. When it was over, beads of blood dotted Giovanni's skin. "I was in—marked for life," Giovanni says. "Nobody could tell me anything."

Days later, in January 2006, Giovanni was arrested again, this time for violating a city gang injunction. A tactic pioneered in LA and challenged with periodic success on constitutional grounds, gang injunctions expanded the reach of public-nuisance laws—giving the city attorney's office the authority to "abate" a gang's activities. In 2005, just as Giovanni was finding his way in, the Columbia Lil Cycos were hit with one. The injunction described their behavior as "injurious to the health" and "indecent and offensive to the senses," and it barred not just criminal conduct but all sorts of everyday interactions, creating a pretext for police to detain virtually anyone deemed gang affiliated. Every Columbia Lil Cyco was prohibited from "standing, sitting, walking, driving, gathering or appearing" anywhere in public with another Columbia Lil Cyco.

Giovanni had been on his way to the 500 Building, a two-block walk from his apartment. As he approached the rear alley, the LAPD came barging through the front. It was some sorry luck. Giovanni bolted. Officer Hernandez chased him down. "I feel better when he is locked up," Giovanni's mom told the juvenile probation department. "He is a bad influence to the rest of my kids."

Once again, Giovanni's short tenure with the Columbia Lil Cycos was interrupted. He was sent to Camp Afflerbaugh, a juvenile facility in the foothills of the Angeles National Forest. It was his first exposure to 18th Street's geographic reach, to foes from corners of LA he'd never even heard of. In MacArthur Park, the Columbia Lil Cycos mostly concerned themselves with their two closest neighbors, Mara Salvatrucha on the west and Rockwood on the east. But at Camp Afflerbaugh the tattoos on Giovanni's arms meant that he inherited the disdain of dozens, maybe a hundred or more other gangs feuding with 18th Street cliques far from anywhere Giovanni had ever been. "I had to learn real fast who my enemies were," Giovanni says. "Which was basically everyone." He also learned to fight in the covert wrestling posture known to generations of juvenile wards. To stay out of view and ensure a fair bout, he and whichever rival wanted to go at it would drop to the floor, lock legs, and with only their arms, wallop each other. The technique worked. After four months, the staff reported that Giovanni had avoided trouble: "Minor has tried to distance himself from any potential problems that would prolong his camp stay." He turned seventeen behind its fences.

With Giovanni locked up, Reyna reached the dispiriting conclusion that she would have to pack up and move again—the great decisions of her life not so much choices as emergencies. To stay on Burlington Avenue was to accept that she'd lost Giovanni, that the gang filled a void in him she didn't know how to treat. It would be easier while he was away. Reyna would remove Giovanni in absentia, inform him after the fact that he no longer lived among the Columbia Lil Cycos.

If nothing else, maybe she could save his brother. Israel was more of a mama's boy, loyal and watchful. He had defended her the time her latest boyfriend, yet another mercurial drinker, threatened to kill himself with a kitchen knife. Reyna tried to snatch it from his hands, the two adults of the house struggling over the blade, careening between suicide and homicide. Israel, though only fifteen, barreled between them and emerged with the weapon. Giovanni began calling him Scrappy.

Reyna also had her daughter to worry about. Her little angelita had turned skittish and weepy, running into Reyna's bed at the wail of a siren or thwomp of a helicopter. Even a nine-year-old girl could sense the power of the Columbia Lil Cycos, the way the gang thrived on the neighborhood's breakdowns, filling the gaps, compromising her family. The crackle of gunfire outside their door was a nightly indictment of Giovanni; her brother's gang, whether under attack or on the prowl, had them cornered. "She hated living there," Reyna says. "She was so scared all the time."

Before Giovanni earned his release, Reyna made her break, relocating sixty miles north, to a Section 8 apartment in Palmdale. Reyna disliked the high desert barrenness of the Antelope Valley, the blinding sky, the lattice of dusty lots. The streets barely had names, just numbers running north and south and single letters going east and west, like a lunar map. The whole place seemed to have popped up overnight, an exurb of last resort. Reyna had family there, including her Tía Dina, the only relatives in LA who would even take her calls, so Palmdale also provided an answer to the question of where—*where else?*

"I always told her, 'Come over here, it'll be calmer for you and your kids,'" says Reyna's aunt. "By the time she came, it was already too late."

In August 2006, Camp Afflerbaugh sent Giovanni home, to a place he'd never lived. He hated Palmdale more than his mom did. She'd drop him off at the alternative high school that his probation required him to attend, then as soon as she'd drive away, Giovanni would hop the Metrolink train that ran past the campus and make his way back to MacArthur Park, hoping to restore his 18th Street credentials. Reyna didn't know what to do. She'd extracted Giovanni from the neighborhood, hauled him to one of the most distant corners of the county, and yet the Columbia Lil Cycos exerted a gravitational force, drawing her son back to MacArthur Park's orbit.

"I told him a bad word," Reyna says. "I said, 'Fuck them, they're not your family.'"

Giovanni repaid her with another tattoo. It said EIGHTEEN in flowing script. He had it inked on his bald scalp, just above his forehead.

Giovanni still occasionally spent weekends with his stepdad, who'd completed his own six-month jail sentence that summer, for driving while impaired. They hadn't lived under the same roof for several years by then, which took some of the sting out of their relationship. Even as Giovanni built his identity around the Columbia Lil Cycos, Juan loved and accepted him as a son, never drawing familial lines or attributing his delinquency to someone else's genetics.

When Juan met Reyna, in 1991, he was staying with four other guys in a bachelor unit on the top floor of an old apartment house in MacArthur Park, on the corner of Eighth and Alvarado, stitching together a living between restaurant work and a check-kiting ploy. Reyna, who had moved into the building with Giovanni and Israel after their father's death, was rooming with a friend a floor below, subsisting on county benefits. To step into Reyna's life—to assume responsibility for two toddlers, their dad buried in Mexico under mysterious circumstances—had been a noble undertaking. Juan didn't give it a second thought. "I just saw the need that she had," he says. "It was all very improvised."

In the years that followed, Juan often floated the idea of giving the boys his last name, Monroy, especially after their daughter was born and he and Reyna tied the knot downtown, at one of the storefront chapels that line the commercial heart of Broadway. But before formalizing their family unit, Juan thought that Giovanni and Israel should know the truth about their biological dad, and Reyna was never ready to tell them.

What Juan knew about raising kids came mainly from his grandmother, who'd lashed him with a horse whip back in Guatemala. He saw that Giovanni lacked structure and self-restraint, and he blamed Reyna's frailties, the accumulation of upheavals she'd endured, for her inability to impose the boundaries their son needed. But Juan also blamed himself, the weakness for drink he'd come to accept as a family curse. He knew that his binges had fueled the outbursts with Reyna that made their home intolerable—the same violence he'd watched drive his own parents apart. "That's also why I had to distance myself, because I didn't want the kids to see us fight," Juan says. "It's a fucked-up thing to see."

During these easier weekends together, relieved of his duties as disciplinarian, Juan sometimes took Giovanni to mingle with the free spirits of the Venice Boardwalk, and if they encountered a drum circle, Juan would grab some congas and weave his way into the beat. The communal flow of rhythms, meandering, surging, repeating, seemed to transport him to a place Giovanni had rarely glimpsed. "He just went on that little trip, not worrying about nothing, you know, enjoying the moment," Giovanni says. It made him feel good to see his pops like that: unburdened, consoled.

The months after Camp Afflerbaugh had an animating effect on Giovanni too. While doing laundry with Juan at Lucy's Lavanderia, a few blocks south of the park, Giovanni wandered around the corner to a Subway and instantly recognized her: full cheeks, strong forehead, sassy smile. He remembered Mayra Gutierrez from their freshman year at Belmont High. She didn't recall him, not at first, but then he wasn't the same raggedy skater kid; he was Rusty, from 18th Street, with the scalp and ink to prove it. It seemed improbable that a fledgling gangster could wander into a sandwich shop and charm his way into the heart of the teenage girl behind the counter in a single afternoon, but he was making her laugh, projecting a confidence he'd only recently acquired. Giovanni talked to Mayra until the end of her shift, then offered to walk her home. "Which I loved," Mayra says. But then he snapped out of his reverie; there was still laundry to fold. On the spot, Mayra decided, "he was not like other guys."

She lived with her parents and an older sister in a cramped, century-old pink cottage in the shadow of the Harbor Freeway. A brother, who went by Lucky, had joined a clique of 18th Street known as Red Shield, which took its name from a nearby Salvation Army community center. Lucky had been sentenced to sixty-five years to life for a murder few in the neighborhood thought he'd committed—a codefendant had fingered him in a plea deal. Although Mayra wasn't in a gang, she liked Giovanni's look, "probably because I grew up around people like that."

Giovanni fell hard. He doted on Mayra, wrote her poems, bought her lingerie, smooched with her on the Santa Monica Pier. Her parents weren't thrilled about his pursuit of their daughter. But when he wanted to, Giovanni knew how to act proper—to dial up the charm. "I sweet-talked my way in there," he says. Instead of sending him home to Palmdale, Mayra's folks even allowed Giovanni to stay the night, if he remained in the kitchen, on the other side of the curtains that divvied the living room into sleeping quarters. He'd line up some chairs, fashioning a bed from the row of seats. He'd also help with dishes and play with Mayra's young nephew, her sister's son, the product of another 18th Street romance. Giovanni still slipped out to sell dope—he wasn't high enough on the food chain to have traqueteros working for him—but he insisted that Mayra steer clear of that life. He wanted her safe, untainted, though he didn't mind when she tattooed *Rusty* on her bikini line. "He was just, like, a sweetheart," Mayra says.

Romance put Giovanni in a strange bind. His 18th Street credentials had given him an edge with Mayra, but their enchantment was hobbling his ability to live up to the Columbia Lil Cycos' demands. Over the previous year, Giovanni had spent two months in one facility and six months in another, and now free to do the gang's bidding, he was being pulled in another direction. To the extent gangs offered love, it was conditional—hard to earn, easy to lose. The Columbia Lil Cycos maintained their dominance through visibility. They needed gladiators to wear the uniform, patrol the streets, tag the walls, and, for the baddest of them, take preemptive trips onto enemy turf. It was called putting in work, and it was onerous, self-destructive, and nonnegotiable, especially if you were just starting out and hadn't yet demonstrated how crazy and fearless you could be.

During those latter months of 2006, Giovanni's friend Dennis Molina packed his bags, determined to leave LA for a fresh start. He'd avoided gangs, graduating from one of the city's elite public high schools that summer, but still carried the weight of his own family's chaos and felt guilt for failing to keep Giovanni from being dragged down. Dennis paid him a final visit at the new apartment in Palmdale, urging Giovanni to join him in North Carolina. He even offered to buy Giovanni's plane ticket. "Hey, dude, look, I'm leaving," Dennis told him. "Everything here is kind of, like, fucked up. You should come." Giovanni listened, but his mind was elsewhere. "That night," says Dennis, "he was supposed to go to some meeting with some high-ranking 18th Street people, and he missed the meeting to hang out with me."

While Dennis was making his case, the phone rang. "Somebody called him from the gang and started chewing him out, like, 'This is not a game, you know,'" Dennis says. "And his mom overheard it, and being protective, came over and snatched the phone from him and was like, 'How dare you talk to my son like that!'"

Giovanni looked resigned. Dennis did too.

"Dude," he told Giovanni, "you gotta get out of this shit."

6

To Rise above Conformity

U nder Tricky's reign, the vendor tax spread like an algae bloom on the MacArthur Park lake, infecting one block after another without regard for product line. It was too hard to manage collections in the targeted way Baby had envisioned, charging some while exempting others, and too easy to boost revenue by imposing a blanket rule. Los Angeles's municipal code had left the vendors with little recourse, anyway, making it illegal to sell even legal products. The city was taking a cut for itself, too: a fine placed a surcharge on an economic lifeline. The Columbia Lil Cycos were happy to do the same.

The gang started small—five, ten bucks a day—a pinch that most peddlers could absorb without feeling too put out. Many had known corruption in the countries they'd left; if the cost of doing business was paying somebody off, it wouldn't be the first time. It might have stayed that way, a low-key shakedown, except the Columbia Lil Cycos were maximalists: They were so well organized—"like their own government, but on the street," as Officer Hernandez has put it—that the gang inevitably milked from everyone whatever it could. By 2006, the Columbia Lil Cycos were charging an initial buy-in fee to secure a spot on the sidewalk. One vendor paid $400 for her patch of Sixth Street. In the months that followed, the gang also implemented new tax brackets, jacking up the rates to $25 a day, then to $50 on busy weekends. What for many vendors had only stung now brought misery—a loss of maybe half their profits.

Nobody resented this more than Francisco Clemente. He had a dark, leathery face and moist eyes, a trim mustache, and a thick crown of glistening black hair. His voice was low and sputtery, like an idling muscle car, and well geared for the Spanish aphorisms he favored about life and death and God's plans for us, even if he'd switch to English for a useful word like business. "We all have rights, whether you have papers or don't have papers," Francisco says. "We all have the right to have our voice count."

From his youngest days on the streets of Ciudad Nezahualcóyotl, the tempestuous, largely self-built slum on the fringes of Mexico City, Francisco discovered that "life is very hard—very hard is life." After his dad walked out, his mom took a job cleaning government offices, and Francisco learned to fend for himself. In the late 1970s, by the age of eight, he'd begun venturing into the mercado to make himself useful, sweeping floors, hauling trash, and retrieving water, earning a peso or two for his labor. Later, he hopped buses, hawking newspapers and magazines on the fly. School bored him. In Ciudad Neza, Francisco says, "it was one of two things: work or steal." In the 1980s, as a teenager, he crossed the border at Ciudad Acuña, jumping off the international bridge and into the marshy outskirts of Del Rio, Texas, before the border patrol could spot him. For the next decade, he worked in San Antonio: ice factory, lawns and gardens, body shop.

Francisco came to LA in 1998 and found a place in the lowlands of Silver Lake. He continued to refine his automotive skills—hammering out dents, spraying on layers of gloss—and eventually opened a one-man stall near the banks of the Los Angeles River that he called Transformer Auto Repair. He dreamed of expanding, of someday buying and selling used cars, but lacked the capital to build an inventory. "When you start at the bottom and don't have money," Francisco explains, "you have to invest." To build a bankroll, he reprised the hustles of his youth and headed downtown, to the cheapie electronics wholesalers near Skid Row. Earphones, MP4 players, iPhone cases—you could buy them by the dozen and sell them individually at a 50 percent markup. And so in the early days of the twenty-first century, Francisco began to moonlight as a vendor, closing up his repair shop at 4 or 5 P.M. and then putting in another four or five hours on the streets between the Toy

District and the Garment District, trusting in his own ingenuity. "I don't like being a conformist," he says. "I've always tried to get ahead, to rise above conformity."

Francisco enjoyed the bustling sidewalks, the clamor of familiar voices, the immediacy of placing a product in a customer's hands and touching their money with his own. The vendors along Los Angeles Street formed a provisional community, congregating and disbanding day after day, and he soon felt himself drawn to one of them, a young woman with sleepy eyes and an elastic smile. "I don't know, I just kept looking at her and looking at her," he says.

Her name was Jessica Guzman, and she was from Mexico City too, raised in the borough of Iztapalapa. Like Francisco, Jessica had worked from an early age, selling sweets outside the men's prison known as Reclusorio Norte. In LA she was on her own, barely twenty, and living in a pay-by-the-week hotel with a friend, Daniela Garcia, who was in an even more desperate state. Just four foot nine and ninety-eight pounds, Daniela had recently become pregnant by another vendor; the minute he'd learned he was going to be a father, he'd run out on her. The two roommates were selling imitation perfume when they crossed paths with Francisco, who was thirty-five, steadier and more reliable than the wolves that prowled the old city after-hours. "For some reason I like this guy," Jessica told herself.

The three of them became a team: Francisco and Jessica started a romance; Daniela—pobrecita, Francisco called her—leaned on them for support. Their nightly tour of the downtown circuit, however, didn't last long. The sidewalks they plied overlapped with LA's gray-market apparel trade, anchored by the medina-like stalls of Santee Alley, a counterfeit fashion mother lode. It was a special enforcement target of the LAPD, which assigned a decorated officer to crack down on outlaw vendors and spruce up the streets. The officer pledged to make shopping there, as he told *California Apparel News* in 2006, "like going to Rodeo Drive." Francisco had several run-ins with this cop, who ordered him to pack up and get out. If he saw Francisco again, he would ticket him—even arrest him, if Francisco kept flouting his commands. "I've always been a man who, if I can avoid a problem, I will," Francisco says.

He told Jessica and Daniela that they should try their luck elsewhere, in a place with more foot traffic and more opportunity, where the hurly-burly of the immigrant economy was harder for the city to contain. They would give it a go on MacArthur Park's chockablock Sixth Street corridor. "Don't stress, if you want to bring your things over there, let's go, I'll take you," Francisco proposed. "There, you're going to sell very tranquilly."

They started a new routine. After a full day at Transformer Auto Repair, Francisco would hop in his truck and make what had become a roundabout commute: a dozen miles east, out the San Bernardino Freeway, to a back-alley tire shop in El Monte. As Daniela's belly swelled, Francisco had taken it on himself to find her and Jessica a cheaper, less erratic place to live than a weekly hotel. A friend he knew from the car business said the women could stay in the laundry room adjoining his shop; it was a pitiful solution, but the price was right. They put a mattress on the floor next to the sink.

It was another fifteen miles west, back to MacArthur Park, a trip that Francisco then had to repeat in reverse at the end of the night. The vending life was struggle enough without adding a fifty-mile loop. "It's not easy being a humble man, an upright man," says Francisco, who was living with his mother at the time. "Believe me, it costs a lot. When you want to act right and do good things, that's often when the heaviest things come your way."

Francisco chose a spot on the north side of Sixth, toward the east end of the block between Bonnie Brae and Burlington, not more than five hundred feet from where Giovanni had lived before his mom's move to Palmdale. It was directly in front of Ace Cash Express, a payday lender that would later fork out $10 million to settle claims that its debt-collection practices created a "culture of coercion." From there a row of other squat storefronts extended west, from Video Mania to Juice Max to H&R Block, which then abutted the International Mall and Unico's Tattoos. Francisco would drop Jessica and Daniela off at the curb, where they would unload their backpacks, then park across the street in the same Food 4 Less lot that Giovanni had explored in his skate days. They laid a red tablecloth on the pavement to display their wares—a routine that both established boundaries and created an instant bale should the police run them off.

Francisco had figured there would be safety in numbers, and compared to downtown, he wasn't wrong. The Sixth Street crowds were so dense, the vendors so tightly packed, his little operation didn't attract much attention, at least not from the LAPD. MacArthur Park offered a lesson in what sociologists call "quiet encroachment" or the "art of presence," the steady creep of ordinary people into disputed spaces when economic survival demands it. A form of silent protest. But noncompliance with vending laws didn't make MacArthur Park a free-trade zone. In the absence of legislation that addressed the precarity of immigrant life—in a country that refused to offer the undocumented a path to legal recognition, in a city that rejected the cultural practice of selling goods on the street—the Columbia Lil Cycos imposed rules of their own. Wherever Francisco turned, there was someone demanding la renta for a swatch of public sidewalk.

The gang didn't have to work hard to enforce its scheme. Sixth Street came with an invisible map, one that outsiders would have mistaken for chaos. To sell there was to place-make, to construct an unplanned city with its own mechanisms for allocating space and assigning rights. Repetition pre-empted most boundary disputes. By reassembling week after week, year after year, the vendors already knew who was most senior, who belonged where, and who was trying to horn in. A newcomer who didn't offer tribute to the Columbia Lil Cycos was just as likely to be outed by the other vendors as pegged by the gang itself. It didn't take long for everyone on Sixth Street to know Francisco as el chilango, the headstrong Mexico City dude.

"If we have to pay something to do business, I think really it would be the government we're accountable to," Francisco says, "not somebody who's nobody."

To avoid handling cash in public view, the Columbia Lil Cycos dragooned newer immigrants into collecting rent from the Sixth Street vendors.

Sometimes the gang enlisted the vendors themselves to serve as collectors. A paisa would be easy to overlook, easy to replace.

The Columbia Lil Cycos installed one guy known as Barrios, who'd begun selling DVDs in MacArthur Park shortly after his arrival from Mexico in 2003. The gang framed it as an opportunity: collect rent and have your own rent waived. The LAPD had already cited Barrios for illegal vending in 2005—sticking him with a fine of $150, a restitution fee of $100, and a court security assessment of $20—so the gang's proposal would at least offset the cost of any future tickets. Whenever Barrios approached the trio of Francisco Clemente, Jessica Guzman, and Daniela Garcia, he adopted the roundabout language of la mordida, familiar to anyone who's ever bribed their way out of a jam in Mexico. "He would say to us, 'Hey, what happened with the stuff for the soda?'" Jessica says. "'What happened with the delivery?'"

The other rent collector, known as Atlas, was recruited by Baby. Atlas wasn't a gangster or a vendor. He worked for a demolition company: gutting commercial interiors with picks and hammers, breathing in drywall dust and insulation fibers. In his early thirties, Atlas had a jowly face, with cheeks out to his ears, a helmet of black hair, and a matching mustache. A devotee of Guadalajara's underdog soccer team, the Atlas Fútbol Club, he'd often show up at a Sixth Street billiards hall in a red, black, and white jersey or a cap with an embroidered *A*, which was enough to cement his nickname. "Just a regular dude," Baby says. "A guy with a job."

At one point Baby asked if he could join Atlas's demo crew; he needed to show his probation officer that he'd been working. "I did it, I got him hired," Atlas says. But after one sixteen-hour day, Baby was wrecked. "He got off work and couldn't even walk," Atlas says. "He wasn't accustomed."

Atlas had lived something of a double life: tough and industrious yet malleable and rash. Since arriving in the US as a teenager in 1989, he'd done the work that machines couldn't on their own—thread trimmer at a garment factory, polyethylene resin handler at a plastic bag manufacturer, executioner at a pork processor—sacrificing his body to repetitive tasks. Atlas also chased quick money. Although Baby saw him as an immigrant laborer, Atlas had been a mule, unloading bags of cash from a plane in Georgia and retrieving a truckload of cocaine from Arizona. He'd played the squatter in an auto insurance scam, cutting off cars and bracing for the impact. Back home in Tecalitlán, Jalisco—the cradle of mariachi, he was forever reminding folks—Atlas had harvested both corn and cannabis. He was susceptible to epileptic seizures, like his father, who'd died after suffering a convulsion on the job at a lumber mill, but that hadn't stopped Atlas from strapping himself to the back of a bull and competing on the Mexican ranch circuit. "I still remember the scolding my mother gave me: 'Devil child, what the hell are you doing?'" Atlas says. "'Don't be a pendejo, you little cabrón. Can't you see that an animal like that can kill you!'"

Without quite understanding what he'd signed up for, Atlas started making the Sixth Street rounds sometime between 2005 and 2006, mainly the one-block stretch between Burlington and Bonnie Brae, from Ace Cash Express, with its giant yellow PAYDAY LOANS banner, to the International Mall, where the phone number for Unico's Tattoos was stenciled on the white brick facade. He saw himself more as a facilitator than a taxman. The vendors already knew they had to pay up—Atlas was just around to help keep them current. "I never mistreated anyone," he says. "I never used crude language. I always tried to make sure people felt comfortable and not intimidated." To demonstrate his finesse, he pantomimes one hand slipping folded bills into the other while shaking it at the same time. "And they were all happy with me."

Whenever a vendor was short on cash, says Atlas, he'd even try to cover for them. "They'd say to me, 'Right now, I don't have any,' and I'd tell them, 'That's fine, don't worry. If somebody asks, just tell them you already gave it to Atlas.'" As he saw it, the Columbia Lil Cycos were never that precise about how much they were due; they cared more about their dominance over the neighborhood than the pocket money the vendors generated. Of the $700 he'd collect most weekends, the gang would pay him $150—and even then, he'd break off a bit more for himself without anyone being the wiser. The vendors greased Atlas with freebies: CDs, tacos, whatever else caught his eye. "I did like watching movies, so sometimes they'd say, 'Hey, you want this disc? It's the very latest.' And they'd give it to me—always of their own volition."

If Atlas imagined himself a moderating force, maintaining the equilibrium out on Sixth Street, Francisco Clemente was proving to be a vendor unlike any the Columbia Lil Cycos had ever encountered. Francisco ponied up at first. Sometimes he offered partial payments. More than once, he promised to pay after he'd made a few sales and had profits to share. But he'd scrapped for too many years, endured too many indignities, to now surrender to a shakedown by Atlas and Barrios—people who looked like him.

As a man of faith, it would not have been lost on Francisco that the rent collectors of MacArthur Park had a biblical analog: the tax collectors of ancient Rome. They were loathed two thousand years ago, lumped in with thieves and prostitutes and other sinners not just because they were squeezing a distant province on behalf of a militaristic empire. The tax collectors were traitors, sticking it to their own countrymen. "Many people accept injustice," Francisco says. "At times, you don't have any other choice. But a moment arrives when you can't. You just can't. It's too much."

7

Do Something

A year into gang life, Giovanni was a washout. He didn't have the icy soul of a combatant or the financial moxie of a racketeer. Giovanni mostly enjoyed belonging—kicking it, as he'd put it. For him, the Columbia Lil Cycos were the ultimate fraternity, a secret society that served his need for kinship and release.

Tricky wasn't having it. As shotcaller, he drew his power from what he could extract from those beneath him, from people eager to commit violence or extort money. The little homies "can't just stand around here and not do anything—you know, live off the neighborhood," Tricky says. "You've got to put in your work. You've got to basically come up." He couldn't see what Giovanni was doing for him or for the hood; the kid didn't even live there anymore. Tricky considered Giovanni so ineffectual, he'd begun chewing on the possibility that this rookie on his team might be a snitch—beholden to the cops. Or at least Tricky found an advantage in spreading that rumor. It steamed Giovanni. All he could think was that someone had spotted him speaking with Officer Hernandez—the gang cop was forever pulling up on Giovanni, warning him that he still had time to avoid trouble. Giovanni hadn't ratted anyone out. Still, being labeled a snitch was a slur that he couldn't easily disprove, one that jeopardized his place in the Columbia Lil Cycos, putting him at risk of banishment or worse.

When Giovanni showed up at Unico's Tattoos after his release from camp, Tricky booted him out. On an October day in 2006, Giovanni tried calling.

"Unico's Tattoos," Tricky answered.

"Hey, fool," said Giovanni.

"Who's this?" asked Tricky.

"Me, Rusty, fool. I'm going to drop by your shop right now, alright?"

"For what?"

"To go kick it, fool."

"What? Nigga, you better go gangbang around the hood or do something instead of coming over here."

"Uh, damn. Are you mad at me?"

"You call me fool and you talk nonsense on the phone, dog. Instead of being outside gangbanging, homie—you're trying to make friends and shit."

"No, fool, no—"

"You know?"

"—hey, fool, well, I—"

"What, what, what? Come on, dog. Get the fuck with it, fool."

It was a low point for Giovanni. He felt slighted, misunderstood. But there was bigger trouble. Tricky's phone had been bugged. The FBI was listening in.

8

I Am Real

At the very moment that Giovanni was straining to gain Tricky's favor, Tricky was laboring to win an endorsement of his own, and from a patron he'd never met. Tricky called him Tío. Others have known him as Dad. To some, he is Pancho Villa. Because he has a strawberry splotch over his left eye that bears a faint resemblance to Mikhail Gorbachev's birthmark, a few call him Gorby. Or the Spanish word for a blemish: Mancha. The one name that everybody knows Francisco Ruiz Martinez by is Puppet. It is usually uttered in voz baja, whispered as if it could place a curse on whoever were to invoke it cavalierly.

In 2006, at the age of forty-three, Puppet had a beaver pelt of a mustache, a square buzz cut that had begun to gray, and a gaze so icy even a photo of him could make you squirm. The ink across his torso announced a messianic commitment to the life he'd constructed: a two-headed serpent coiled into the letter *M* tattooed across the base of his throat, a weeping, thorn-crowned Jesus on his right breast, the *XVIII* logo in the center, and over his abdomen, an approximation of the Aztec deity Tonatiuh, tongue out and clawed hands gripping human hearts.

"Men and loyal soldiers aren't made or borrowed," Puppet once told the Columbia Lil Cycos in a letter from prison. "We're born that way. True from birth."

Anywhere from 10 to 30 percent of the rent the Columbia Lil Cycos collected—from the vendors, the traqueteros, the miqueros, and everyone else in MacArthur Park subject to the gang's machinations—went every week to Puppet, even though he hadn't set foot on those streets in more than a decade. Puppet controlled the whole scheme from a thousand miles away, from the most restrictive environment the federal government could devise: ADX Florence, the Alcatraz of the Rockies.

Home to a murderers' row of terrorists and traffickers, from the Shoe Bomber to (at the time) the Unabomber to (more recently) El Chapo, the prison—known simply as Supermax—stood on thirty-seven acres of lonely, treeless scrub in Florence, Colorado, about a hundred miles from Denver. It had the look of a Martian colony: interlocking steel triangles ringed by mirrored-glass gun towers and connected by subterranean corridors. A twelve-foot razor wire fence encircled the complex, rigged with motion sensors, pressure pads, and 1,400 remote-controlled doors. Puppet spent twenty-two hours a day alone in a twelve-by-seven-foot soundproof cell with a poured-concrete bed and a four-inch-wide window that revealed only the sky. His meals were delivered through a slot. He bathed alone under a time-controlled shower-head. His mail was screened, his calls were taped, and his visits, even with his lawyer, were conducted in front of a camera. The whole arrangement was designed to defeat and disorient, to clinically shrink the world of its inhabit-ants. A former warden called Supermax "a clean version of hell."

The psychological effects of prolonged solitary confinement have been well documented: obsessive thoughts, memory loss, panic attacks, and paranoia, often culminating in psychosis and suicidal ideation. Supermax breaks men. But not Puppet. It was almost as if the more dehumanizing the strategies of the government's penological experts, the more clarity Puppet gained. Confinement simplified his goals, focused his imagination.

"Life is what you make of it," he wrote in a 2006 letter. "You will run into a few bumps, but that's when you continue to learn and move forward."

Puppet, the puller of the Columbia Lil Cycos' strings, derived power from his membership in the American prison gang that calls itself the Mexican Mafia (or la Eme, Spanish for *M*). Founded in the 1950s by Mexican Ameri-can inmates seeking to defend themselves against racial violence in California's prisons, the Eme functioned as a gang of gangs, an alliance of street gang members from across dozens of rival Los Angeles barrios who agreed to set aside local beefs and band together as a united force behind bars. To become an Eme carnal—a soul brother, of sorts—a candidate had to demonstrate ruthlessness and devotion. This meant a willingness to kill on command: to shank another inmate without knowing or asking why. It also required an expansive view of what the human body could conceal; a soldier who learned to "keister" a blade in his rectum would never be caught unarmed.

Some Eme carnales learned Náhuatl, Mexico's principal Indigenous tongue, to communicate among themselves without tipping off guards. Others taught themselves American Sign Language. One Eme boss specialized in blanketing his outgoing correspondence in thick pencil marks that when erased by the recipient, revealed messages in tiny, fine-point ink. The reading list required for initiation—texts such as Sun Tzu's *The Art of War* and seventeenth-century swordsman Miyamoto Musashi's *Book of Five Rings*—speaks to how the syndicate sees itself: as battlefield strategists and underworld psychologists, as masters over conflict. "I mean, these are things that our corporate leaders read," says Richard Valdemar, a retired sergeant in the Los Angeles County Sheriff's Department who spent years infiltrating the Eme. "It's our mistake to think that they're just stupid thugs."

There were never more than three hundred to five hundred inducted Eme members, but their zeal for warring with white supremacist and Black militant organizations promised a measure of protection to the rest of the Latino inmate population. The Eme's readiness to turn against its own, meanwhile, helped limit internal dissent. The threat of violence also allowed the Mexican Mafia to control the hyperinflated market for drugs that thrives in California's jails and prisons: to both direct the traffic in contraband and levy a tax on the traffickers. In an environment without formal procedures for enforcing property rights and restraining opportunistic behavior, the Mexican Mafia served as an "extralegal governance institution," in the parlance of political economists. It was an analytical, albeit brutal, response to a genuine demand for order.

As California's prison population surged, quadrupling between 1980 and 1990, Latino inmates reached a plurality of 45 percent. A younger Eme cohort—they came to be known as the Pepsi generation—saw an opportunity to exploit their demographic clout and flex their muscle beyond prison walls. Southern California comprised six hundred to seven hundred Hispanic street gangs, from Los Angeles to Riverside, Bakersfield to San Diego, and as many as a hundred thousand street gang members, spreading incomprehensible misery. LA gangs alone killed upward of eight hundred people a year in those days. If the carnales could impose order on that chaos, pushing the gangs to prioritize financial gain and requiring them to kick up a share of their earnings, the Eme would transform into a true mafia. "It was then that I realized, this is a gold mine, a real gold mine," says Rene "Boxer" Enriquez, an Eme defector who helped conceive of the expansion. "We were high school dropouts, but we were implementing these *Fortune 500* business practices: horizontal leadership, vertical integration, profit sharing, franchising, brand recognition, market exclusivity."

The Mexican Mafia rolled out the plan in the early 1990s, summoning thousands of street gang leaders to conclaves in parks across Southern California. As an organizing effort, it was beyond audacious: armies of nihilistic young people had to be convinced to surrender a portion of the drug money passing through their neighborhoods to an insular circle of mythical figures based in far-off institutions who operated largely out of sight. The Eme couched the maneuver in ethnic pride. It ordered the gangs to stop drive-by shootings; reckless violence hurt communities and attracted police attention. Business thrived on stability. Every carnal would be granted his own domain, often the same turf on which he first earned his gang bona fides, and every gang would have to tax itself on behalf of a carnal if it wanted to remain in good standing. There was really no choice. As long as the Eme controlled life on the inside—and as long as gang members recognized that they or their loved ones faced a reasonable chance of incarceration—the Eme could also control life on the outside. The Mexican Mafia wasn't going anywhere. If a homie on the streets refused to break bread, the carnales would be waiting.

Puppet had come up through 18th Street's founding clique, in the Pico-Union district, near the namesake street itself. Compared to other Mexican Mafia overlords, who tended to be US-born graduates of old-time Chicano gangs, Puppet was from Mexico. "A bit of a paisa, very little education, with a thick accent," says Rene Enriquez, who met him in 1984 at the San Joaquin Valley's Deuel Vocational Institution, where Puppet was serving his first prison sentence, six years for manslaughter. Neither was a made Eme member at the time, but both were auditioning. When the carnales ordered the duo to carry out a hit, to punish another inmate for some unspecified act of disrespect or cowardice, Enriquez found their target on the handball courts and perforated him with the sharpened tip of a paint-roller handle, while Puppet held the victim in a bear hug from behind.

Puppet returned to prison on a car theft case in 1992, just as the Eme was leaning on the gangs to pay tribute. He initially resisted the drive-by ban, believing it both impractical and antithetical to a warrior mentality. But when violence dipped in the aftermath of the edict, and the carnales began carving up gang turf like prospectors, Puppet came around. He grasped the economic potential of a neighborhood as thickly populated as MacArthur Park, and while he'd never directly belonged to the Columbia Lil Cycos, he had 18th Street cred and the blessing of an older Eme boss with Marine Corps training. By the time Giovanni started kindergarten, Puppet had installed himself as the Columbia Lil Cycos' godfather.

Puppet had come to the US without papers, and upon his parole in 1994, the government deported him to Mexico. Of all the attempts to stymie Puppet, this might have been the most futile. He returned within days. The police soon learned he was staying in the working-class suburb of Huntington Park, at the home of his wife, Janie Maria Garcia, a zealous facilitator known to the Columbia Lil Cycos as Mom or Lady Boss. Most carnales had a woman on the outside—a network of señoras—to serve as a go-between: communicating orders, safeguarding cash, assessing loyalties. "I got involved in his world," Janie Garcia would say in an online Christian testimonial. "I was running amok." When the cops raided the place, they found a Colt .45, a bulletproof vest, and a stun gun. Puppet told officers that if he'd known they were coming, he "would have shot it out" with them.

Back in custody, Puppet was indicted on weapon and immigration charges. He took a deal, pleading to a sentence of about seven years, and was shipped to a series of federal pens: Oxford, Wisconsin; Oklahoma City, Oklahoma; Marion, Illinois. The government believed that removing carnales from California and spreading them around the country would help splinter the Eme. It only broadened the Eme's reach.

In 2000, as his release date neared, Puppet was indicted again, this time in a case that made headlines—a federal RICO prosecution against twenty-six members of the Columbia Lil Cycos that revealed the wealth he'd siphoned out of the neighborhood. It was the first time that the Racketeer Influenced and Corrupt Organization laws, designed during the Nixon years to combat Mob-related crime, had been used against a Los Angeles street gang. The RICO Act gives the feds a powerful penalty enhancer, allowing them to piece together seemingly unrelated crimes that alone might not have triggered long sentences and to prosecute them under the banner of a broad conspiracy. An individual defendant could thus face a severe prison term for "carrying on" an organization's pattern of racketeering, even if he didn't commit a particular crime himself.

RICO cases took years to investigate. That made them well suited for the FBI, which didn't have to chase radio calls like a municipal police force. The LAPD—which believed it could handle anything—typically didn't appreciate being bigfooted by an organization that answered to Washington. To Los Angeles cops, FBI agents were "accountants with guns." The feds often recruited local officers for assistance, but there was no doubt about who was in charge: even before the FBI dug into the Rampart scandal, agents had probed the LAPD's 1991 beating of Rodney King. They hesitated to bring "cowboys" into sophisticated investigations.

Starting in 1998, the FBI set out to dismantle the Columbia Lil Cycos, "piece by piece, brick by brick, street by street, corner by corner, house by house, room by room, person by person," as the federal prosecutor in the case would tell a Los Angeles jury. Agents conducted surveillance, bugged phones, intercepted mail, and posed as scavengers to sift through trash cans. They parsed Puppet's letters, eavesdropped on his conversations. They tracked deliveries of rent money from MacArthur Park directly to Janie Garcia's house in Huntington Park and another she owned in the largely Asian suburb of Monterey Park. They learned that Puppet taxed everything, even the settlement that a Columbia Lil Cyco received for a beatdown at the hands of Rampart officers. The city had paid the gangster $231,000; Puppet demanded $20,000 of it. When the FBI finally secured warrants to search his wife's houses, agents expected to find a hidden safe or a trapdoor under the carpet. Instead, Puppet's bankroll was tucked away in an upright vacuum cleaner parked in the closet; more was in a cardboard box next to the dresser. The top bill in each bundle had the name of the street captain who'd collected it scrawled on the face, a gangster accounting technique. In all, Puppet was hoarding $450,000 in cash.

The raids provoked spasms of paranoia. Puppet became convinced he had a snitch on his hands. The finger-pointing finally landed on the Columbia Lil Cycos' shotcaller of the day, a steadfast camarada named Termite whose business sense had grown the neighborhood's revenues and padded Puppet's riches.

"Se tiene que fumigar," Puppet wrote from prison. Termite had to be fumigated.

It didn't take long for Puppet's loyalists to riddle Termite's car with bullets as he and his driver left S&A Auto Sales on LA's south side, a dealership Termite had set up to launder the gang's earnings. Shot in the leg, wrist, and hand, Termite didn't die. A week later, when Puppet called Janie Garcia from prison, the FBI was listening.

"You know how the house has termites?" Janie asked him. Oldies hummed in the background: *Young girl . . . You better run, girl.*

"Yeah," drawled Puppet.

"You know, they fumigated it, but I don't know—I think the termites are back," she said.

"Yeah," Puppet said again.

Before Puppet could finish the job, the FBI swooped in and arrested Termite, convincing him to testify for the government. Puppet's misplaced suspicions had created a nemesis.

In 2002, when the RICO case went to trial in Los Angeles federal court, only four defendants sat at the defense table: Puppet, his wife, and two lieutenants. The other twenty-odd targets had taken deals. Puppet's lawyer argued that his client couldn't possibly be controlling the streets of MacArthur Park from a penitentiary, much less one out of state. "When you're in prison, you're literally in the dark," the lawyer told the jury. "Once you're inside those walls, a very harsh environment, that's a situation, a case of survival, mere survival in the most hostile, vicious environment you can imagine or maybe can't imagine." He went on: "It's brutal. You are certainly concerned enough with your own survival in prison to where the street isn't anymore a concern of yours, nor are you anymore the concern of the people on the street."

Half of this was true: prison leaves no room for error. But the lawyer (who'd later die in a murder-suicide after shooting his paralegal) sold his client short. Puppet—who ended up receiving life plus sixty years—had uncommon abilities as a communicator and a manipulator, a talent for pushing buttons and smoking out frailties. Running a complex, multimillion-dollar organization while incarcerated takes more than brute force. "It's about interacting and networking with people, cultivating relationships, and fostering loyalty, and Puppet's quite frankly really good at it," Rene Enriquez says. "That's just being, like, a people person."

Puppet wrote hundreds of letters a year, usually to remind his people in MacArthur Park that he still called the shots and to line up replacements when his regulars fell short. He mixed Spanish with English, elegant cursive with jagged printing, and concocted his own coded terms: an "affidavit" was a report on his revenue streams, a "higher court judge" meant a fellow Eme brother, and a "magazine"—as in the ones he expected to arrive by mail—stood for $100.

To keep allies close, Puppet did a lot of buttering up. He assured one of his shotcallers: "Like I said before and I'll say it now, even though I'm gone, in my heart you will always be." To a female associate mired in a toxic relationship, he noted that "any man in their right mind would appreciate a good lil lady such as you." Puppet was especially adept at guilt trips. "It seems you no longer have time for your godfather or am I imagining things?"; "Just a lil worried about you. I'm still alive"; "What do you want your uncle to think if you leave him hanging?"; "Thank you for your letter. I was very happy to hear from you since you had disappeared." And he wasn't above a little humor at his own expense, noting that in his current state, without "vicios o viejas"—vices or chicks—"I could even be a priest."

But when Puppet turned serious, there was no camouflaging the menace: "I am real and will always do what is needed when needed."

He knew that shotcallers were fungible; they came and went. Puppet had never even met most of them. So he was forever nudging each new proxy to put business first, to give it their all before the odds caught up with them. "I never change," he proclaimed in one letter. "You guys are the ones who change." After ascending to shotcaller, Tricky often wrote back to Puppet, vowing to stay focused, updating his phone number, apologizing for his poor Spanish. Tricky wanted Puppet to see his potential—to recognize him as a carnal in training, worthy of an invitation to the Mexican Mafia.

"I hope things are better in school," Puppet wrote to him in 2006, an oblique nod to Tricky's ambitions. He used long dramatic strokes for the tails and arms of his letters, especially the *y*'s and *t*'s, which made every sheet of paper look as if it had been slashed. "You know that if you don't do good in school you're not going to get ahead," Puppet added, "but I know you'll make it."

It was classic Puppet: paternal yet ominous, supportive as long as his interests were served. He signed it: "Love always, your uncle."

9

Why Do We Have to Pay?

There was one vendor nobody charged, a fourteen-year-old girl with round cheeks and a strong chin who worked the sidewalk outside the International Mall. The Columbia Lil Cycos considered her off-limits. She was five foot one. Everyone called her Shorty.

Shorty was the daughter of Guatemalan vendors who'd ventured to Sixth Street from the Akateko-speaking highlands of Huehuetenango, eight thousand feet up in the misty Sierra de los Cuchumatanes—a journey out of genocide. Guatemala's military dictatorship, with training from the CIA, had waged a scorched-earth campaign against the region's Indigenous communities in the 1980s, seeking to eradicate a base of support for the leftist insurgents who called themselves the Ejército Guerrillero de los Pobres. The sister municipalities that Shorty's family left, San Miguel Acatán and San Rafael La Independencia, suffered repeated massacres. On an August day in 1981, the army slaughtered fifteen villagers in San Miguel Acatán after forcing them to dig their own graves; that October, the military stripped and tortured nineteen men from the hamlets around San Miguel, then executed them in an old copper mine. Shorty was born in Los Angeles eleven years later.

Shorty's mom, Juana Matias, rented a stall at the Selecto, an indoor swap meet on the southeast corner of Sixth and Bonnie Brae that faced the International Mall, an investment that qualified her as a brick-and-mortar merchant. The shop was even registered with the Los Angeles office of finance. But she and her husband didn't distinguish between a licensed booth under a roof and the ad-libbed marketplace of the pavement outside, and so they did both, officially conducting business as Juanita's inside the Selecto while also setting up several unsanctioned outposts on the Sixth Street sidewalk.

Shorty had been out there with them, selling cut-price electronics, ever since she was in kindergarten. On weekdays, she joined her parents after school, from four-thirty to nine; on weekends, she started at 11 A.M. Whenever the LAPD's Edgar Hernandez cruised by, he'd see her and stop, marveling at the sacrifices that MacArthur Park's immigrants made just to get by. "She had a little chair, and she was always doing her homework, like, on the sidewalk, always there," Hernandez says. He'd shout to her parents: "Hey, what are you doing? Take her home."

Shorty wasn't a gang associate or anyone's girl, but she knew all the Columbia Lil Cycos, at least their monikers. They treated her with a mix of protectiveness and flirtation. Baby had a younger brother—an 18th Streeter known as Clever—and he more than anyone showered Shorty with attention, offering advice, even slipping her money. "Nothing sexual, just trying to take care of her as a sister," says Clever, who was then eighteen. "Mostly encouragement, like 'Go to school, stay in school, hard work pays off.' It's funny, I was talking about education, and I wasn't even getting one myself."

Shorty walked a fine line: chatty with the police, obliging to the gang. Officer Hernandez would use her as a scout. "Just me asking her, 'Hey, have you seen this guy? Who was he with?'" says Hernandez, who as a gang officer didn't concern himself with the city's anti-vending ordinance. "She never thought she was helping me out. She just thought she was being friendly." The Columbia Lil Cycos played the same game, asking Shorty which officers were on duty and when she had last seen them. The vendors, who had their own issues with the police, relied on Shorty too: whenever the LAPD's beat cops ratcheted up their cat-and-mouse game, she'd serve as a lookout, alerting the Sixth Street vendors to the patrols. "'Cause the cops, they used to go bug people that did illegal vending," she says. "Cops used to come after us." At one point, Atlas and a member of the Columbia Lil Cycos approached Shorty's dad for money. Andres Matias chided the gang for shaking down the vendors instead of helping the vendors avoid the police. "You're not even taking care of us or, you know, nothing of LAPD, nothing," he told them. "So why do we have to pay you?"

Because of Shorty, the Matiases could get away with deflecting the Columbia Lil Cycos. But not Francisco Clemente. The more he balked—stalling, dodging, haggling, protesting—the more he frustrated and embarrassed the rent collectors. His resistance threatened their authority as emissaries of the gang; it would be better for them all to avoid an escalation. Atlas, in keeping with his self-image as an affable go-between, tried to talk him down, but Francisco refused to play along. "He got too big for his britches," Atlas says. "He wanted to be the hero."

Francisco was trying to build a business, to prove that anyone could get ahead with some sweat and pluck. He also felt protective of the two young women he'd introduced to MacArthur Park, both more vulnerable than he. Daniela's baby would be due soon. The father still hadn't surfaced. Jessica couldn't be certain yet, but her body was telling her she might be pregnant, too—a first for her and Francisco. Whatever they made on Sixth Street was no longer just about the three of them; they'd have to stretch their earnings to now sustain two little ones.

Alerted to the problem, the Columbia Lil Cycos sought the chilango out. Francisco refused to be intimidated. They told him to pay up. He told them to get lost.

"The street is for everybody," he proclaimed. "The street is for whoever is there."

It was a small act of defiance, unseen beyond that one block of Sixth Street, but a stand as courageous as anyone, anywhere in Los Angeles, likely took that day. Francisco didn't know which members of the Columbia Lil Cycos he'd addressed, but they couldn't possibly have imagined that a mere paisa, an "illegal" immigrant doing "illegal" work, would spurn a squad of tattooed soldiers, much less in a public manner. Francisco's resolve inspired

Daniela to get in a jab of her own. She cradled her belly. "Can't you see I'm pregnant?" she scolded. "You want to take money from my baby?"

The gangsters, likely stunned, offered a rote warning: "Everyone pays. If you're not going to pay, then get out, and we'll put someone here who will."

That probably would have been enough to convince another vendor to move along. There was no way to take on the Columbia Lil Cycos single-handedly and not suffer some kind of repercussion. Maybe if the hundreds of vendors on Sixth and the hundreds more on Alvarado felt empowered to rally behind Francisco and his two companions, if the whole mass of them had the civic footing to unite and resist, then he might have stood a chance. If LA had not criminalized street vending decades earlier—if he hadn't already been harassed downtown by the cops—then maybe Francisco would have turned to the LAPD. Instead, Francisco dug in his heels. He was so invested in the righteousness of his cause, in a version of manhood that did not allow for retreat, he blinded himself to the showdown that loomed.

The Columbia Lil Cycos again spotted Francisco with Jessica and Daniela out on Sixth Street. A group, maybe six or seven of them, surrounded him, glaring and taunting.

"Give me fifty bucks, motherfucker," one of them growled. If he didn't pay or leave, the gangster said, they'd jack all his stuff.

"I'd like to see who's going to be the first person to take my things," Francisco replied. "If you strip me of them, then they're yours, you can take them. But believe me, I'm not going to allow you to take anything. Because this is mine, and I'm the one who paid for it all."

One of the gangsters got up in Francisco's face, poised to throw the first punch. Francisco pulled a knife from his front pocket. He sliced the air. *Fwsshhh, fwsshhh.*

"I don't want problems," Francisco said.

Another gangster started to make a move. Francisco pivoted.

"And you, cabrón?" Francisco snapped.

By drawing a knife, Francisco might as well have declared war. He was standing his ground, an act of self-defense, but also publicly provoking a crisis, challenging the whole odious scheme. The Columbia Lil Cycos backed off when they saw the blade, but they had to be wondering: Was the chilango really prepared to kill for the right to do business on Sixth Street? Was he prepared to die?

10

The Drama

At the end of 2006, a month after Tricky hung up on him, Giovanni was arrested again—his third case in little more than a year. He'd been riding with a crew of 18th Streeters when the LAPD stopped their car in Hollywood. Giovanni was already on probation for violating the gang ordinance. The juvenile court gave him another six months, this time at Camp Mendenhall, a detention facility in the Sierra Pelona, where the Pacific Crest Trail bends toward Mojave.

LA's juvenile camps bordered on the dysfunctional, plagued by years of excessive force, sexual assault, and substandard medical and mental-health care. The US Justice Department's civil rights division had begun investigating the Los Angeles County Probation Department that same year, ultimately obliging the agency to accept a federal consent decree—just as it had done to the LAPD. Giovanni made the most of his time. The staff praised his "positive attitude"; he took anger management classes, enrolled in GED prep, and accepted a job in the kitchen. He also thought constantly about Mayra, concocting grown-up scenarios that featured her at his side, perhaps someday with a baby. "Well, about me going back to my old ways . . . ," Giovanni wrote to her. "When I get out, I'll try my best to stay away from my barrio."

Maybe Palmdale wouldn't be so bad if Mayra was with him. She'd be a good reason to shape up. Giovanni turned eighteen on June 11, 2007, his second birthday in a row behind barbed wire, and he didn't want to do it again. His mom agreed. "I thought he'd stay home," Reyna says, "if I let her move in." Giovanni was released on June 27. Although her parents protested, Mayra left for Palmdale within a week or so. Reyna even gave them their own bedroom; she could sleep with Giovanni's sister. And for a month or so, it worked.

They went to the movies together as a family. They barbecued. Mayra was hired at the Subway inside the Antelope Valley Mall, where Reyna had found work as a janitor. Giovanni landed a legit job, too, stocking the shelves at a nearby discount store called Factory 2-U. He blew a whole paycheck on some Air Jordans, the Black Cat edition: one pair for him, a matching pair for Mayra. "I was responsible for the first time, making decent money, staying out of trouble—and I had my girl," Giovanni says. "We had a good little thing going."

Still, the pull of the Columbia Lil Cycos—the need to be recognized by them, to be redeemed in their eyes—proved irresistible. Giovanni added more 18s to his body. Worse, he'd gone and inked something like devil horns on his scalp, two bare triangular points at the hairline, which made his efforts to go straight feel fraudulent. He'd also tattooed a demon's face on the rear of his head, its eyes looking behind him. "My guardian angel," he'd called it. "Like somebody watching over my back."

By August, Giovanni had left home again, heading down to MacArthur Park with Mayra. Between his various juvenile sentences and the move to the high desert, he'd been missing in action for roughly sixteen of the previous twenty-two months. He needed to reintroduce himself—remind the Columbia Lil Cycos that Rusty had not forgotten his oath—and prove that Tricky had gotten him wrong. Yes, he'd been away, but he'd reemerged: a legal adult now, with new ink, who'd chosen the Columbia Lil Cycos over his mom.

Yeah, alright, I'm back, Giovanni thought. *Back where I belong.*

For all his devotion to the 18th Street cause, Giovanni knew almost nothing about how the gang worked. He'd never heard of Puppet. He had no idea what the Mexican Mafia expected of the Columbia Lil Cycos or what might await his homies if they failed to kick up rent. It was a testament to 18th Street's potency as a social institution—its gift for selling self-reinforcing fictions—that someone consigned to the bottom of that ecosystem could still imagine a future of advancement and approbation without having the slightest clue what he was up against. In Giovanni's mind, the gang's top organizational layer, whatever went on there, was the realm of "politics," and best not to be disturbed.

To announce his return, Giovanni chose an extreme caper. That August, armed with a nine-millimeter, he went patrolling on the eastern end of Columbia Lil Cycos territory, at the border with Rockwood's turf. It was likely the first time Giovanni had gone out by himself strapped and looking for enemies, the closest he'd come to the military skirmishes he'd contemplated as a middle school kid. Near Sixth and Union he spotted a rival slipping— walking alone, minding his own business—and from a reckless distance, Giovanni "started unloading on his ass."

His target, rather than fleeing, ran straight toward Giovanni. "I was like, what the fuck?" says Giovanni, who did an about-face and bolted. Then he remembered that he was the one who'd brought a gun to this mission, its weight and power all at his fingertips, and he turned again to chase his pursuer, both of them sprinting and ducking through traffic as Giovanni popped off more rounds. It was some crazy, heart-pounding urban combat, the kind that had been missing from Giovanni's gangster life.

The bray of an LAPD helicopter interrupted his stunt. Giovanni dove into some bushes near Wilshire Boulevard. He pawed the earth and tried to bury the weapon. Fearing he'd be tested for gunshot residue if he were caught, Giovanni undid his pants. He'd always prided himself on his talent for impro- visation. The piss landed hot on his hands. He rubbed them together. It was unnecessary—the cops never found him—but Giovanni had drowned out the evidence.

On less suspenseful days, Giovanni sold dope, posting up in a parking lot at the intersection of Sixth and Alvarado. Hidden behind a shopping complex called the Grande Mall, the second-story lot had become a Columbia Lil Cycos marketplace, a ready source of cash and camaraderie. Giovanni's hunger for fellowship gave him traction; he enjoyed filling orders, being in demand. "It was a rush, hell yeah," he says, "'cause I knew what they wanted." He cashed in, too, trading crack for favors. A rock for a late-night sandwich. Or, once, for a romp with a former MacArthur Park neighbor—a middle-aged woman too addled to recognize him—on the floor of a nearby laundry room.

The drug spot fell under the command of a MacArthur Park newcomer, an 18th Streeter who went by Face. A thirty-one-year-old former boxer from Mexicali, Face projected self-importance: rakish smirk, cocked eyebrow, lace-up fighter's gloves tattooed on his right arm, "which means commitment to excellence," he would say. Although he'd come up through a South-Central clique, the Wall Street Gangsters, and stayed at an 18th Street crash pad in South Gate, just across the railroad tracks from Watts, Face saw the money to be made with the Columbia Lil Cycos and, in 2007, managed to lateral his way in without any pushback.

It helped that Face had a baby mama in MacArthur Park, a pregnant ex whose comings and goings he monitored, which gave him an excuse to visit the neighborhood. He'd given his number to Shorty—that's how friendly the teenage vendor was with the homies—instructing her to call anytime she spotted the woman out on Sixth Street. Face also saw an opportunity to hitch his star to Tricky, who was expanding his reach beyond Columbia Lil Cycos turf and jockeying to handle the business of other 18th Street cliques across LA's Westside. Tricky continued to fantasize about earning his way into the Mexican Mafia, to serve as Puppet's heir, a position without limits "to where I can go, what I can do," he says, "as far as in the gang and in politics that surround the gangs in LA." As Tricky ascended, he anointed Face to fill his shoes: "I gave him the keys to Columbia."

Unlike Tricky, Face had no history with Giovanni and no reason to judge him, so he seemed happy to tutor an impressionable understudy, and Giovanni relished the opportunity to play adjutant to an older gangster. "He wasn't from here, and I thought if I walked around with him, people would recognize me and that would let them know it was cool, that he was okay," Giovanni says. Face often wore dress clothes to avoid attracting unwanted attention—slacks, fitted shirt, 310 Motoring shoes—and because he'd recently inked an 18th Street insignia above his left eye, he'd also taken to dabbing it with makeup before heading out to handle business. Giovanni mimicked Face's diversionary tactic, swabbing his scalp with Mayra's CoverGirl concealer.

Face gave Giovanni his first glimpse of the vending racket. On Sundays they'd walk down Alvarado to the Yoshinoya Beef Bowl, where a paisa from Honduras, a vendor turned rent collector, would meet them in the parking lot. The guy had once sold cigarettes and batteries, paying the gang $50 a week for a scrap of sidewalk. Now he kept a ledger, a lined sheet of notebook paper with two dozen names penciled in—Chapiz, Mamon, Elotero, Pimpo, Novelas—showing which street vendors and document peddlers had made their rent for the week and which would require a nudge. He'd wrap the cash in rubber bands and hand it to Face in a blue zippered deposit bag.

Face didn't offer any money to Giovanni, and Giovanni didn't ask. "The vendor thing, that ain't my thing," says Giovanni, who didn't even know about the tax "until I started kicking it with Face."

Face also gave Giovanni his first taste of what might happen to a vendor who flouted the rules. While making their rounds on Sixth Street one day that 2007 summer, Face and Giovanni were alerted—by a rent collector or another vendor—that an interloper was attempting to sell without ponying up. "So me and Face talked to this guy and told him, 'Hey, you either pay rent or you got to get out of here,'" Giovanni says. "He said, 'I ain't going to do nei-ther.' So I told him, 'Alright, you got five minutes to leave,' and I kicked his car, and Face threw—kicked his things around and told him, 'We're serious.' He said, 'Alright, I'm leaving.' We stayed there till he left."

Giovanni stopped returning to Palmdale. Reyna reported him as a run-away. In Face, Giovanni had exactly what he'd longed for, everything that had eluded him. "He gave confianza, you know what I mean?" Giovanni says. "He told me, 'I'm gonna carry you under my wing.'" Face brought Giovanni back to the crash pad, a drab stucco ranch house with a clay-tiled roof, the decor a blend of 2Pac posters, rosary beads, valentines, and a matching scorpion-etched decanter, shot glass, and ashtray set. Face didn't even object when Giovanni asked if Mayra could stay there too; most nights they'd grab a pile of blankets and knock out on the living room floor.

The first time Tricky came by to retrieve the rent money and found Giovanni there, it was an unpleasant surprise for them both.

"What the fuck is he doing here?" Tricky demanded.

"The homie's cool," Face replied.

"He's a little punk," Tricky said.

Giovanni retreated. "I didn't want the drama."

One day that summer Giovanni walked out of the South Gate house, head down, hands stuffed in his pockets. He was wearing his black Jordans, over-the-knee black shorts, and a swap meet T-shirt silkscreened with a pair of ghostly "smile now, cry later" masks. A telephoto lens captured the moment. Twice now, Giovanni had crossed paths with the FBI.

He still wasn't anybody, a temp on the Columbia Cycos' factory floor, but in the span of just a few weeks, Giovanni had found an ally in upper management. Face seemed to think him useful, maybe even to trust him. Giovanni felt like he was going places, unaware he'd chosen the worst possible time to make a fresh impression.

Two years into the vendor tax, the Columbia Lil Cycos had at last met an unmovable force: a paisa with attitude. Francisco Clemente had dared to stand up for himself. He'd raised the stakes by pulling a knife on the gang, and rather than fearing what might come, he'd crowned himself the victor. "If you have a problem with somebody and you fight and you beat them," Francisco says, "that person has to respect you and say, 'OK, you know what, you were a badass, shake my hand.'"

It fell to Tricky to evict Francisco. Although he considered the impasse beneath him, Tricky knew that all of Sixth Street was watching, that a failure to dislodge one vendor threatened to embolden everyone who paid tribute to the gang, and that any dip in revenue would require an explanation to

Puppet. The Columbia Lil Cycos were running a tax racket, but they were also subject to one: the Mexican Mafia always got paid.

Sometime that August, Tricky marched out of the International Mall and down Sixth Street, to the spot in front of Ace Cash Express where Francisco had installed himself. He delivered an ultimatum. "You need to get the fuck out of here," Tricky snarled. He vowed to return in twenty minutes. "If you're still here," Tricky said, "I will send you to hell."

Then Tricky found Atlas. He'd personally drawn a line. It had to be enforced. "If the vendor comes back acting stupid, just go ahead and call Face," Tricky told the rent collector. "So he can take care of it."

Francisco took a short break. Poor little Daniela, the third wheel of their vending troupe, had reached her due date, and because the bueno-por-nada father still hadn't surfaced, Francisco and Jessica felt responsible for her and the child she was bringing into the world. On August 23, 2007, on the afternoon Daniela's son was born, they joined her in the maternity ward of Hollywood Presbyterian, where the wood-paneled rooms on the third floor point west, offering a direct view of the sapphire-blue Scientology campus. Daniela named the boy Luis Angel.

Then it was back to work: first Francisco and Jessica, and barely three weeks after giving birth, Daniela. The night she returned to Sixth Street, the third Saturday in September, she brought Luis Angel, whom she'd swaddled in a striped Baby Dino onesie and tucked inside a stroller. If it seemed awfully soon to be introducing a newborn to a congested sidewalk, a nocturnal swirl of cash and food and exhaust, Daniela didn't know what else to do. "She had to go sell," Jessica says. "She had to buy things for her baby."

That was the night Face got the call. "Get dressed," he told Giovanni. They were all at the crash pad, a dozen miles south of MacArthur Park. Giovanni had spent the day obliging Mayra, doing his best to erase his dalliances and reassure her that she remained his everything. "I was barely starting to get back on her good side," he says. It was evening already. Giovanni put on nice clothes—long-sleeve black shirt, khaki slacks—the kind he wore when Face wanted them to avoid raising suspicions. If not for his bald head, Giovanni could have passed for one of the jesucristos who gathered on weekend nights to chant and stomp in the storefront temples clustered around the lake.

"What's happening, fool?" Giovanni asked.

"Don't trip," Face told him. "You'll find out when we get there."

11

The Right Guy

S eptember 15 was el Día de la Independencia for a million Central
American–descended Angelenos. For millions more Mexicans and
Mexican Americans, it was Independence Day eve. A weekend for barbecues
and beer bashes and black-market skyrockets. Sixth Street buzzed with
commerce—vendors and shoppers alike packing the sidewalk, spilling over
the curb—while from the MacArthur Park bandshell the oomph-chicka-
oomph-chicka of cumbia diva Vilma Díaz and La Sonora Dinamita echoed
across the water:

Es-cán-da-lo, es un escándalo.

The rest of LA hardly noticed. Hillary Clinton, seeking to stay one step
ahead of a young senator named Barack Obama, had arrived at Magic
Johnson's Beverly Hills home the night before to secure the former Laker's
endorsement. The following night, at the Shrine Auditorium, *The Sopranos*
would cap its final season by taking the 2007 Emmy for best dramatic series.
After a week of deliberations, the jury in the Phil Spector trial had gone home,
soon to announce it was deadlocked. O. J. Simpson was giving interviews, trying to explain away the Las Vegas altercation that would see him arrested for
armed robbery within a day. Jamie Foxx had just received a star on the Walk of
Fame. And an octogenarian Carol Channing, in town for a guest Hollywood
Bowl performance that weekend, had her $150,000 beaded Bob Mackie dress
stolen and returned all in the span of twenty-four hours.

LA was not just preoccupied with fame; it was awash in grift and hubris.

The *Los Angeles Times* had fallen into the hands of a carpetbagger, Sam
Zell, who was taking the paper private in a buyout that he funded by raiding
the employee pension plan. His plunder of the country's largest metropolitan

daily triggered a spiral of cuts to the staff and the newspaper's pages, eventually pushing the *Times* into bankruptcy.

The Los Angeles Dodgers, maybe the one unifying force in a vast, balkanized landscape, had also been commandeered by out-of-town charlatans—parking-lot mogul Frank McCourt and his wife, Jamie, an unlikely presidential aspirant—who proceeded to treat a civic treasure like an ATM. When their marriage crumbled in a burlesque of ego and consumption, all the lawyering, at $50,000 a day, enshrined the divorce as the most expensive in California history.

The mayor, Antonio Villaraigosa, a rising star in Latino politics, was forced that summer to acknowledge he was having a secret relationship with a Spanish-language TV reporter—a woman who'd broadcast the news of his separation from his wife on air. Telemundo suspended her. The mayor kept his job, but apologized for being a "distraction to the people of Los Angeles."

And then there was the LAPD, a more accountable agency post-Rampart scandal, yet on May 1, 2007, officers had overreacted to a largely peaceful immigrant rights march in MacArthur Park—swinging batons and firing rubber bullets while journalists documented the melee. In the end, nineteen officers were disciplined, and the city paid out $13 million in settlements.

Giovanni, son of LA, outcast of 18th Street, was sober on September 15, just as he'd been when he visited Tricky for his first tattoo. Although he wasn't sure what the Columbia Lil Cycos had in store for him, he knew there was "something that had to be done"—a mission that would require the kind of coldness everyone seemed to doubt he could summon. Whether Tricky really believed that Giovanni was a rat or was just badmouthing him for leverage, it worked: Giovanni didn't have the luxury of asking for details or negotiating his role. If he backed out, he'd likely become a target himself. Face, his keeper, would put it this way: "He was a homie, but he was questionable."

A little after 8 P.M., Face and Giovanni piled into a gray Dodge pickup truck, a dude named Silly at the wheel and three other 18th Streeters crammed in the back. If it seemed unwise to implicate so many compatriots in a vile expedition, there were about to be even more. Face had sketched out an extravagant plot, choreographing assignments as if he were leading a special ops team. When they arrived in MacArthur Park, Silly kept the truck idling on Fifth Street, at the rear of the International Mall, while Face guided Giovanni around the corner to USA Donuts. There, Face summoned Atlas, whom he'd called five times in the previous few minutes, and the other rent collector, Barrios. They were joined by two other Columbia Lil Cycos, Big Guy and Lil Primo. Huddling under the glowing "Vida Loca" mural, they held a misa—literally, a Mass—to go over their marching orders.

Barrios produced the pistol. Giovanni had never seen the guy, but he did recognize the gun: a cheap .22, the classic Saturday night special. The Columbia Lil Cycos had owned the piece for a while, passing it around to whichever dope spot needed some low-profile protection. It wasn't the grade of weapon you'd choose for the biggest test of your life.

"What the fuck is this for?" Giovanni asked.

"Didn't I tell you you were gonna do something?" Face said.

"To who?"

"A vendor."

"Oh, hell no," Giovanni said.

"You know how it goes," Face said.

It was no surprise that he'd been recruited to pull the trigger. If he was being honest with himself, Giovanni had known in his gut that he would be called on to take a life that night, to prove his 18th Street allegiance once and for all. But to shoot a vendor—a civilian? There was no rivalry involved, no tribal fury. Face was using him as a sicario, a hit man. Giovanni didn't even know the fool he was supposed to kill.

That's where Atlas came in. He'd be the one to point out the chilango. Giovanni didn't know Atlas either. All these strangers collaborating on a murderous plot—directed by Face, a newcomer to the neighborhood, at the behest of Tricky, a Mexican Mafia wannabe, for the ultimate benefit of

Puppet, the caged wizard of MacArthur Park's underworld—made the Columbia Lil Cycos seem less like a gang than a cult. Money may have brought events to a head on Sixth Street that night, but it didn't explain what Giovanni was doing there. He heard Tricky's voice in the recesses of his teenage brain: *He's a snitch. He ain't no good. He doesn't do shit.* Giovanni could choose to be a trembling creature. Or he could prove them all wrong.

He took the gun from Barrios. Once the deed was done, Giovanni was supposed to hand it to Lil Primo. Big Guy—whose mom was a vendor—would then take the weapon and dispose of it.

"Hey, Face."

It was Shorty. She was right there in her usual spot, outside the International Mall, watching the six of them—four gangsters, two paisas—wend their way through the crowd. Even though she'd barely entered ninth grade a couple of weeks before, Shorty had spent so many years greeting and chatting and winning hearts on that patch of concrete, she might as well have been the prom queen of Sixth Street. Face stopped to hug her.

"What's up, baby girl?" he said.

Something seemed different to Shorty. Maybe it was Face and Giovanni (she knew him as Rusty) in their churchgoing outfits. Or the way they seemed to be parading in unison with the rent collectors, Barrios and Atlas, neither of whom dared collect from her. She also knew Big Guy and Lil Primo, stone-faced on a festive Saturday night. They were heading east, toward Burlington Avenue, the corner her dad chose for displaying his wares. Whatever was unfolding, it worried Shorty, so she shadowed their steps.

Face turned on his heels and stood in her way. Shorty craned her head to one side, trying to peer around him, then to the other. Face mirrored her moves, juking like a dance partner, doing his best to block her view. His eyes said it all: *You don't want to see.*

Giovanni kept walking, past Juice Max and Video Mania, and as he neared the end of the block, past Ace Cash Express. Then he turned to Atlas. "I told him to make sure to tell me, let me know who was the guy, to describe him to me because I didn't know him," Giovanni says. Atlas pointed to a copper-skinned man twice Giovanni's age. He was standing near a pay phone, bobbing his head to music. "We walked in front of him and walked back and forth a little bit," Giovanni says. "So he could be sure that that was the right guy."

"That's him," Atlas said.

Atlas ducked into Video Mania. A handwritten sign in the window advertised DVD XXXS: $1.00 LA RENTA. If he stayed in the shop, maybe Atlas could tell himself that he didn't know what was going to happen, remove himself from the terrible crime he'd helped bring to fruition. Atlas didn't realize that a surveillance camera had already captured his image a few hours earlier at Juice Max, where he'd flirted with a cashier, handing her his phone number. And he couldn't have known that she and her Juice Max coworker had overheard him speaking to another man about the trouble with Francisco Clemente, how every vendor had paid "except the chilango." Then either Atlas or the other man—the two Juice Max employees couldn't agree—responded:

"Don't worry, we're going to fix it."

Giovanni joined Atlas in Video Mania. He wanted to gather his thoughts one last time. "Debating whether or not to do it," Giovanni says, "to do it or not to do." He took some deep breaths. His head pounded. It was a monstrous thing to even contemplate. He knew nothing about this man out on the sidewalk, wished him no harm. The guy had never done anything to him. But the decision wasn't his. Higher-ups had made the call.

Giovanni didn't have the emotional tools for seeing the vendor's humanity, for recognizing his own. He thought instead about what would happen to him, maybe his mom too, if he didn't have the stones to go through with it. How 18th Street might make his family pay for his timidity. Giovanni had left himself with two bad choices, either one of which stood to irrevocably alter the course of his life, but on that day, in that moment, at that age, one seemed just a little less shitty.

Alright, I'm going to do this. No ifs, whats, or buts, no turning back.

The gun was already loaded and cocked, a bullet in the chamber. Giovanni took the safety off and swung open the Video Mania door. He held the weapon with two hands, his arms outstretched and elbows locked. He marched right up to Francisco, raising the gun when he was just a step or two away, and pointing at his head. "To make sure he was dead," Giovanni says. He felt like he was in a movie: the picture slowed, the sound grew hushed. "Tunnel vision," he says. "I didn't want to get distracted by anything else. Just get that thing done right."

He pulled the trigger—*pop pop pop pop pop*—five times. Then he ran.

Giovanni zagged through the Sixth Street crowd, back past Video Mania and Juice Max, to the edge of the International Mall. He shoved the gun into Lil Primo's hands, then dashed through an alley on the side of the building, across the rear parking lot, and hoisted himself over a fence onto Fifth Street. The truck was still there, idling.

"Let's go, fool!" Giovanni gasped.

No pissing on his hands this time. Safely back at the crash pad, Giovanni jumped straight in the shower. It felt good to get out of his dress clothes. He piled them in the yard and doused them with lighter fluid. *Phooshhhh.* The flames danced. So did Giovanni. He gulped a Corona and shimmied around his little bonfire. When gangs commit violence, their actions mask a language—the vocabulary of the despondent, as Los Angeles priest Gregory Boyle, founder of the gang recovery program Homeboy Industries, likes to say. Each bullet speaks not to conflict but "a lethal absence of hope."

Gangs sniff out those vacant places. They fill the wounds. Under their spell, a damaged kid can believe the lie that killing is a kind of alchemy: pain transformed into approval. Giovanni hadn't wanted to, but he'd risen to the occasion. Because of him, the whole organization would have a smoother time collecting rent—the consequences of nonpayment couldn't be starker—and here he was, living to tell about it. Nobody could talk shit about him now, least of all Tricky. In one cold-blooded flourish, he'd shown he was no snitch.

He'd faced his fears, and he'd conquered them; he could be counted on to do whatever, whenever. It was a feeling more intense than anything the square world, with its rote tasks and rigid schedules, could offer. "I dirtied my hands for them," Giovanni says. "That's supposed to bring you closer together, make your bond even stronger."

Giovanni woke up the next day to a visit from Tricky.

"You fucked up," Tricky said.

12

The Price You Pay

T he last thing Francisco Clemente saw was fire. A flash in the dark. He lurched. Jessica Guzman grabbed her boyfriend, shoving him to the ground. She curled into a fetal position, covering her head. Francisco touched his shirt and felt heat. The blue cotton was turning dark and wet. He wheezed, his breath escaping from somewhere deep inside.

Everyone on Sixth Street seemed to be fumbling with a phone, racing to call 911, Jessica included. The operator told her to stop Francisco's bleeding as best she could, to press hard until paramedics arrived. "We were all there like crazy people, calling for the ambulance," Jessica says. "It seemed like hours." She placed her hands over Francisco's wounds: his chest, his jaw, the corner of his head. He dripped onto the sidewalk. Brass shell casings formed a crescent around his body. "It was very ugly," Jessica says. "Very, very ugly."

The Los Angeles Fire Department delivered Francisco to County-USC Medical Center at 9:53 P.M. The 1933 Art Deco structure on LA's Eastside (featured in the *General Hospital* opening credits for decades) treated about a thousand gunshot patients a year—military surgeons often trained there before heading to battle. The old joke was that if you got shot, County-USC would save your life; if you went there for anything else, it'd kill you. A Chicago Medical School grad named Cameron Nouri, nearly bald in his mid-thirties with a goatee soon to be flecked gray, was working the main trauma room that night. It was the fourth and final year of his residency in emergency medicine. Francisco had lost consciousness. Dr. Nouri recognized that his wounds were "life-threatening at that point and needed immediate attention."

He observed two gunshots to the right side of Francisco's chest. One had punctured the lung. The first order of business was to insert tubes, to reinflate Francisco's lung and drain it of trapped blood. "A gunshot wound to the right side of the chest resulting in collapsing of the right lung not only compromises, obviously, your oxygen delivery, it can develop into what we call a tension pneumothorax to the point where basically the other side would also collapse and you would go into cardiac arrest," Dr. Nouri says. Francisco's stomach was also "very tender," raising suspicions that the second bullet had traveled south and penetrated the abdomen. He was rushed into the operating room. Surgeons performed a laparotomy—a fancy way of saying excavation—from his belly button to his solar plexus. "You have to open up that cavity," Dr. Nouri says, "to see what kind of damage has been done." The bullet had torn through Francisco's liver, spleen, pancreas, and intestine.

A CT scan showed a third bullet caught in his jaw. A fourth had grazed his temple, causing only superficial damage. The surgery went on for hours. "It was quite, quite, quite hard," says Francisco, who didn't wake up until the next morning. "In truth, I thought I wasn't going to exist anymore."

Floating in and out of consciousness, his belly left open to seep and aerate, Francisco had visions that both confused and comforted him. "I saw what is life and what is death," he says. "Believe me, I experienced many things. I had many, many, like, dreams. I don't know if it was the drugs they give you in the hospital or what, but I saw many things, things that are hard to understand." He was trying to make sense of what he had done, and of what had been done to him. His words could have flowed from the pages of a Steinbeck novel. "You have to accept that there is good and evil, and if you do evil, evil is going to be the price you pay. It's better to do things as best you can and fix now what you can fix. Because when you die, you're not going to be able to do anything. God's going to come, and He's going to say to you, 'Let's see, what did you do? Did you behave badly? Did you do wrong to somebody? Or to the contrary, were you an arrogant man?'"

As Francisco grappled with the strangeness of his own survival, another horror was sinking in. Without the benefit of parental leave or sick days or childcare, Daniela had brought her twenty-three-day-old son to work—to the sidewalks of MacArthur Park. She'd already lost more than a month of vending income, and while California's Women, Infants, and Children program could provide an indigent mom with about $40 a month in nutritional assistance, Daniela's safety net couldn't sustain Luis Angel. If not for Jessica's solidarity as a roommate and Francisco's show of gallantry, Daniela was about as alone as someone in a city of millions could be. Returning to Sixth Street, exposing her baby to the only employment she could access, wasn't really a choice.

When Francisco collapsed under Giovanni's bullets, Daniela instinctively reached for Luis Angel. He'd been asleep. She pulled him from the stroller and clutched him to her chest. He didn't make a sound.

"My baby!" Daniela wailed.

She thought maybe the shock had overwhelmed him—he'd begin crying any second.

"Look at him, look how he is!"

Luis Angel didn't cry. Blood foamed from his mouth. Daniela moaned. Shorty watched aghast. "She went crazy," says Shorty, who'd followed the gang down the block, up to the moment Giovanni opened fire. "You go crazy seeing your own son getting shot." Daniela was still cradling Luis Angel, her white cardigan stained red, when paramedics arrived. They took the baby to California Hospital, a downtown LA trauma center that treats mostly uninsured and Medi-Cal patients. Doctors tried to resuscitate him, pumping him with a cocktail of cardiac drugs. Luis Angel didn't respond. Twenty minutes after arriving, he was pronounced dead. An autopsy would show that a single bullet—maybe the fifth one Giovanni fired, maybe the one that glanced off Francisco's head—had entered Luis Angel's chest. It was still there, lodged behind his heart. The .22 might have been just measly enough to save Francisco's life. But it still had the firepower to take a baby's. A pathologist removed the projectile and placed it in a manila envelope.

As Daniela unraveled and Francisco teetered, Tricky laid into Giovanni. Back at the crash pad that Sunday, September 16, there was no more cele-bration, no chance for vindication. With the vendor alive, the Columbia Lil Cycos now had a witness to contend with. Francisco would surely remember that Tricky was the one who'd vowed to send him to la chingada. Giovanni's failure to finish him off left Tricky at personal risk—he'd counted on the vendor being gone.

Then there was the matter of Luis Angel, a debacle of the gravest sort. Giovanni refused to believe it. He'd seen no baby. Even though he didn't think it needed to be said, he wanted it known: he wouldn't have shot a baby if he'd seen one. Never.

"I know what I did," Giovanni said. "I didn't kill no baby."

"Well, this is what they're saying," Tricky told him.

Giovanni didn't know what Tricky was up to, what mind games the Columbia Lil Cycos might be playing with him. It seemed like a setup—like he'd been made the fall guy for some other scandal, for someone else's breach. He continued to protest, until Tricky threw up his hands and struck a reassur-ing note. He told Giovanni not to trip; the Columbia Lil Cycos would blame the bungled shooting on their neighborhood rival, the Rockwood gang. Giovanni just needed to lay low for a bit.

"Don't worry about it," Tricky told him. "I'll try to fix it."

Still feeling defensive, Giovanni left the crash pad, retreating to Mayra's house, the cottage by the Harbor Freeway, to sulk. He kept playing it over in his mind. There had to be some mistake, some exaggeration. How could a child have died right in front of his eyes without him knowing? To avoid thinking about it, Giovanni joined Mayra's nephew in front of the TV. The boy was five or six. They stuck a tape of *The Lion King* into the VCR. It helped Giovanni forget, even when Scar tricked Simba into believing the cub was responsible for his father's death. Simba pleaded: it was an accident.

When the movie ended, Giovanni flipped to the news. Monday, Septem-ber 17, two days after the shooting, there was the mayor, standing at a lectern, next to other political figures and police officials. His brow creased and his face drained, Antonio Villaraigosa seemed to be peering out from the screen and straight into Giovanni's soul.

"The cold-blooded murder of a tiny, defenseless newborn baby is a crime that we just can't tolerate and won't tolerate in the city of Los Angeles," said Villaraigosa, adding that he had met with the baby's mother, who was "in terrible pain," and had held her hand.

The words sucked the air out of Giovanni's throat. He doubled over and held his head in his hands. It was true, then, all true. Giovanni cried so hard he thought he would pass out.

As offensive as killing a child was to every legal and moral principle on this planet, it constituted a special atrocity within the gang world, something akin to a war crime. There was a code, albeit one that allowed for all manner of carnage—a line that still determined what was off-limits and preserved some frayed vestige of honor. The penalty for Giovanni's sin was dictated by the Mexican Mafia, and it was automatic: a green light. That meant open season not just on Giovanni but potentially every member of the Columbia Lil Cycos, a license to attack anyone, anywhere, on the street or behind bars.

Tricky stuck to his invented story. He sent word to Puppet that "Rockwood had passed by and shot at one of the homeboys and accidentally had killed the baby." It was a dangerous game to play: misleading the Columbia Lil Cycos' godfather to preserve his own reputation. But Tricky needed to buy time, "to take the attention away of what really happened and what really went down." The LAPD was papering Sixth Street with flyers seeking information in connection with the MURDER OF AN INFANT. The reward, a larger-than-usual $75,000, might be enough to loosen lips. With all that heat, the gang's rent collections were going to lag, and as Tricky recognized, he would have to explain to Puppet why "there was going to be a change in the money situation."

He also needed to preempt the green light, to act before the truth emerged. As LA's largest gang, 18th Street already had a surplus of enemies. If everyone on Columbia Lil Cycos turf were fair game, business would only get riskier. Homies doing time would have targets on their back. And Puppet wouldn't do a thing to protect them, not if the Columbia Lil Cycos didn't make things right themselves. It was a perverse brand of tough love: the patriarch's willingness to sacrifice his own progeny, if necessary, to instill discipline and grow the Mexican Mafia's mystique. Tricky channeled Puppet. "I was given the blessing from Puppet to make sure that everything I did—everything, the way I acted, the way I talked—was basically . . . on his behalf," Tricky says. "I was being referred to as Little Puppet, being him on the streets."

In the end, Tricky had only one way to avoid the green light, and he'd known it all along. The Columbia Lil Cycos spoke of it in euphemism. They would have to clean their yard. The trash would have to be taken out.

Part Two

2007

Photo by Guillermo Buelna

13

Something Bigger than Yourself

At every step of Giovanni Macedo's gang life, from the beatdown that initiated him in 2005 to the catastrophe he triggered in 2007, the federal government was tailing the Columbia Lil Cycos. The dust had barely settled on the first RICO case, the one that in 2002 condemned Puppet to a lifetime behind bars, when a second investigation took shape. The Columbia Lil Cycos were that resilient, the profitability of the narcotics trade that inflated, incarceration that inadequate a strategy: the FBI could deliver a death blow and then, just as Giovanni was joining the gang, start all over again.

Special Agent Paul Keenan recognized what this said about the limits of suppression, of what a war on drugs or gangs could accomplish. The Columbia Lil Cycos had taken everything the government could throw at them, then gone right back to business. He didn't think the FBI could just look the other way, though, and wish the good people of MacArthur Park luck. There was still virtue in putting up a fight, a societal cost in surrendering to cynicism. "We're not going to stop crime completely," Keenan says, "but that doesn't mean you stop working."

RICO was powerful but hard to prove. It involved more than making arrests or enforcing injunctions. The goal wasn't to solve a particular crime. To build a racketeering case against the Columbia Lil Cycos, the feds had to decipher the organization: identify patterns, connect dots, show how otherwise piecemeal offenses served the interests of the whole enterprise. Keenan had done the work. Starting in 2005, using hidden cameras and confidential informants and marked bills, he'd penetrated the mechanics of the gang's dope and tax game. He'd mapped its reconstituted hierarchy. He knew all about Tricky. He was on to Oso and Baby. He'd even started to puzzle out

Puppet's secrets, to chart how a dollar on the streets of MacArthur Park made its way to Supermax. By the summer of 2007, Keenan was ready to move—to "take them all down at once."

Now it was all blowing up in his face. He learned about the hit on Sixth Street the same night it happened, September 15, just before twelve. A vendor gunned down, a baby shot dead—and right there between Bonnie Brae and Burlington, a block he'd staked out countless times. It made his stomach hurt.

Keenan raced to the Rampart station, convening a team of FBI agents and LAPD officers. His mind spun with woulda-couldas and what-ifs. He'd been so careful and methodical. It sickened him to think the murder might have involved the same people he'd been investigating. Keenan would have to scramble now to put together evidence for a grand jury, to get indictments issued before his targets made more of a mess. "I mean, I didn't have a crystal ball," he says. "Obviously, we didn't know this was going to happen." The timing hadn't been entirely up to him. Every cop understands the tension between investigators and prosecutors, between those who think they've got the goods and those who have to prove it in court. The federal government rarely took cases to trial—the Department of Justice expected defendants to fold—which is why an investigation had to be fastidious, airtight. "FBI, we always want to do it faster—the US attorney's office always wants more evidence," Keenan says. "You always think your case is the most important, but they have other cases they're working. So there's always that back and forth. It's a balancing act."

He had to admit, he'd never taken note of the struggles that MacArthur Park's street vendors faced. Drugs were the Columbia Lil Cycos' main revenue source, the FBI's swiftest route to long sentences. Even if Keenan had caught wind of the vendor tax, the federal government hadn't invested all this time and money to thwart some low-rent shakedown. "The bang for your buck wasn't there," he says. "I mean, it sounds a little cold or calculated, but it was an easier method to get these guys in jail through drugs and through violence than it was through the collection of rent from street vendors."

Paul Keenan was a Southern California kid, but before taking on the Columbia Lil Cycos, he would have struggled to place MacArthur Park on a map. He'd grown up in a different Westlake—the master-planned community of Westlake Village—in a Brady Bunch–style four-bedroom, two-bath house about forty miles to the northwest, in the foothills of the Santa Monica Mountains. Westlake Village was safe, affluent, educated, and very white, with a high percentage of military veterans, like his father, a retired navy commander.

Keenan, who sprouted to six foot four, shined as a forward on the Westlake High basketball team. In his senior year, 1987, he became the first player in school history to score more than four hundred points in a season. He also led his squad to the playoffs for the first time, a run that culminated in a California Interscholastic Federation championship game at the Los Angeles Sports Arena, then home to the NBA's Clippers. Keenan wasn't a "showboat" or a "holler guy," as his coach put it. He played with selfless intensity, finding ways to contribute even when his shot wasn't dropping. "I've always been a kind of protector-type personality," Keenan says. "Which lent itself to playing on a team, being part of something bigger than yourself."

UC San Diego made him its number-one freshman recruit that fall, but a blown Achilles derailed that season and hobbled his attempts at a comeback. After transferring to Indiana University and majoring in political science, Keenan returned to Southern California in the 1990s with the hope of becoming a cop, but a back injury while training for the academy put that plan on hold. He went to work instead in the hospitality industry: first as the general manager of Kachina Grill, a Southwestern restaurant in the corporate fortress of downtown LA's Bunker Hill, then as the bar manager at Dublin's Irish Pub, a club on the Sunset Strip. He honed his Spanish by b.s.-ing with his staff; Latino workers, especially immigrants from Oaxaca, kept the city's kitchens running. And he refined his intervention and de-escalation techniques by cutting off customers who'd had one too many. "Hard conversations," he says, "that translate well to law enforcement."

After two failed attempts, he made the DEA, which took him to New York and Las Vegas, and then in 2003, he transferred to the FBI, which brought him back to Los Angeles. It was a different bureau than it had been just a few years earlier, transformed by the intelligence failures of 9/11. The agency that had once put crime-fighting first now reassigned some two thousand agents to counterterrorism work. Drug cases plummeted. Mafia investigations stalled. The LA division shed nine of the fifty-two agents working gangs. Keenan understood the shift, but it didn't match his skills or passions. "When I think of the FBI, I think of organized crime," he says. "So working gangs in LA, for me, is one of the best places you can be."

Assigned to the Criminal Enterprise-5 unit, the "Hispanic gang squad," Keenan embarked on the second RICO investigation of the Columbia Lil Cycos while the first one was still working its way through the courts. The FBI's office was on Wilshire Boulevard—the western end, nearer the ocean—so to get to MacArthur Park, Keenan would drive the boulevard east, around the Los Angeles Country Club and Beverly Hills, through Museum Row and the La Brea Tar Pits, past the consulates and the mayor's mansion, until ten miles later Wilshire reached the park and curled around the lake, revealing an urban American borderland. "It's a different world," Keenan says. "If you take surface streets, it's really a stark difference."

Despite his respectable Spanish, Keenan was about as conspicuous as any outsider could be, a giant Irish gumshoe with big green eyes and a balding forehead. One of his partners, Tiburcio Aguilar, an FBI agent of Mexican descent who could disappear into MacArthur Park's throngs, christened him Pablo. "Yeah, he could not, you know, just get out of the car, stop, walk in somewhere, and kind of blend in," Tib Aguilar says. MacArthur Park hummed on anyway. If Pablo Keenan walked past the corner of Seventh and Alvarado, the touts who congregated there, in front of Botica del Pueblo, would hiss "micas, micas"—Mexican slang for a laminated identification card—just as they have for decades. "It doesn't matter who you are or what you look like," Keenan says, "they'll try to sell you an ID."

Early in the investigation, in 2005, he and another agent thought they'd grab lunch at a seafood place in a Sixth Street mini-mall called Playas de Tijuana. It had a menu board in the window advertising sopa de caracol and siete mares next to a homespun painting of a big-clawed lobster. "When I sat down, everyone looked at us, like, 'You know this isn't really a restaurant?'" Keenan says. "They literally didn't have any food in there." One of his first moves was to put Playas de Tijuana under surveillance. The proprietress was selling crack for the Columbia Lil Cycos out of a phony Coca-Cola can.

The FBI gained another peek into the gang's tactics that year when the owner of a botanica reported that the Columbia Lil Cycos were extorting her. The gang wanted to place a traquetero inside her second-floor store—an emporium of herbs and charms—perched atop Payless Shoes in a retail-residential complex built in the aftermath of the 1992 riots. The Columbia Lil Cycos ruled the building. They'd installed a middle-aged Salvadoran man, a former security guard who'd also worked as a busboy and a special-needs caregiver, as the on-site accountant. His job was to collect $600 a week from the botanica's owner until she allowed drugs to be sold. Keenan set up a sting. The next time she was strong-armed, the shopkeep had marked bills and a closed-circuit camera to capture the exchange.

Keenan kept doing stakeouts, snapping photos, tailing suspects, building an org chart. It didn't take long to figure out that Tricky was calling the shots. Several times a week Keenan drove his government-issued Ford to the Food 4 Less parking lot, the one on Sixth Street that Giovanni had once skated across, and sat there, sun visor down, watching to see who might be headed into Unico's Tattoos. Whether out of discretion or entitlement, Tricky didn't spend much time on the streets. He'd just as soon cyber-bang inside the shop, pecking out boasts and threats on an 18th Street chat page that the gang had set up on the web hosting service angelfire.com. It was the beginning of the gangster social media age. Tricky devoted hours to dissing rivals online, especially Rockwood. He delighted in calling the neighboring gang Cockwood—an insult that came with traces of a compliment.

To tie Tricky to the Columbia Lil Cycos' schemes, Keenan needed someone on the inside, an informant who could connect him to the mariscos joint and the botanica. After some months, he found the ideal candidate, a Cuban asylee who'd been selling and smoking crack in MacArthur Park since shortly after the Mariel boatlift of 1980. A theatrical Afro Caribeño who favored silk slacks and guayaberas, he was known, appropriately, as Cuba. He had been around so long, he'd supposedly hit the pipe in the park with Richard Ramirez before Richard Ramirez became the Night Stalker.

Cuba was in it for the money; a confidential witness in a federal investigation could earn ten grand, easy. He had no qualms about wearing a wire. He just had to be coached into dialing down his natural flamboyance. "He wanted to talk more than listen, to kind of show his knowledge of the game and impress people," Keenan says. "So we were always trying to get him to just shut up and let the subjects do the talking, because that's where your evidence is going to come from."

The first time Cuba went undercover at Tricky's shop, in 2006, he ordered $1,000 of crack. Tricky's wife, Morena, slipped out to an apartment on Burlington Avenue, half a block from where Giovanni's mom had invited the cops to roust her son the year before, and returned with a Styrofoam cup. The product was inside, under a lid and straw. "Tricky had a certain charisma, or arrogance, like he knew he was the boss, and I think he liked it," Keenan says. "But, you know, his wife, she was the one who was really keeping track of the numbers: who sold what and how much people owed and how much dope they were receiving and how much they should be paying. She was really the brains behind the operation."

Cuba returned to the shop four more times. His work eventually helped the FBI secure a wiretap of Tricky's and Morena's phones—four of them altogether—which is how Keenan happened to be listening when Giovanni called that fall day in 2006 and Tricky chewed him out. The conversation meant little at the time. "The feeling I got was, like, 'Why are you bothering me? I'm the shotcaller and you're, you know, a pooh-butt gangster,'" Keenan says. The more Keenan listened in, the more it appeared that Tricky suspected he was under surveillance. Tricky told one caller there was "a bird on the wire," and to resume the conversation on his burner phone. But the possibility that a law enforcement agency may have been circling him wasn't enough for Tricky to go dark. Like most legacy enterprises, criminal or not, the Columbia Lil Cycos had only one way forward: keep the machinery running and the revenue streams flowing, even in the face of an external threat. "What are they going to do?" Keenan says. "If the way you make your money is selling drugs and collecting rent and extorting people, you can't stop. Especially when Puppet needs his money."

In February 2007, after more than a year of surveillance and months of wiretaps, the FBI made a move. Keenan wanted to see if he could flip Tricky, to pressure the shotcaller into giving up the whole organization. Armed with a search warrant, the FBI raided Tricky's house. They found wads of cash jammed in pockets and drawers, about $10,000 altogether, and small baggies of crack stuffed in the woodwork. The letter from Puppet urging Tricky to "do good in school" was in a picture frame, behind a photo of one of Tricky and Morena's kids.

The search gave the FBI an opening. Agents cuffed Tricky and led him to the rear unit, where his mother lived. "Tricky is a talker," Tib Aguilar says. "You could hear that from the wiretaps—he would just ramble on and on." Aguilar sat him down and made the pitch: how Tricky could help them and help himself at the same time if he wised up and agreed to cooperate.

"In good-type words," Tricky says, "I told him to fuck off."

The FBI chose not to arrest Tricky. Keenan wanted more evidence against him or more information from him. He warned Tricky that his troubles weren't over, though, that the FBI was playing the long game. They'd be back— maybe the next day, maybe in a couple of months, maybe in a year. Then the agents walked out, leaving Tricky as he was, free to resume the Columbia Lil Cycos' business.

14

The Suspect

O n September 15, 2007, at 10:43 P.M., Shorty's phone rang. It was barely an hour after the shooting. She recognized the number: Face.

"You see anything happen tonight?" he asked.

Shorty had only a second to calculate her response, to come up with something artful. She'd spent too much of her life on Sixth Street to just blurt out what she'd witnessed, but she was still so young, having turned fifteen only a month before, and suddenly in way over her head.

"You should know," Shorty replied, "you were there."

Face said he hadn't seen anything. Shorty told him not to act dumb, then she hung up. Face called her again at 11:59, this time after dialing *67—the code for blocking caller ID. And again at 12:01. She stopped answering after that.

The next day was a Sunday, the commercial pinnacle of the week. By 11 A.M., Shorty was back on Sixth Street, right where she'd been the night before, in her knee-high folding chair outside the International Mall next to a sandwich board advertising Unico's Tattoos. So were her parents: mom near USA Donuts and dad down at the Ace Cash Express end. No matter what had happened the night before, Shorty's folks couldn't afford to skip a weekend. Above all, Shorty couldn't afford to act scared. She'd witnessed everything: the moment Giovanni pulled the trigger, the instant Francisco collapsed, the eternity Daniela spent pleading with Luis Angel to make a noise. In another kind of workplace, Shorty might have been offered grief counseling or a security detail, told to take all the time she needed. Instead, she put up a front.

"If I would not have gone back, people would be saying that I knew what happened that night and maybe I opened my mouth, and, you know, told the police," Shorty says. "So that nobody would know that I know something, I went back and just act normal, like nothing happened."

Not long after Shorty set up shop that Sunday—laundry basket overflowing with five-packs of cotton socks, plastic-wrapped headphones stacked high—a car pulled into the International Mall alley. It was the same corridor Giovanni had used as an escape route less than twenty-four hours earlier, the spot where he'd handed off the gun to Lil Primo. Behind the wheel, five seven and two hundred pounds, with a frosty glare and a ragged mustache, was Lil Primo's cousin, a Columbia Lil Cyco named Grumpy. He called Shorty to his window.

"I know you know what happened," Grumpy said.

"I don't know nothing," Shorty said.

"If you snitch," Grumpy said, "something might happen to you or your family."

The next day, Grumpy was back, this time with Raven, whose name matched her jet-black mane, and whose boyfriend, Big Guy, had taken the murder weapon from Lil Primo and made it disappear. They called Shorty into the alley again; when Shorty hesitated, Raven got out and dragged her by the shirt.

"I know you were there," Raven said.

"I don't know what you're talking about," Shorty said.

Again, they told Shorty that if she spoke to police, something would happen to her—to her or her family. They had a gun and made sure she saw it.

Then it was Tricky's turn. He summoned her into the International Mall. "I know you know something," he said. Shorty again insisted she didn't. Tricky needled her about her chumminess with Edgar Hernandez, the LAPD's 18th Street specialist; the gang knew he was forever chatting her up, fishing for tidbits. "You better not go snitch to your padrino Hernandez," Tricky told her. "Or something's going to happen."

Shorty's life—her family's livelihood—was one extended balancing act, a dance between the cops and the gangsters, the ticketers and the taxers. She'd grown up trying to accommodate them all and, to an astounding degree, succeeded. Now she faced the greatest test of her survival skills. "I was scared and shocked," Shorty says. "I couldn't sleep or do nothing." When the police canvassed Sixth Street in the days after the shooting, she stuck to the script. "I told them I wasn't there that day." She claimed that she'd had soccer practice, that she'd been in the park. "I lied."

On Tuesday, September 18, a day after asking the public for help solving the baby's killing, the mayor announced an arrest. "We've found the suspect," Antonio Villaraigosa said, breaking the news during a vigil on Sixth Street. Mourners, activists, and clergy had been converging on Ace Cash Express since the weekend, offering prayers and singing hymns. They'd left stuffed animals, red roses, votive candles, wax saints, and sympathy notes, wishing comfort for the infant's mother, scrawled on cardboard. The Buddhist teacher Thich Nhat Hanh would even make an appearance that month, leading a thousand people on a march around the lake. "My message is, go home and take care of yourself," the monk said. "Don't be a victim of the environment you are in. You can drown, be carried away by your environment, and you can lose your peace."

The mayor's phrasing—his reference to *the* suspect—came as a surprise to police, who were still combing for witnesses and didn't know who'd pulled the trigger. The name the mayor revealed also surprised the Columbia Lil Cycos. In custody and charged with capital murder was Luis "Clever" Silva, Baby's kid brother. The night of the shooting, Rampart gang officers had interviewed Francisco's girlfriend, Jessica, and her description of one Columbia Lil Cyco extortionist—slender build, fade haircut, *1* and *8* on his forearms—made police think of Clever. At two in the morning, they showed Jessica a six-pack of photos; she picked Clever, adding that she'd seen him just before the bullets struck Francisco. Officer Hernandez took Clever in that same Sunday morning—no warrant, no raid—just showed up at Clever's door on Fifth Street and told him to come on out.

"What seems to be the problem?" asked Clever, doing his best to sound courteous.

"There's somebody who wants to talk to you," Hernandez replied.

Clever's mind was elsewhere, lost in a grief of his own. His mom—Baby's mom—was in hospice, succumbing at fifty-one to a brain tumor. On the evening of the shooting, Clever had visited her at Good Sam, the same hospital that had tended to Giovanni's mom after her overdose, and returned home in tears. "That was the first time I experienced stress like that," says Clever, who went straight to bed. Later that Saturday night, he consoled himself with gulps of foul chemical smoke from a meth pipe.

Hernandez took Clever to the old Rampart Division detective building, a former credit union on Third Street. He was greeted with taunts. "Everyone started telling me, 'You fucking baby killer,' you know, blah, blah, blah," Clever says. "I was looking at them like, What the fuck?" There was no denying that Clever was from 18th Street, that he had a *1* and *8* on his arms just like Giovanni, that he served dope in the hood. He was also a regular at Video Mania, stuffing quarters into a World Cup arcade machine, so he would have been forever passing the patch of sidewalk where Francisco, Jessica, and Daniela set up shop. "I was always around that area just, you know, being a knucklehead," Clever says. But he wasn't part of any homicide, and he didn't know who was.

"I told them the truth, and they were, like, refusing to understand me," he says. Then, according to Clever, the cops took turns smacking him, "smacking me like a motherfucker," he says, "trying to smack the truth out of me." He sat there, hands cuffed in his lap, tucking his chin to avoid direct blows.

"Why'd you do it?" the cops demanded.

"If I would have done this shit, I wouldn't even be here," Clever told the cops. Between the drugs and the fear, his mouth felt too dry to swallow.

A police report described Clever's reaction to the questioning as "one of disinterest and insensitivity."

Officers took Clever downtown, to the old Parker Center headquarters. Anyone who grew up on *Dragnet* would recognize the midcentury modernist garrison, all right angles and ceramic facades. Clever was held in a glass cell, where he slept some more, then picked up the built-in phone and dialed out to check on his mom. He reached his brother Baby, who was at the hospital with their whole brood of siblings, enough of Bernice Napoles's kids to field a soccer team. From his cell Clever could hear the sobs in her room, and he started crying too; their mother was dead.

Clever's name was all over the news that night. In the morning he was on the front page of the *Los Angeles Times*. Spanish-language daily *La Opinión* put him in the headline: "Suspect Arrested for Murder of Baby: Luis Silva, 19, Could Be Sentenced to Death."

Clever felt like the most hated man in LA, the scapegoat for a barbarity nobody was willing to believe he didn't commit. He understood he was in more than legal peril. His arrest exposed Tricky's smoke screen—the Columbia Lil Cycos could no longer blame the crime on a rival hood—which meant the green light was on. Anyone wanting to play avenger on behalf of the Mexican Mafia would be hunting for Clever. The police moved him to Men's Central Jail, a dank, decrepit bunker that civil rights groups have compared to a medieval dungeon. Just the year before, a federal judge ordered the creation of a reform panel after touring the facility, calling conditions there "not consistent with basic human values."

The windowless cells, the permanent twilight, the mold-blackened showers, the roar of metal bars and mad howls: Men's Central pushed everyone to the brink. Clever was placed in K-10, the "high jail security risk" unit, home to several hundred of the most violent or disruptive inmates, usually killers headed to prison or returning from prison to appeal their convictions. "High-profile cases, lifers, big bad dudes," Clever says. He was a skinny 160 pounds with a pained frown and a lost gaze. He'd been arrested once before, briefly taken into custody while posted up on Fifth Street with a Columbia Lil Cyco bagman, but this was Clever's first time in jail. He wanted to scream to everyone that it wasn't him, that he was a victim of mistaken identity, but the old heads warned him to stay quiet; it wasn't personal, it was politics. "I was the youngest one in that unit," Clever says. "I was trying to hide as much as possible."

Baby knew how exposed Clever was. His brother needed more than a lawyer. As the instigator of the MacArthur Park vendor tax, Baby felt an awful weight—a burden, he says, "that is going to haunt me for the rest of my life." He'd set something dreadful in motion, invented a racket that had turned grotesque, and now all he could think of was to save his brother, to exonerate Clever before he was killed. "I was basically, like, insane," Baby says. "I wasn't thinking rationally. I knew how serious this was."

Baby tracked down Atlas, his hand-picked rent collector. He dragged him to the top of the same Fifth Street building, with the barred windows and wrought-iron fire escape, where Clever had been living. It was four flights of stairs up to the normally off-limits roof, a nest of compressors and vents. The railing couldn't have been more than waist high. Baby pushed Atlas to the edge and pulled a gun.

"You better tell me what happened," Baby thundered.

For a time, he and Atlas had been running buddies, the bald gangster and the shaggy paisa. They'd gone to concerts and boxing matches together, partied at the Indian casinos, played soccer. But as Baby began withdrawing from the neighborhood and Atlas started reporting to Tricky, Baby noticed a change—how Atlas grew to covet the attention that his position commanded. "It gave him a sense of more empowerment around there," Baby says. "It elevated his ego." Baby was itching to pull Atlas back down to earth. He felt him shudder, struggling for traction in his tire-soled huaraches.

"Tell me what happened," Baby demanded, "or I'll throw you off the roof."

Other than those few minutes on Sixth Street a couple of days earlier, Atlas had never seen Giovanni, so he couldn't tell Baby much. "The truth is, I didn't even know his name," Atlas says. "But Baby didn't believe me."

"Tell me, was my brother involved or not?" Baby asked.

"I guarantee you, your brother wasn't there," Atlas said.

Baby loosened his grip on Atlas. Fearing that the Columbia Lil Cycos weren't done with him, Atlas packed a bag and booked a flight. By the end of the week, he was once again in Mexico—his eighteen-year odyssey in the US over—determined to never look back.

Baby went searching for Tricky. They met outside a bowling alley near Koreatown. "I just told him that, you know, my brother—I know my brother wasn't involved—and he confirmed it," Baby says. "I just wanted to get the right person that was involved and turn him in." Tricky told him it was Giovanni who'd messed up, who'd brought disgrace to the hood. He also warned Baby to stand down—Giovanni was being "taken out."

Baby felt like his head was exploding. Without the right suspect, he'd have no chance of clearing Clever's name. That meant getting to Giovanni first. "I needed to find him before, you know, they—they kill him," Baby says, "because I wanted to turn him in to the police."

He enlisted the help of another homie, a friend whose brother had a child with one of Mayra's sisters—the same kid who'd coaxed Giovanni into watching The Lion King—so he had an idea of where to look. They drove to the cottage at the edge of downtown, Baby preparing to play bounty hunter. "I'm just thinking, like, what can I do?" says Baby, who knew he was stepping out of line, inviting trouble for even thinking of handing over a fellow 18th Streeter to the police. He hadn't really contemplated how he would do it—at gunpoint?—or what would stop the LAPD from arresting him instead. Baby was already planning a funeral for their mother; he couldn't bear the thought of losing his brother at the same time. "I'm like, whatever I have coming, fuck it, let's do this," he says. "I didn't have too many options."

When they reached Mayra's house, Baby's heart sank. He was too late. There was no sign of Giovanni.

15

No One Sees Nothing

T he detectives of the LAPD's Robbery-Homicide Division all wear suits. It's a sign of professionalism and panache: as the top murder investigators in a city renowned for celebrity-entangled mayhem, they're conscious of looking the part. It's also a way to communicate respect for the victims, to say *Your loss is worth dressing up for.* Some detectives go all in, dropping a week's pay on a set of tailored Italian threads. David Holmes usually bought whatever was on sale: 3 Day Suit Broker, Macy's semiannual clearance. "Decent enough," he says, "to get the job done." With the help of a nimble dry cleaner, he didn't have to replace too many. "She sewed up pockets and seats in my pants, I don't know how many times over the years," he says. "My cleaner, she kept me in business."

Detectives Holmes was a Robbery-Homicide newbie. He'd joined the LAPD in 1998, a patrol officer in the San Fernando Valley. After a year and change, he moved to an undercover burglary detail, tracking prowlers, which introduced him to the detective bureau. When a suspect turned up dead, Holmes earned a transfer to the Devonshire Division's homicide team, just three years after putting on the uniform. "I loved chasing people," he says. "I was like a kid in a candy store." In 2007, after five years on the murder beat, he was tapped for Robbery-Homicide, the exclusive citywide squad. That meant a desk downtown, on the third floor of Parker Center, where the LAPD's best detectives cherry-picked the cases most likely to command resources and the spotlight, from Charles Manson and the Hillside Strangler to the Night Stalker and the Grim Sleeper. "It was like starting all over again," Holmes says, "all *yes, sir, no, sir.*"

The first case assigned to him was one the old-timers didn't want to touch: #0702–26094, the murder of Luis Angel Garcia.

Gang cases tended to be messy and frustrating, a morass of reluctant witnesses, and this one, as public and brazen as it was, appeared to have almost none. In Central America, where survival has long depended on forgetfulness, the strategy has been reduced to a saying: ver, oir y callar. See, hear, and keep quiet. "You knew a ton of people saw," says Holmes, "but then you get down there and no one sees nothing."

Although he'd worked 18th Street murders in the Valley before, Holmes didn't know MacArthur Park well. The sagging flophouses with their sardine-can studios, some without kitchens or even a private bathroom, where a dozen laborers might sleep in a single room on wall-to-wall mattresses, resembled the Lower East Side of nineteenth-century New York more than Southern California. The sidewalk commerce, pulsing with the sizzle of bacon-wrapped hot dogs on pushcarts and the crackle of pirated Los Tigres del Norte CDs on overburdened speakers, reflected a fortitude that he realized he'd never quite appreciated.

What most astonished Holmes was the gangster mural on the side of USA Donuts, its unabashed branding of the 18th Street aesthetic. "I'm thinking, 'How in God's name is the city allowing that?'" he says. "I mean, you go try to interview some of these people, and they're living in barely pantry-size apartments, and there's a ton of people in there just trying to make ends meet, you know, trying to cook the food or do whatever they bring out on the streets, and they are absolutely terrified that the police are even at the front door. And then the fact that they've got to walk by this mural every single day—it's just hammering home, you know, what's going to happen to you if you say anything. I didn't look at it as art or whatever. I looked at it as the full-on intimidation of the people that were living there." His first instinct was to gather some officers and paint over the thing. Supervisors warned, if he did, he'd be "starting World War Three."

Holmes grew up in the rolling hills of eastern San Diego, one of seven children born to devout Catholic parents, a Vietnam War medic and a nurse, who'd met while working at Balboa Naval Hospital. Like them, Holmes married young; within a year of graduation, he and his high school sweetheart had a kid on the way. "Being so young, I guess we could have taken the easy way out, but that was never an option," he says. "We were having a baby." The after-school job he'd worked at Price Club since he was sixteen became his career. For eleven years, Holmes would scratch his way up, eventually becoming a Costco floor manager after the two companies merged. It taught him good organizational habits and customer service skills, how to be detailed yet personable. He might have kept ascending at one of America's best workplaces but for two events he couldn't get out of his head.

In 1986, a twenty-year-old San Diego State University student named Cara Knott was pulled over by a California Highway Patrol officer on a dark, isolated off-ramp along Interstate 15. It was the same spot he'd chosen for making creepy overtures to other women drivers. When she resisted his advances, the officer grew enraged, strangling her with a rope and heaving her body off an abandoned bridge. Cara Knott had been Dave Holmes's babysitter.

Then, in 1993, a thirteen-year-old boy named Charlie Keever disappeared while riding his bike with a nine-year-old friend down a riverbed trail near the southern tip of San Diego Bay. Two days later, their bodies were found in a makeshift fort, each sexually violated and strangled. Charlie Keever's sister worked for Dave Holmes at Costco.

"Things like that, you know, that are kind of close to home, not just something that you see on TV or hear about—it was just kind of something always in the back of my mind," he says. "I mean, murder is just the ultimate crime." A thought began to form, one that has since crystallized into a mantra: "Only God gets to play God." Leaving Costco in his late twenties for the LAPD meant taking a pay cut, but Holmes felt there's "just a lot of evil in the world."

Like Special Agent Keenan, Detective Holmes stood out on the streets of MacArthur Park: close-cropped sandy hair, conservative tie, the broad shoulders of a onetime member of Valhalla High School's top-rated water polo program. But unlike Keenan, who needed to coordinate with the Justice Department back in Washington on a case as sensitive and complex as a RICO investigation, Holmes didn't have to be diplomatic. His job was simpler and less political—solve murders—and he was flabbergasted to learn that the one now on his plate had occurred right under the federal government's nose. "To say pissed off would be an understatement," Holmes says. He thought that Keenan had put together a "damn good case," but that the lawyers had held it up, "playing ping-pong back and forth." That's how a bureaucracy maintains a pristine conviction record, overwhelming defendants and discouraging them from going to trial. "You can't try to make it perfect," Holmes says. "You're not baking a cake for a wedding. It's crime. It's criminals." At the least, he thought the feds could have charged Tricky with something when they'd had him in cuffs earlier that year—taking him off the streets before the Columbia Lil Cycos went gunning for Francisco Clemente.

"You're getting people hurt by waiting," he says. "I thought this baby got killed because of the delay."

While Keenan raced to tie up two years of investigative work on the Columbia Lil Cycos' drug business, Holmes set out to find the killer of Luis Angel. On September 17, the Monday after the attack, Holmes started interviewing the survivors. Francisco was still heavily medicated and unresponsive; Holmes thought he was "touch and go at that point." Jessica kept vigil at his bedside. Just twenty-two, she seemed to grasp that Francisco's wounds had rearranged their lives, that she'd now have to summon enough tenacity for the both of them. In whispered pleas, she vowed to remain his partner—to raise the child in her belly together—if only he'd pull through.

Jessica did her best to describe the shooter: thin, young, fair-skinned, bald, with a wisp of a mustache, and "very well dressed." Although she thought she'd seen him once before out on Sixth Street, he'd never been among the gangsters who'd demanded rent. When Holmes showed her a six-pack of photos that again included Clever—still the only suspect the LAPD knew of—she circled his picture. Jessica thought he looked like a guy who'd been with the shooter that night, someone who'd shouted "hurry up" just before Francisco crumpled.

Holmes went to see Daniela Garcia at Guanajuato Tires, the cut-rate llantera in El Monte that Francisco had arranged as lodging for her and Jessica. The shop was little more than a driveway, tucked behind a stucco arch, just west of the paved San Gabriel River. The shop's approach to extending a tire's life depended more on faith than technology. "I remember watching the guys, and they would hand-carve the tires—take tires and literally carve tread into them," Holmes says. "It was crazy. Go in and get a tire for ten bucks, fifteen bucks, that somebody else threw away. But, you know, it was a business."

The three vendors had planned to spend Mexican Independence Day at Guanajuato Tires, along with the owner, who'd taken a liking to Daniela. They should have all been firing up the grill, fussing over the newborn. Instead, Francisco was entwined in tubes, and Luis Angel lay in the morgue.

Daniela had gone numb. "She had that thousand-yard stare," Holmes says. "She really didn't have much to say, rightfully so." When he showed her a six-pack of photos that included Clever, she recognized him—he was a regular at Video Mania—and on the back of the display, she wrote: "For the way he dresses up, looks like a gang member." But unlike Jessica, Daniela didn't remember him being there the night Luis Angel was killed.

Holmes's first concern was finding shelter for Daniela and Jessica. He'd be relying on them as witnesses for months, maybe years, if the Columbia Lil Cycos didn't get to them first, which meant not just ensuring their safety but freeing them from the tire shop, inching them back from the margins. "It was important to let them know we were basically going to take care of them," Holmes says. He checked Daniela and Jessica into a long-term hotel called Extended Stay America.

When at last Francisco came to, he still had two bullets in him: one suspended behind his lung, too close to his spine for doctors to safely remove; the other lodged in his jawbone, which made it difficult for him to open his mouth or talk. He'd been sharing a room at County-USC with at least three other patients—surviving a headline-making gang hit was no guarantee of privacy at the hospital of last resort—so when Holmes visited, he asked to have Francisco wheeled away from his neighbors.

Before Holmes could ask a question, Francisco began to cry. He tried to speak, but between his broken jaw and his pent-up tears, the words stayed stuck in his throat. It took Holmes a solid fifteen minutes before he realized what Francisco was trying to get across. Francisco said it again:

"It was my fault."

"What do you mean?" Holmes asked.

"I should have just paid them," Francisco said.

The detective was at a loss. "You could just see the guilt in his face," he says. "I walked out of there thinking, 'This guy probably wishes he were dead.'"

Of all the Sixth Street regulars who claimed to have seen nothing, there was one whose denials rang the hollowest. It was hard to imagine that Shorty, the alternately savvy and naive teenage lookout, hadn't been working on a Saturday night. Having watched for years as she triangulated the interests of cops and gangsters and vendors, the LAPD's Edgar Hernandez refused to believe that the girl who "tried to be everyone's friend" had been off playing soccer. "If someone's gonna know, it's gonna be her," Hernandez says. "So I told the detectives, 'I know she was there.'"

On September 27, twelve days after the shooting, the police brought Shorty to Parker Center, to Holmes's office. She wanted to be anywhere but a police station. The barrage of threats—the incentive to play dumb—remained fresh in her mind, even if she didn't breathe a word of it that day. If she was scared, she was also "extremely upset about the baby being killed," says Holmes, "and that was a motivation for her talking to us."

Shorty tried to have it both ways, offering clues while insisting she hadn't been present. She claimed to have heard who was involved, but couldn't say for sure—she was sticking to her story about soccer practice. "We could tell she was there because she was starting to give detail, and when we asked her about it, she immediately looked to the ground," Holmes says. "She couldn't look us in the face. You knew she wasn't telling the truth." Shorty did let a couple of names slip: Face and Rusty. But she insisted she was just passing along rumor, repeating what others were saying. Holmes recognized the monikers; he'd spotted them spray-painted on the side of a Bancomer branch at Sixth and Burlington, around the corner from the crime scene. "We just kind of left it alone," he says. "I didn't want to push her."

The next day, the phone rang in Holmes's office. He'd set up a hotline, to encourage anyone with information to call. Hernandez was with him, so they put the tipster on speakerphone.

"I want to make an amom-, an amom-um, an amomynous call," the voice on the other end said.

Hernandez looked at Holmes. It was a young girl, speaking accented English, stumbling over a word she'd probably never in her whole life had the need to say. They each stifled a laugh.

"Shorty?"

Click. The line went dead.

16

A Change of Plans

T he Wednesday after the shooting, September 19, Giovanni heard a
honk. Face was outside Mayra's house in a white SUV. Giovanni had
done as instructed: laid low, stayed off the streets, given Tricky time to cover
their tracks. But four days had gone by, and Giovanni was going to need cash
if the Columbia Lil Cycos expected him to do it much longer. He jumped in
the truck, figuring Face had brought a little something to tide him over. "I
trust people," Giovanni says. "If I just meet you, I feel like I would trust you
until you show me different. I don't know if that's a good quality or not, but
that's how I am."

Face had been a saving grace that summer, ready to defend Giovanni
against Tricky's aspersions. Whatever had gone wrong out on Sixth Street,
they were homies. Face had *XVIII* in one-inch numerals stamped above his
left eyebrow; Giovanni had the number spelled out across his scalp. They
were dieciocho por vida. Forever. Face headed for the freeway.

"Where are we going?" Giovanni asked.

"Mexico," Face said. "You can't be here."

Giovanni told Face he didn't want to go. Face told him they had to get out
of town, that people "were dropping a dime on us." Giovanni told him to slow
up. He needed to alert Mayra, who'd been in the bathroom; he'd walked out
the door without so much as a goodbye. He also didn't have a phone on him or
even his ID. He wanted to go back, to at least see if his girl would come along.

"Nah, that can't happen," Face said. "Nobody can know where we're going."

Instead of heading out of town, Face took Giovanni to South-Central, to a
six-unit apartment house on Eighty-Third Street. The owner of the SUV lived

there. Five feet tall, she went by Midget. She'd belonged to Face's clique of 18th Street, the Wall Street Gangsters, since she was twelve. "They were my family," says Midget, whose mom had relinquished her after arriving in the US from El Salvador as a pregnant teen. "I grew up in the street." Midget had thin, penciled eyebrows and long, auburn-tinted hair; her smile was tight-lipped, at once wily and cautious. Thirty-one by then, a single mother of five boys between the ages of six and seventeen, Midget was doing her best to be their rock—to repair what she could and inch toward something better. She'd nearly completed a nursing program at American Career College.

Face had been on her that evening about borrowing the truck. He kept insisting that he had to drop someone off in San Diego—a homie who "needed to keep low-pro because he was being looked for," Midget says. She objected. Because of her messed-up credit, the 1997 Chevy Tahoe wasn't in her name. Another 18th Streeter had signed for it, and when he learned that she'd been loaning the truck out around the hood, he threatened to return it to the dealer. Midget couldn't afford to kiss her only transportation goodbye, not with a brood of kids. To pacify Face, she told him that she'd drive them to San Diego herself, even though she felt like she was being "sweet-talked into doing some shit that I shouldn't be doing."

When Face arrived with Giovanni, Midget thought he looked familiar. She often drank beer at the same South Gate crash pad where Giovanni had taken up residence that September. Face told Giovanni to stay at the apartment while he left with Midget to gather some clothes for himself. Four of her children were there, asleep; it was a school night and close to twelve. None of it added up: Face needing to pack, Midget bailing on her kids, and Giovanni wondering why he wouldn't need more than the checkered shorts and Sean Jean shirt he had on.

It occurred to Giovanni that he could walk out the door right then and there, vanish into the night. He'd heard that the police had arrested Clever; it wasn't right, but it was convenient. If the cops thought they had the killer, maybe they wouldn't come looking for him. Giovanni didn't want to go to

Mexico, especially without Mayra, who was surely fuming about his disappearance. He didn't want to add to his mom's heartbreak either; he hadn't spoken to her since leaving Palmdale in August, and his silence would now be extended for who knew how long. But to get up and split, to defy Face and upset the plan the Columbia Lil Cycos had devised for him, wasn't something likely to be forgiven. He'd be running out on the hood, squandering whatever goodwill his audacity had earned him over the weekend. Maybe putting his life in danger. It seemed safer to play along. "I had a feeling," Giovanni says, "but I didn't listen to it."

He did seize the chance to use Midget's landline, to call Mayra and explain why he'd left so abruptly. "She's like, 'What the hell, where you at?' I'm like, 'I'm in South-Central, I'm going on the run.' She said, 'What the hell you mean you're going on the run?' I said, 'Yeah, I'm gone, you know.' And she started crying. So I told her, 'Hey, look, if you want, you could come with me, I'll take you if you wanna go.' And she agreed."

While Giovanni stayed put, Face made preparations. He and Midget drove fifteen minutes east, to the South Gate house, where Face gave the Tahoe a once-over: oil, water, fluids. His thoroughness exceeded what a trip down Interstate 5 would demand.

Face also brought another 18th Streeter from South-Central into the mix, a homie named Ranger. Two months shy of his thirtieth birthday, Ranger had a puggish nose, a heavily creased chin, and eyes that seemed to look straight through everyone. Ranger and Midget went way back, to the early '90s. "We used to hang around together and party," she says. "We pretty much grew up together." In her teens, Midget had a fling with Ranger; she'd also hooked up with Ranger's brother, the father to one of her sons.

Ranger had trouble staying out of jail. As a scrawny sixteen-year-old, he killed a woman in a drive-by: shot her in the chest as she smoked a cigarette outside a friend's house. The victim looked butch—cropped hair, shirt buttoned to the top—and witnesses speculated that Ranger had mistaken her for a male rival. Tried as a juvenile, he was out by twenty-four. That year he caught a trespass case and went back to jail on a parole violation. A year later he was arrested for vandalizing a neighborhood market and a few months later for possessing a firearm. He got busted for stripping a stolen car of custom rims. In 2006, when he was twenty-eight, Ranger was arrested for snatching a fifteen-year-old girl off the streets and holding her captive to extract a $500 ransom from her dad. Charged with attempted extortion, he paroled on September 5, 2007. The address Ranger gave his parole agent was Midget's apartment; he was supposed to be starting a job as a carpet installer.

By the time Face and Midget returned, now with Ranger, Giovanni had spent an hour unsupervised. He didn't ask Face what he'd been doing. He didn't question Ranger's role. Giovanni's head was back at Mayra's place. He told Face he'd called her.

"You did what?" Face said.

"Yeah, she's gonna go."

"Hell, no," Face said.

For a second time that night, Giovanni left Mayra hanging.

Midget wrote a note for her kids, explaining that she'd be home in the morning to take them to school—a glimmer of maternal concern before a preposterous errand. Without traffic, it was two hours to San Diego. If they hit rush hour on the return, maybe three hours to get home. Midget asked Face to leave some money for the kids' bus fare, "just in case we didn't make it back." Then she whispered to one of her sons: "I'm going to be out." And they left.

Ranger and Giovanni climbed in the back seat. Face drove with Midget at his side, a crucifix dangling between them from her rearview mirror. Along the way, they stopped for gas and beer. After another hour or so, as they neared San Diego, Face broke the news to Midget.

"There's been a change of plans," he said. They had to go all the way to TJ.

Midget protested. She needed to be in LA by sunrise to get her kids ready for school. Face told her it would be quick. "He said we were going to drop

Rusty off and just come right back," she says. She'd gone too far to make a fuss at that point. Better to be a sport.

They reached the border, some twenty miles past San Diego, around two in the morning, illuminated green arrows pointing them across the international line. There is no greater reminder of the asymmetry between the US and Mexico than the experience of rolling unimpeded into Tijuana—no questions, no documents—while cars queue up for hours in the northbound lanes of the San Ysidro crossing, the busiest land port in the western hemisphere. Nobody thought twice about the four 18th Streeters from LA as they cruised down Avenida Revolución.

17

Make Him Feel at Ease

ricky left for Tijuana not long after Giovanni arrived there. He was still the number-one target of the FBI investigation, but the feds needed time to indict him, to present evidence to a grand jury, so there was nothing to stop him from heading for Mexico to orchestrate Giovanni's death. Except maybe Morena. "I didn't go and tell my wife, 'Hey, baby, I'm going to go to Mexico, and I'm going to kill this fool,'" Tricky says. He invented a story instead about bringing his van there to be painted. Low-cost auto work, like marked-down dentistry and half-price plastic surgery, brought hordes of bargain seekers to TJ. Even while executing a murderous plot, the ruling family of the Columbia Lil Cycos valued domestic tranquility. "I mean, that's my wife," Tricky says. "I'm not going to just get up and leave and not tell her where I'm going."

Tricky, of course, could have arranged for Giovanni to be disappeared just about anywhere: desert, mountains, the lake at MacArthur Park. But in his jaded, American gangster view of Mexico, the border beckoned like some all-purpose dumping ground. "It's easier to kill them in Mexico because so many people are killed over there, and they don't even know who they are. They don't know whether they're from the United States or whether they're from over there," Tricky says. "We kill him over here, the cops are going to be on it."

On September 20, Tricky parked on the US side, in the long-term lots of San Ysidro, and walked through the revolving one-way pedestrian gates into Mexico with $30,000 stuffed in a backpack. He was picked up by an exiled shotcaller, the one ousted over his fishy brothel deal several regimes earlier. It's unclear how the money fit into Tricky's plans. He spoke of using it to disguise the plot, to keep Giovanni calm until the particulars could be ironed

out. "Making him feel comfortable in having confidence that there was nothing out of the ordinary that, you know, he was just in Mexico to party—you
know, get drunk, have some broads with him," Tricky says. "Just make him
feel at ease that, you know, everything was going to be alright." More likely,
the cash would fund a backup plan if Face chickened out—perhaps entice the
ex-shotcaller to help Tricky kill Giovanni, and maybe do away with Face too.

Either way, Tricky looked at this excursion as a triumph in the making, a
testament to his leadership abilities and organizational control. He didn't
need to consult Puppet about it. "One of the main reasons why he sponsored
me," says Tricky, "was because of my business personality that I had with how
to control the business aspect of the enterprise." If he could extinguish the
green light without having to involve Puppet, maybe even before Puppet
learned the full extent of the blunder on Sixth Street, then Tricky might be
on his way to Eme induction. "That's what I was being groomed for," he says.
"Eventually, one day, I would become a Mexican Mafia member."

Giovanni didn't know much about Mexico. He'd gone once in his early
teens to attend a quinceañera for a family friend. And he'd gone once as a
toddler, so long ago the memory had been erased. That trip marked a turning
point, a journey steeped in shame and silence: the family's original sin. In
December 1990, when Giovanni was a year and a half, his mother took him
to Guadalajara to say goodbye to his dad. Then she made that man—the story
of his life, the circumstances of his death—a secret.

Roberto Macedo was a scamp, the product of hard knocks, surviving on
little more than wit and nerve. Born in the remote ranching town of Cuautla,
about three hours from Jalisco's capital city, he'd been cast aside by his
mother—"a very fierce, super fierce woman," says his older sister, Teresa
Macedo. "What we wanted was love and affection, not blows, and life gave us
many blows." As a teenager, Roberto headed into Guadalajara to fend for
himself. He had Indigenous features: high cheekbones, thatch of black hair,
almond eyes, smooth chest. In the central city's hive of street commerce,
between the graceful granite-slabbed plazas of downtown and the narrow

lanes entwining Mercado San Juan de Dios, he trafficked in fayuquita—counterfeit baubles—fobbing off phony jewelry on unsuspecting customers. "He was just out there trying to make his little living," his sister says. "At least he wasn't robbing. If the people allow themselves to get screwed, well, that's another thing. He was great at crooked business."

At the end of 1978, when Roberto was twenty, he hooked up with a sixteen-year-old girl. She became pregnant with a son, but Roberto was gone, off to the US before the boy was born. "When he left, he said he was going to better himself, to give a better life to my mother, which, well, he never gave, because he never sent anything," says the son, also named Roberto, who works the graveyard shift at a Guadalajara glass factory, molding tequila bottles. "The truth is, I didn't know if he existed or not."

As a young man in Los Angeles, with little education and no papers, Roberto Macedo gravitated to MacArthur Park, then in the throes of its cultural transformation. He dealt some drugs and played some dice. "He was a gambler, my brother," Teresa Macedo says. "You have to be intelligent to play those games. I think he did well, too, because as far as I know he didn't work." In the 1980s, Roberto got popped by the LAPD at least twenty times, mostly for gambling. He'd go to court, post—and forfeit—the $50 bail, then head right back to the park.

In LA, he had two more kids, twin girls, with a Puerto Rico–born woman named Ramonita Montañez. Raised in Brooklyn by a churchgoing social worker, Ramonita began running away the minute she hit adolescence—"a very strong, power woman," says her younger sister Elisa. "I don't think no one could stop her from the things she wanted to do." Ramonita started getting high. She spent time in juvenile detention. When she was about twenty, Ramonita surfaced in LA, intent on kicking what had become a heroin habit.

Nobody is sure how Ramonita met Roberto, but after the twins were born in 1982, her sister visited their apartment, in a building with conquistadors carved into the window arches, on a leafy street near Koreatown. Compared to the other men in Ramonita's life, Roberto was "a wonderful husband to her and a great, great, great father," Elisa says. The twins were a blend of both parents, two precocious café con leche girls with big heads of curls, and in every photo that has survived, Roberto is cradling them, one in each arm, or hoisting them, one on each shoulder.

In 1986, Ramonita fell ill. She returned to New York with the twins. Elisa tended to her big sister, feeding and bathing her as she grew frail, "skinny like a toothpick." At the beginning of 1987, Ramonita Montañez died of AIDS. So extreme was the stigma at that time, so limited the medical guidance, a sheet of glass was placed over her open casket at the R. G. Ortiz Funeral Home. "You could view her, but through glass," her sister says. "The virus was so new. People were scared."

It's hard to know what Roberto understood about HIV in that era, but when he met Reyna Flores in 1988 on the MacArthur Park lakefront, he sanitized the details of his previous relationship. "He told me she died of cancer," Reyna says. "I didn't know. I guess I believed him." Every summer the twins flew out to LA to see their dad. They had to be tested twice a year, to be sure they weren't carrying their mother's virus, but nobody mentioned that to Reyna either. In 1989, the girls met their newborn baby brother, Giovanni, and in 1990, Israel. Roberto, on the strength of his dope game, had moved Reyna and the boys into a nicer place, a turn-of-the-century Italianate fourplex near the USC campus, and filled it with new appliances. When the girls visited, he took his expanding family to the Exposition Park Rose Garden, thousands of blossoms deep, and to Knott's Berry Farm, a bastion of Peanuts-branded amusements, where they posed with a giant Lucy mascot. In the photos, Reyna looks sullen. Roberto beams, flashing a thumbs-up in his Le Tigre polo.

The summer of Israel's birth, the girls had to cut their visit short. "It broke their hearts," Elisa says. "'My papi is sick,' they kept saying, 'Papi is sick.' And I'm, like, 'Oh, my God. This can't be happening again.'" By fall 1990, Roberto's face had turned blotchy. He shook with fevers, retched if he tried to swallow food. When he refused to see a doctor, Reyna called 911. At County-USC, they told her that Roberto had full-blown AIDS, that he'd be gone within two months. The news shattered Reyna. It infuriated her. "I was so angry," she says. "I didn't know what to do." Roberto grew morose, threatening to kill himself—he kept a gun near their bed—or worse, kill Reyna and the boys too, to put them all out of their misery. Reyna couldn't think. The shock, the deception, the fear that she and her two babies would be next—it was all too much. She was nineteen.

Roberto determined that he should die in Mexico. He sold every possession he could and left for Guadalajara, taking refuge in his sister's house in the Hermosa Provincia district. He'd been away almost twelve years. Some of their old friends hoped to conjure a miracle, "running around, trying to figure out how to cure him," Teresa Macedo says. "Even looking for a shaman." For the first time Roberto met his eldest child and namesake, presenting him with a mariner's cross—Jesus atop an anchor.

Reyna flew down a month later with the boys. Although she'd by then secured her green card, allowing her to travel, Reyna never shook the sense that her place in the US was provisional; that some bureaucratic glitch, or a misstep of her own, could one day undo her privileges. She felt nothing for Roberto. The trip wasn't to find peace. Reyna had hoped that Roberto's years on the hustle would at least deliver a windfall, something to help restart her life. But whatever money he'd accumulated, according to his sister, went to "expenses," including doctors and funeral arrangements. Reyna returned to LA to collect her WIC check, afraid she'd lose her benefits if she were out of the country. She took Israel, still an infant, but agreed to let Giovanni stay with his father through Christmas. When she returned two weeks later, Roberto was dead, buried in the Panteón Guadalajara under a white granite crucifix. "She came back for Giovanni and left," Teresa Macedo says. "The boy didn't want to go. After all, he hadn't seen her for a while. At the airport, he cried and cried. I said, 'No, he should go with his mother, pobrecito.'"

Now Giovanni, almost seventeen years later, was returning to Mexico like his father to die. It was too late to do much of anything that first night in

Tijuana. Giovanni's offing would have to wait. Face chose a motel, a mission-style dump a few blocks from the lurid, neon glare of the main drag, with its discount pharmacies and beer-by-the-bucket clubs and showgirl palaces. The Hotel Leyva inhabited a border-adjacent nook known as the zona de tolerancia, where sex servers in spandex and pumps lined the sidewalks outside Bar Adelita and La Gloria. The bare-bulb rooms were stuffy and dank, and the clip-clop of heels echoed down the long terrazzo corridors at all hours, but you could score a bed for $20, no ID needed. Face paid for a double. Giovanni had to share a mattress with Ranger.

They woke up on Thursday, September 20, late morning. Face left in the truck with Ranger. "They said they were going to go look for the address where we were going to drop Rusty off," Midget says. "And me and Rusty stayed in the room." Once again, Giovanni had a chance to bolt. Tijuana's streets teemed with supplicants and peddlers and troubadours. Giovanni could have camouflaged himself in that world, bought himself time. Midget couldn't have stopped him. Instead, Giovanni waited and trusted. They found a mini-mart, bought chips and soda, then returned to the room. They made small talk.

Midget told him that her eldest was almost his age. Giovanni told her about his mom and his girlfriend, how he hoped he'd be able to return before the end of the year and spend Christmas with them. Midget didn't ask what he was running from: "Knowing stuff that you are not supposed to gets you in trouble." But she did reassure him that getting back to the US wasn't a big deal.

"I told him that if he was a US citizen, he wouldn't have a problem," Midget says. "That all he got to do was just cross the border with his ID or birth certificate."

Giovanni explained that he had nothing on him, no ID, no proof of anything. He'd been forced to leave in such a hurry. He told her: "Face just kind of like kidnapped me."

When Face and Ranger left the motel, they went to see Tricky. They met a few minutes outside town, where the border meets the beach, in the Playas de Tijuana neighborhood. Face parked the SUV and rolled down the window.

"This is the homeboy Ranger, from South-Central 18," Face said.

"Mucho gusto," said Tricky, reaching inside the truck and shaking Ranger's hand.

They talked about Giovanni's mental state, whether he suspected what was coming, and how much longer to let the charade play out. "The way I figured it, if it went the way I wanted it, I'll take him, I'll keep him, I'll feed him," Tricky says. "I mean, that was my intention. Yeah, you know, overseeing him for a minute." Tricky's attempt at paternalism, as if a leisurely approach to Giovanni's final hours were the mark of a discerning leader, didn't jibe with an international kidnap-murder plot. Even Face could see that.

"Fuck it," Face told Tricky, "I'll take care of it."

He pried back the truck's AC vent and pulled out a gun—a .357, Tricky thought.

The show of bravado put Tricky's mind at ease. "So basically," he says, "that cleaned my hands of having my hands dirty." Tricky drove off, confident that he'd remedied the Columbia Lil Cycos' crisis without having to do anything distasteful himself. He needed to get back to LA the following day anyway. "That happened to be my wife's birthday," says Tricky, who wanted his return from Mexico to be a "surprise."

When Face and Ranger arrived back at the motel, Midget asked to use Face's phone. She couldn't get reception in Mexico with her own, and she needed to find someone to pick up her kids from school that afternoon. Face agreed. But when Giovanni asked if he could make a call, Face again shut him down. "He just told him that he couldn't use the phone because he was supposed to be keeping low-pro," says Midget, "and he couldn't have nobody know where he was at." Giovanni felt dejected, sure that Mayra would blame him for this silence, and anxious about what his months of purgatory would entail. He'd need clothes, food, a bed somewhere, yet the details remained hazy. "I was being told to just chill," Giovanni says. "I couldn't get a straight answer from nobody."

Face proposed they hit Avenida Revolución that afternoon, to have a good time before Giovanni went into hiding. Ranger seemed withdrawn. "He was pretty quiet—quieter than usual," Midget says. "Usually he was joking around." The four of them wandered the dance clubs, the titty joints, the dives, encouraging Giovanni to take advantage of Mexico's eighteen-year-old drinking age. Face told him that "he better drink up," says Midget, "that, you know—that probably—that he could only party like that once." Giovanni didn't need much prodding. Whatever his misgivings, he was the toast of this little 18th Street detachment, the center of their grown-up attention.

After a few beers, Giovanni grew bolder. He chatted up a prostitute near the motel. In TJ slang, streetwalkers were called paraditas, a play on words for a woman on her feet and a hard-on. Giovanni figured he was in for a long dry spell. "He kept on bugging Face about, you know, being with her, giving him money to be with her," Midget says. Face laughed it off at first, but then saw opportunity. He bought a fifth of vodka. Back at the motel, Face told Giovanni that he'd give him money for the paradita if he drank the whole bottle—taunted him, actually, telling Giovanni he couldn't handle that much liquor.

"Well, I'll show you," Giovanni announced.

Nobody else touched the vodka. Giovanni chugged it. He was going to make Face pay.

Giovanni drank at least half the bottle, maybe two-thirds, something like ten to twelve shots. "He was pretty pumped up," Midget says. She and Ranger took Giovanni back out on the town, while Face stayed in the room to sleep. Giovanni found the woman he liked and asked how much: $25. It was more than Face had given him. Ranger left to retrieve more money. Giovanni tried to keep cool as he waited out on the streets of the world's most visited city to get laid, the prospect of no-strings gratification tantalizingly close. But his head had started to spin, and then his stomach. Giovanni barfed right at his would-be companion's feet. "Splattered all over," he says. "I think I even ruined her high heels."

Giovanni staggered away. Midget draped his arm over her shoulder, and together they weaved back to the Hotel Leyva and up the stairs to the room. As soon as she and Giovanni stumbled in, Face and Ranger split again. Once more, Giovanni was free, at liberty to walk out the door and save himself, if he could have snapped out of his stupor long enough to realize that 18th Street was throwing him a Tijuana bachelor party only because he'd never live long enough to have one. Instead, he turned his attention to Midget. "He was already pumped up because he wanted to go be with that one prostitute he had seen," she says. "So he started telling me, you know, to have sex and stuff." Midget told him no. Giovanni didn't listen. She was a homegirl—one of their own; if Face and Ranger kept leaving them alone, there had to be a reason. Midget lied and said she had a thing with Ranger. Giovanni climbed on top of her. Midget, who'd already been manipulated into making a trip to Mexico for 18th Street's benefit, relented yet again.

"He insisted, and after a while, I gave in," she says. "I just gave in so he would leave me alone."

Face and Ranger returned. It was maybe 1 A.M. They asked Midget to step outside to the courtyard and have a talk in the truck. It was then that they made explicit what Midget had begun to suspect, that all the drinking, the daring, the stalling—it was a warm-up for the main event. "They told me that they weren't going to drop him off nowhere, that it was a hit," Midget says. "That they needed to get rid of him because he had messed up. That either it was him or a lot of other homeboys because the hood had a green light."

Midget had to think quickly. She'd been used by Giovanni. Now she was being used by Face and Ranger to chauffeur them to Giovanni's execution. Midget didn't protest or try to back out. She didn't warn Giovanni. She figured she'd be risking her own life, or jeopardizing her kids' safety, if she tried to intervene. Her mind raced ahead—she'd surrendered to sex with a dead man. If she wasn't yet a nurse, Midget at least knew about DNA.

Before it was too late, she needed her homeboys to make Giovanni take a shower, to clean himself off. She had so little control, it was the best she could come up with to protect herself. "I knew that if anything happened to him and he was found," says Midget, "my fluids would be on him."

18

Headfirst into the Deep End

Shorty had gone to a pay phone outside Children's Hospital, the same East Hollywood facility that had treated Giovanni for his panic attacks. She didn't plan on talking to the cops, let alone making a confession. But she had known Clever for years—knew he hadn't been on Sixth Street the night of the shooting—and felt obligated to speak up for him. "They got the wrong person inside jail," she says. "It was not fair to have the innocent person inside and having the shooter outside."

Shorty's act wasn't entirely spontaneous. Clever's family insisted that she make the call; they drove Shorty to the pay phone to ensure she went through with it. Shorty had hoped she could blurt out the truth without answering any questions or saying her name—"and just get it over with." She hadn't banked on giving herself away.

On October 1, 2007, three days after Shorty hung up on him, Holmes paid her a visit at school. She'd just started her freshman year at a troubled South-Central LA campus bursting with more than four thousand teenagers, less than 15 percent of them proficient in English. An administrator pulled Shorty from class and brought her to the counselor's office. "She was scared to death," Holmes says. "I mean, to the point where she was shaking." His manner in these moments tends to be folksy yet forceful, a kindly uncle who just caught his favorite niece in a lie. He speaks in down-home phrases, turning his *you*s into *ya*s and *g*-dropping his *-ing* verbs, while conveying the inevitability of a confession—a languid, help-me-help-you vibe. "David is just so humble, so levelheaded," says Laura Evens, his Robbery-Homicide partner. "I talk like a truck driver."

Holmes coaxed Shorty into divulging almost every name he could have hoped for: Face, the choreographer; Rusty, the triggerman; Barrios and Atlas, the shakedown artists; Lil Primo, the weapon collector; and Big Guy, the evidence dumper. She told the police about Tricky. About Grumpy and Raven too. Although she'd set out only to exonerate Clever, Shorty was cracking the case, exposing the whole boneheaded scheme.

"A small, little girl," Holmes says, "but with the courage of a lion."

He then visited her parents, to commend them for their daughter's bravery and prepare them for the backlash it would provoke. Their place was a long, narrow three-bedroom rectangle with barred windows and spiked fencing at the foot of a towering freeway noise barrier. The Matiases had bought the house in 2005, during the boom in subprime mortgages, qualifying for a $324,000 loan while simultaneously taking out a second deed of trust for $81,000, both at adjustable interest rates with the potential to soar into the mid-teens. Holmes explained that he'd have to move them to a safe location, for a month or two, maybe more. Shorty couldn't be vending out on Sixth Street either. Andres Matias, the patriarch, was sixty, his face hard and serious; Juana Matias was shorter and stouter, a follower of charismatic Catholicism, a Pentecostal movement sweeping Latin America. Holmes's words appeared to have no effect. "They were mad at her for talking to the police," he says, "which ticked me off. She got a lot of pushback. I mean, they used her to sell stuff, to help put food on the table, and they were angry with her not being able to go out anymore."

Even after Shorty's act of conscience, the authorities did not release Clever. They believed that she was trying to protect him—"for whatever reason," Detective Evens says. "She was so smart at that age. So smart but so dumb. I mean, she literally thought these guys and gals were her friends." Clever looked too familiar to too many people. He had to fit in somewhere.

So Clever stayed in jail, without bail, a sitting duck. Although *La Opinión* quoted an LAPD spokesperson in late September saying that Clever wasn't the shooter, he remained the only suspect publicly linked to Luis Angel's death, and because he hadn't confessed or cooperated, he wasn't placed in protective custody. Whatever the Columbia Lil Cycos were cooking up in Mexico, it wouldn't do Clever any good unless word of Giovanni's elimination reached Men's Central. Once a week or so, Clever's unit earned a visit to the caged rooftop exercise yard: a chance to escape the clatter and gulp some noninstitutionalized air. It was also an opportunity to handle business. Not long after his arrest, as the men lined up to return to their cells, Clever was ambushed. "That's when I got touched," he says. "Boom boom boom boom boom boom boom boom boom boom."

It wasn't just one guy, or one gang, enforcing the green light but seemingly every inmate on his floor. "It was all of them," Clever says. "Grown men." They jumped Clever, engulfing him in a cyclone of fists and feet. Clever tried to twist away, but they had him pinned. He buckled. His face burned. He'd barely seen it coming, but it had to have been a blade, likely extracted from a disposable razor and melted into a plastic toothbrush handle. It carved a gash from the base of his left ear to the corner of his lip. Blood gushed. His teeth poked through the serrated flesh. "They were all saying I was the one who did it," says Clever, "the one who killed the kid." He felt his mother present, her spirit watching over him. It was the only explanation he could muster for why he didn't die.

Deputies peeled him off the floor and threw him in his seven-by-nine-foot cell. No medical aid. As Clever was beginning to learn, his third-floor module served as the breeding ground for a gang of sheriff's deputies known as the 3000 Boys—jailers who subjected inmates to "the kind of stuff you imagine seeing in Saddam Hussein's Iraq," as one civil rights lawyer has put it. The 3000 Boys were among nearly a dozen secret cliques across the Los Angeles County Sheriff's Department whose decades of brutality, inside the jails and on the streets, have cost taxpayers upward of $55 million in abuse payouts. "I was like, 'Something's wrong here, you know, these guys are different,'" says Clever, who felt as threatened by the guards as by his neighbors. Despite his injury, he told himself: "You gotta ride it out." He took a white T-shirt and balled it up, pressing it against his left cheek. He tried to sleep. The shirt turned the color of beets. After two days, a deputy noticed his condition and transported Clever to the jail ward of County-USC. It was on the thirteenth floor of the old General Hospital—a source of gallows humor for the medical staff—an unlucky combination of lockup and infirmary. There behind the barred windows, doctors worked to clean his festering wound. They sealed the skin with medical glue.

"One of the fucking deputies was like, 'Treat him up—he's never gonna get out,'" Clever says. "'Because he murdered a kid.'"

During the few hours that Clever spent in the hospital, it's likely that Francisco Clemente was still there, under the same roof, recuperating from the bullets that the Mexican Mafia attributed to Clever. All told, Francisco would spend close to three weeks hooked to IVs, waiting for his abdomen to close, growing "skinny, skinny, skinny, so skinny," says Jessica Guzman, who traveled back and forth to visit him, from the Extended Stay America, which was near the South Bay, twenty miles up the 110 to County-USC.

Francisco wasn't well enough to attend Luis Angel's funeral, but he grieved as if the baby were his own. Many times he would say that he should have absorbed all the bullets, that he would have preferred to give his life if it meant sparing Luis Angel's. "It hurts me so much, that poor child," Francisco says. "He wasn't to blame for anything." Jessica did what Francisco couldn't, helping Daniela with arrangements no parent should have to imagine: the miniature oak coffin for the baby's body, not yet nine pounds, the lacy white bereavement gown. Jessica went to the morgue "to dress him in his little clothes," she says. "Where they had him all cold. Frozen."

The service was held on September 24 under tight security at a virtually empty Saint Vincent Catholic Church, the same ornate sanctuary where Arnold Schwarzenegger, California's governor at the time, had battled a gooey, arthropodan Satan in *End of Days*. Luis Angel's casket was wheeled past the vacant pews atop an adjustable church trolley, its accordion-design

X's squeezed tight to fit the small box. The owner of the used-tire shop served as a pallbearer. He'd been so taken by Daniela that he'd bought a crib for her baby, but his affections went unrequited. In the glow of the stained glass, he wore dark shades, a gold cross, and a black aloha shirt emblazoned with flames. The other pallbearer, Howard Dotson, was a US Army veteran, art therapist, and community outreach pastor who had vowed that year to memorialize every homicide victim in the Rampart Division. He tried to live by a motto: "Out of tragedy comes hope."

Just a few days earlier, the LAPD had asked him to comfort Daniela, who'd been summoned to police headquarters for more questioning. He sat with her in an interrogation room, every surface etched in graffiti, including the scrawls of the gang that had killed her baby. "Like, literally there's 18th Street tags on the walls," says Reverend Dotson, who was serving at First Congregational Church of Los Angeles. "If anyone deserved a shepherd at that moment, it was her." Daniela's grief was so disabling, there was little Dotson could say. It wasn't the time for scripture. Instead, he told her that she needn't fight her tears: "Sort of like when you feel nauseated and you throw up, you feel better," as he put it, "those tears are going to help you feel better." At the service, he hugged her tightly. Daniela wore a white shawl over her head, and she wept as a white mortcloth was draped over the casket.

Dotson accompanied her to a private burial at Forest Lawn, in the Hollywood Hills, where a grassy slope called Precious Love is reserved for the youngest departed. He led Daniela, her admirer, and Jessica in a round of "De Colores," the folk anthem of activists and dreamers across the Latin world, after which he prepared to offer a final prayer before Luis Angel's casket was lowered into the earth. It was then that Daniela asked to see her baby one last time—to open the box and kiss his ashen forehead. Following her lead, they each took a turn, everyone except Dotson. "I've had PTSD ever since then," he says. "That tore me up."

After the funeral, Daniela did her best to forget. Whether reverting to old habits or adopting new ones, she drowned her pain in alcohol, suffocated it in crack. Jessica and Francisco, who was home from the hospital by then, looked on in alarm. With the bit of aid she was receiving from a victim services fund, Daniela became an attractive target for men they'd known from the streets, "bad guys," says Francisco, who were only too happy to drag her down. "They got ahold of her," he says, "and she fell."

Francisco suggested to Jessica that they begin to distance themselves from Daniela, "so that she can fix her problems, and we can fix our own." He worried that Jessica might be tempted, in solidarity or sympathy, to join Daniela in whatever escape she'd surrendered to. "She opted for a bad path," Francisco told Jessica, "and I don't want you, as her friend, to later go, 'Oh, look at this, look at that, who knows what.' Better to cut it off here."

It didn't take long for Daniela's desperation to upend her life even more than her sorrow already had. On the afternoon of October 18, 2007, less than a month after kissing her son goodbye, she walked out of the Extended Stay America, across a parking lot, and into a Walmart. Security caught Daniela shoplifting two pairs of earrings. When officers searched her, they found two ziplock baggies of cocaine in her shoe. In her coat pocket, she had two Social Security cards, plus a Visa Platinum debit card, none in her name.

"I was so angry when I got that call," Holmes says. Victims didn't need to be perfect, and Daniela had every reason to want to self-medicate, but it would be hard to put her on a witness stand or even foot the bill for her relocation if she was out committing felonies. Like Francisco, Holmes thought it would be best to separate Jessica from Daniela. "I mean, the whole thing with the baby and everything else, I just don't think she knew how to cope with it," he says. "She dove headfirst into the deep end."

Daniela spent a total of forty-two days in jail, mostly for repeated failures to appear in court on her one rash attempt to turn jewelry into drugs. Holmes worked to get her help, enrolling her in a live-in treatment program and appearing alongside her at a probation interview to attest to her satisfactory progress. A judge accepted Daniela's plea to cocaine possession in exchange for the state's dropping the other charges and deferred entering judgment for eighteen months to give her an opportunity to get clean. But the system, even at its most benevolent, exacted a price. Daniela was ordered to pay a $150 diversion fee and a $20 court security surcharge. When she was a no-show at two more hearings and placed on formal probation for three years, the court assessed her a $200 lab analysis fee, a $200 restitution fine, and another $20 court security surcharge. "It's fucked up," Laura Evens says. "But at some point, we just couldn't help her anymore."

During Daniela's time behind bars, the two detectives paid her what would prove to be a final visit. They were thinking ahead, to the prospect of a trial, to evidence that prosecutors would want when it came time to impress the weight of her loss on a jury. Holmes asked Daniela if she had a photograph of Luis Angel, a picture that would at least remind the world that her baby was real and human and unique. He was unprepared for her response. Daniela had nothing. "David was beside himself," Evens says.

Holmes thought about his own two kids, the record of their lives he and his wife had amassed, the privileges they'd inherited. He was frustrated not to have a suitable image for the courtroom but also, as a father, indignant that the only proof of Luis Angel's existence would have to come from the coroner. An autopsy photo of his gray little body, eyes closed and mouth frozen midbreath, was all there'd ever be.

19

As If All Were Alive and Dead

I t seemed odd to Giovanni that anyone should care whether he'd showered or not, especially in the middle of the night, but he couldn't argue that he needed to. He was sticky with TJ funk: booze, sweat, puke, the cotton-candy body spray of the pole dancers. He'd wrested sex from Midget, too. It never occurred to Giovanni that she might object or have a right to set boundaries; he assumed 18th Street was just looking out for him.

Once Giovanni had hosed off, Face explained that it was time to leave, to transport him to his hideaway. They lumbered into the darkness, out of the Hotel Leyva and toward Vía Rápida, Face at the wheel of the SUV next to Midget and Ranger beside Giovanni, slumped in back. Their route followed the Tijuana River, past the airport and the Otay Mesa crossing, and through the industrial hinterlands east of town, where globalization has drawn hundreds of thousands of assembly-line workers to the maquiladoras that churn out US-bound electronics and toys. After twenty minutes, the sprawl of shanties and gravel roads faded, and they reached the tollbooth that signals the start of Carretera 2D, the gateway to La Rumorosa.

"FELIZ VIAJE," the sign said.

From there, Midget took the wheel, steering them across an arid expanse of ranchlands and foothills, the road rising as it paralleled the US border. Some seventy miles in, Carretera 2D transforms into a geological odyssey, snaking through a prehistoric eruption of escarpments and ravines that resembles few places on Earth. Around each treacherous curve looms another formation of sunburnt stone, hypnotic and impregnable. Had it not been night, the four would have seen the cascades of cars—bellies up, noses down, tires shredded, windshields shattered, airbags discharged—littering the maw below, too worthless or inaccessible to be retrieved. Highway engineers have improved the road in the years since, but it remains easy to underestimate. A Facebook Live streamer driving a Corvette on a rain-slickened afternoon would later broadcast his own death here; as the car flips and disintegrates, his cellphone captures a glimpse of his upside-down face, still not comprehending the miscalculation he's made. Wherever travelers have been surprised by the horseshoe turns and roller-coaster grades, there are clusters of descansos, the roadside shrines that stand as both an intensely personal catalog of individual misfortune and an anonymous predictor of future calamity.

The casualties have morphed into folklore: shadowy figures, glowing specters, the ominous sense that even in the void, someone or something is watching. There is the legend of the lost nurse, a silent apparition in white, perpetually wandering the shoulder in search of an accident victim she can't find. Another tale features the driver of a wrecked car who flags down a passing motorist for help getting a message to his wife—to please explain to her that he's had an accident but is OK. The Good Samaritan agrees to deliver the news, only to learn from the woman that she's a widow; her husband's been dead for years.

Near the summit, where the wind howls the fiercest and snowfall periodically halts traffic, a turnoff leads to the ruins of Campo Alaska. An early twentieth-century military installation, it later served as a mental hospital and tuberculosis ward—a place of banishment for the crazed and contagious. A Tijuana-born poet, José Javier Villarreal, has contemplated the sanitarium's secrets: "At Campo Alaska there are those who are not here anymore, those who didn't arrive, those who never made it, those who left, those who are not visible, what was and what wasn't, what could be and its fantasies. It's as if all were alive and dead. Such is reality, the everything."

By then it had begun to drizzle. Face directed Midget to pull over. She parked along a slender pocket on the left side of the highway, the cliffside. Face and Ranger stepped out to pee. They smoked a cigarette. When they returned to the SUV, Face roused Giovanni and told him to move to the front, to help keep Midget awake, while he caught some z's in the back. "So I moved to the front, front passenger side of the car," says Giovanni, "and then tilted my seat a little bit back so I could still be relaxing."

His gut told him again that something was off. "I felt weird," Giovanni says. But again, playing along seemed like his safest bet. Even if he trusted his instinct, there was nowhere to go in La Rumorosa, nobody to call. He'd been transported to a magnificent gulag.

If Face really had a gun stashed behind the AC vent, as he'd indicated to Tricky, he left it there. For reasons nobody has explained, he chose a more cinematic approach, one that echoed the execution of Luca Brasi, *The Godfather* enforcer, whose eyes bulge and tongue flaps as a rival garrots him from behind with piano wire.

The rope appeared from the corner of Giovanni's left eye. It flew over his head, looping around his neck. It felt thick on his skin, "the kind of rope you'd use to string up a piñata," Giovanni says. Face held one end and Ranger the other, and they'd doubled it, so two ligatures were now gripping his throat. Giovanni tried to pry a finger under the rope, to gain some breathing room, but the two older 18th Streeters were clutching it too tight. The demon inked on the rear of his head, the eyes watching over his back, stared straight at the killers, offering no defense. "I felt helpless and powerless," Giovanni says. "It sent this chill down my back to my guts."

They yanked so hard, they pulled Giovanni halfway over the armrest. He fought them, clawing the rope and kicking the dashboard. Blood poured from his nose and mouth. It stained the door. It soaked into the back seat. As his brain lost oxygen, Giovanni was less afraid than resigned; he didn't want to die but couldn't deny that maybe he deserved it. "I felt that coldness of something that was taking me straight to hell for everything bad I've done," he says. "Those were my exact thoughts before passing out. I was going to hell to pay." Face and Ranger kept throttling him, squeezing his trachea shut.

"Die, motherfucker," growled Ranger, who'd known Giovanni for all of a day. "Die."

Of the more than 18,000 US homicides in 2007, strangulation accounted for only 637—just over 3 percent. Women were twice as likely as men to be strangled, a crime associated with intimate partner violence, not gangster hits. A gun allows a murderer to operate at a safe remove, to shoot and run, as Giovanni had on Sixth Street. Strangling someone requires a bestial fury, a physical and emotional investment in the victim's demise. While pressure on the windpipe can render someone unconscious in as little as thirty seconds, it takes maybe four to five minutes of sustained compression to finally kill off brain function—an eternity to snuff out every last flicker of life.

"You're a good homie," Face announced, "but you fucked up."

They felt something in Giovanni snap. His body softened. Midget, paralyzed in the driver's seat, stared straight ahead. "I kind of like was froze," she says. "I couldn't—I couldn't move. And I'm thinking they are going to do the same to me." Midget prayed the sun would come up, hoped her passengers would be less likely to turn against her if it were lighter out and anyone passing by could see the mayhem contained in the SUV. Face told her to check Giovanni's pulse. "I had been going to nursing school, so I learned it there," Midget says. She put her fingers on Giovanni's wrist. He remained splayed over the console, the rope still wrapped around his neck. "I told them that I felt a pulse," Midget says. Face chided her for being jittery. He leaned an ear to Giovanni's chest and told her that "it couldn't be because, you know, he was already dead," she says, "that it probably was my pulse that I was feeling because I was nervous."

Face swung open the left rear door behind Midget. He looped his arms through Giovanni's and tugged him from the SUV. Midget hopped out and grabbed Giovanni's feet. She tried to lift as Face pulled, but Giovanni was too heavy. "So I just put him down," she says. Ranger walked around from the right side and took over. He and Face lugged Giovanni out of the truck. They shuffled as he sagged between them. Midget returned to the driver's seat. "I didn't want to look," she says. "I just wanted to get out of there."

A retaining wall of stone and mortar, maybe three feet high, guarded the gorge. Face and Ranger swung Giovanni back and forth, then heaved—over the edge, into the emptiness. They listened and heard nothing. They'd done it: cleaned the yard. The green light could be called off.

With Midget at the wheel, they continued east, wending their way down the other side of La Rumorosa, descending a thousand feet every ten minutes or so. Face and Ranger wiped the rope dry and flung it out the window. At some point they passed an ambulance heading up the mountain, its siren screaming, and Midget felt the drumbeat of panic. "I was, like, maybe somebody found him, maybe that's for him," she says. Face and Ranger laughed her off. "They just told me that it can't be—that he was dead for sure."

The road flattened out, taking them across the vast alkaline Laguna Salada, and into the gray quilt of junkyards and tire shops that mark the beginning of Mexicali. Face had lived some portion of his childhood there, and he guided them through the big desert city to his uncle's house. When they arrived, Midget found a rag and tried to mop the blood inside her SUV. Face bought them all new clothes at a supermarket. They doused their tainted outfits in gasoline and burned them in a dirt yard.

Even in those days, years before talk of a wall became a political flashpoint, an ugly barrier separated Mexicali from its US counterpart, Calexico. Made of surplus Vietnam War landing pads—corrugated metal sheets once used for temporary airstrips—the fourteen-foot-tall fence enforced the division between the sun-dulled maze of the Mexican side and the brilliant green rectangles of California's Imperial Valley, one of the largest alfalfa-growing regions in the world. They reached the checkpoint about one-thirty that Friday afternoon, September 21. They'd been in Mexico for roughly thirty-six hours.

The US Customs and Border Protection officer who took their IDs and ran the plates—the first line of defense, as he would put it, against "any discrepancies or anything that just doesn't seem normal"—asked what they'd been doing in Mexico. It seemed strange to the officer that a passenger, not the woman at the wheel, was the one who answered, and that he'd said they came to party and eat tacos. "That kind of seemed not normal," the officer says. "It wasn't a normal party time. It was still early in the day. And it just didn't make sense why they would drive all the way from LA to Mexico for a couple of hours to party and eat tacos, when not only are there plenty of places to be in LA; but, again, that long drive. It just—it just really didn't make sense." He referred them to secondary inspection, a chance for another set of officials to search the SUV and revisit any stories that didn't add up. Dogs sniffed the truck. But even with the heightened scrutiny, with all the resources that the federal government brings to bear on border security, nobody noticed the blood that had soaked into the back seat fabric or found a reason that the three travelers, after a sleepless, murderous expedition across La Rumorosa, should not continue on their way north.

When they reached LA that evening, they stopped at a Jack in the Box south of downtown, just around the corner from Sam's Hofbrau, the topless bar that Tricky favored. While Ranger used the bathroom, Face told Midget that she'd done good—"that I had took one for the team," she says. He reminded her to keep her mouth shut and promised to help her get Giovanni's blood out of the upholstery. Then he asked: "You want me to mention your name?" It was an invitation to receive credit for putting in work, to ensure that "the big homies," in the echelon above the streets, knew the sacrifices she'd made.

Midget grimaced. Better to leave it all behind, forever. "I don't want nobody to know," she told him. "I wasn't there. And that's it."

20

Get Something on Paper

The shooting on Sixth Street put the touchy relationship between the FBI and LAPD to an unexpected test. The consent decree that the Justice Department had extracted after the Rampart scandal still hovered over the LAPD in 2007; a federal judge, just the year before, had castigated the city for its incomplete record of reforms, extending the monitorship until 2009. Now, in one appalling stroke, the Columbia Lil Cycos had dragged both agencies into the same mess.

Paul Keenan recognized the sensitivities. When he'd first joined the FBI's Los Angeles office, his colleagues were still reassuring their LAPD counterparts that "we're not public corruption agents, we're gang agents." Given the overlap between the RICO case he'd been building and the murder case the police had now opened, he approached Robbery-Homicide and pledged to cooperate. Detective Holmes's supervisor told him: "I've been burned by the FBI before, but I take everybody at face value, so I'll work with you." Keenan couldn't ask for much more. "I understand," he says. "We've all been burned by other agencies." He also needed the US attorney's office to expedite his work, "to drop everything else and get the case indicted." Prosecutors would have to go with what they had at that point. "When you have something as impactful and tragic as a child like this getting killed," Keenan says, "it's all hands on deck."

In the weeks that followed, Keenan organized the evidence he'd amassed into a timeline—the "spine" of the case that would be presented to a grand jury. All the undercover videos, all the surveillance photos, all the wiretapped calls, all the marked bills: he categorized them into 158 overt acts, between February 16, 2005, and June 8, 2007, that constituted a conspiracy by the

Columbia Lil Cycos to "control, oversee, and direct" the distribution of crack cocaine in the MacArthur Park neighborhood. Tricky and Morena were the marquee names. The feds had evidence of them working with both the may-oristas and the traqueteros, handling drugs, collecting rent, threatening assaults, and evading police. In its hasty form, the indictment would be just for drugs, not for the full array of extortionary rackets and violent reprisals that Keenan had envisioned, and it didn't implicate all the suspects he'd hoped to reach, but what he'd documented were still federal narcotics crimes that stitched together, could put somebody away for life.

"We just wanted to get something on paper," he says, "and get these people off the street as soon as possible."

While Keenan worked with the US attorney's office to prepare the indict-ment that would become criminal case 07–01172, Holmes expanded the LAPD's investigation into what was known in-house as "the Rampart infant murder." Shorty's decision to speak up had given the detectives a running start. But there were still gaps to fill and monikers to match—nobody seemed to know anyone's real name on the streets. Starting with Face.

The guy was a cipher. The feds had probed the Columbia Lil Cycos for more than two years, and Face hadn't popped up until just days before the shooting. The detectives needed to explore his connection to MacArthur Park, to make sense of his hold over the squad he'd roped into the attack on Sixth Street. Beginning on October 16, 2007, they tapped his phone, recording over sixteen hundred conversations: Face and Morena, Face and Silly, Face and Raven. "Face is such a pompous ass," Evens says. She took pride in handling intercepted communications, "listening to these dumb fucks talk on the phone." Face had returned from La Rumorosa—reported his success to Tricky—and had gone right back to business.

Face was now telling people that he'd been anointed the Columbia Lil Cycos' shotcaller, that Tricky was off "doing something else." The LAPD lis-tened in as Face enforced rent collections on the traqueteros: "Ain't nobody doing no dope slanging for free, dog." He demanded his cut from the corn-on-the-cob vendor too: "Tell him that when I get there I want that fuckin' money, fool." When a homie alerted him that police were circulating flyers about the murder, offering a $75,000 reward for information, Face struggled to contain his curiosity: "They looking for the shooters or what the fuck?" When Face asked if anyone had mentioned "the little kid," he meant Giovanni, not Luis Angel.

On October 19, Face called the rent collector he'd introduced Giovanni to on Alvarado.

"Pizza Loca, can I help you?" the rent collector answered, fishing for a laugh.

"Federal Bureau of Investigation, can *I* help *you*?" Face replied.

To a remarkable degree, the LAPD and the FBI collaborated, waiting on each other, ensuring that each agency had what it needed before moving forward. It would take them five weeks to align their cases—a blink of an eye in bureaucratic terms, ages if you were praying that nothing terrible occurred in the meantime. They chose October 24 for the takedown, a coordinated sweep designed to ensnare more than two dozen 18th Street members and associates wanted in one or both investigations. That would include Giovanni, not that anyone thought he was alive.

Even without knowing about the Mexico trip, both the FBI and LAPD understood the enormity of the green light—assumed that Giovanni had already paid the price. The cops had been listening to calls, trawling for information. If Giovanni were alive, they expected he'd surface somewhere. "No one," says Holmes, "had heard from him."

21

A New Life

Flies buzzed the crumbling slope. Ants scoured the gravel. The air smelled of desiccated sage and spilled motor oil. Everything ached: his neck, his hip, the back of his head. Giovanni welcomed the pain. He'd landed hard on that jagged cliff, but goddamn—he was alive. The desert sun melted the last bands of color from the dawn. It was Friday, a new day.

His adrenaline on overdrive, Giovanni didn't need long to scratch his way up the cliff. He pulled himself over the stone wall, planted his stocking feet on the side of the road. Now what? Giovanni didn't know. He'd never had to contemplate a question like that—to solve the puzzle of his life, much less on the run. If he could have, he would have remained a Columbia Lil Cyco. He wanted that more than anything. It was impossible now. The betrayal broke him. In his most vulnerable moment, when he urgently needed protection and validation, Giovanni had been jilted. "I didn't know who to trust," he says. "I felt like the world turned against me."

His brain burned with vengeful fantasies. That would have been the old Giovanni's first instinct. If he devoted himself to payback, he'd have the advantage of surprise: the killer who'd botched the killing, then survived a botched killing, would sneak back and kill again, only this time get it right. "I'm not gonna lie, I did think of that," Giovanni says. "But then I was like, the violence has to stop with me. If I had more blood on my hands, how would that accomplish anything?" He was angry that the Columbia Lil Cycos didn't see it the same way. They could have easily hidden him out, handed him a thousand bucks and told him to disappear. "If I were them, that's what I woulda done, like, 'We're gonna go back and say we killed you, but we don't want to kill you, so we need you to vanish.'" But they didn't. His mom, for all her shortcomings, had been right. The Columbia Lil Cycos weren't his family. *Fuck them.*

As lost as Giovanni was, it occurred to him that he was also free. An outlandish disaster—all that he'd experienced between September 15 and September 21—had liberated him from the mundane disaster that was his life before. The gang thought he was dead. The police, if they ever learned about him, would conclude he was dead. Giovanni was untraceable: no phone, no credit card. There in La Rumorosa he'd done more than go over the edge; he'd fallen off the grid. *I'm gone*, Giovanni told himself. *I ain't coming back.* It was a dark stroke of luck, one he knew he didn't deserve. But here he was. A certain brand of extralegal justice had been meted out, too. Swift, cruel, biblical. It may not have been the price society demanded, but he'd paid it. He could have died. He should have died. And that would have been the end of it, except now it wasn't.

I'm starting a new life.

A tractor-trailer lumbered down Carretera 2D. Giovanni waved his arms. The truck's brakes groaned. The driver must have thought that the legends were true—an actual ghost was standing there in his socks, pleading for a ride. The pressure that the rope put on Giovanni's neck had burst the blood vessels in his eyes, a side effect of strangulation known as subconjunctival hemorrhage. The white around his pupils had dissolved into puddles of red.

The trailero asked Giovanni if he'd been in an accident. Giovanni said no, that somebody had tried to kill him. It was true and yet impossible to explain without revealing more, so Giovanni left it at that. His rescuer, generous in the we're-all-in-this-together way that Mexico upholds, was unfazed. He told Giovanni to climb into the cab—gave him water, handed him a collared shirt to cover the seeping ligature marks. "I felt like my neck was about to fall down," Giovanni says. The driver pointed him to a small bed tucked behind the seats. As they descended, the truck creeping around the hairpins, Giovanni's eyes grew heavy again, and he allowed himself to doze off.

He awoke in the desert. The eastbound lanes of Carretera 2D went only one place: Mexicali. The trucker wanted to drop Giovanni off at a hospital; Giovanni insisted he was fine. He hopped out near an OXXO, the ubiquitous chain of Mexican convenience marts. A fugitive with more resources, more cunning, might have steered clear of a place sure to be wired with security cameras. Giovanni was eighteen and empty-handed. If he was going to start a new life, he couldn't fathom doing it alone. "That would have meant cutting ties forever," he says. "What would that do to my mom, to her life? I thought that would be selfish. I didn't have the heart." He limped through the store's swinging glass door, still shoeless, eyes worthy of a slasher flick, and said it was an emergency—por favor, could he make a call?

The woman at the cash register looked him up and down. Maybe someone else, somewhere else, would have kicked Giovanni out or called the police. The OXXO lady gave him a handful of pesos and pointed him to the pay phone.

Giovanni knew only one number by heart: Mayra's. She cried when she heard his voice, hoarse from the stricture to his throat.

"What the fuck is going on?" she wailed.

"It's all bad," Giovanni said.

He had little time to talk. What he needed was for her to call his mom, to come rescue him as soon as possible. Three hundred miles away, Reyna Flores had started her Friday morning at the Antelope Valley Mall, wheeling her bucket and mop across the concourse. It had been at least three weeks since she'd seen or heard from Giovanni. Now Mayra was screaming in her ear, trying to explain Giovanni's predicament. Reyna didn't know whether to be angry or relieved. Or privately jubilant. Her wayward son, in his most desperate hour, had turned to her. Giovanni needed his mom.

Reyna rushed to clock out from work. It was still only 9 A.M. She gathered her kids and their birth certificates, including Giovanni's. Then she drove her Toyota minivan down into LA to pick up Mayra and Mayra's older sister. The five of them headed for the border, but instead of taking the most direct route to Mexicali—cutting a diagonal line through the Inland Empire, past Palm

Springs, and around the phosphorous wasteland of the Salton Sea—they followed the same path that Giovanni and his assailants had: south to Tijuana, then east and up, across La Rumorosa.

Reyna had no idea that a precipitous mountain pass stood between her and Mexicali. The otherworldly heights terrified her. "I was so nervous," she says, "I was shaking." Even without knowing that she was traveling past the very spot where, earlier that same Friday morning, her son had been left for dead, it still made her too uncomfortable to continue. She asked Mayra's sister to take the wheel. "As a mother, you get a feeling," Reyna says. "Like, I just knew something was wrong."

Giovanni waited in the OXXO. The kindly manager offered him sandals. She told him to grab whatever he wanted to eat. Giovanni asked to use the bathroom. In the mirror, he finally saw himself. "I looked like shit," he says. "Like I was alive but dead at the same time." He pulled up the collar of his donated shirt. He kept his gaze low. The manager told him not to go outside—if the police spotted him, they'd ask for ID, and if he didn't have it, he'd land in jail. "I tried my best to go unnoticed," Giovanni says. He kept calling Mayra, asking where they were, when they would arrive.

They were lost. It was dark. A monsoonal layer blanketed the night. Headlights ricocheted through the wet windshield. There were hundreds of OXXOs in Mexicali. Giovanni waited for seventeen hours. It was Saturday, two in the morning, when the minivan pulled up. Reyna gasped at his wretched condition.

"It hurt me," she says. "My son, he looked so bad."

"They were all sobbing, and I started to cry too," says Giovanni, "and I just wrapped myself in all of their arms."

"I couldn't understand why someone would do this to him," Reyna says.

"I didn't want her to know that I was the reason of my own self-destruction," Giovanni says. "I didn't want my mom to know that her son had innocent blood on his hands."

They kept asking if he was OK.

He kept telling them not to worry: "The important thing is I'm alive."

Reyna handed him a hooded sweatshirt. Giovanni climbed into the back of the van, scootching close to Mayra. He was in no hurry to tell her about the previous night in TJ. She clutched his hand. When they reached the border, Reyna told him to act like he was asleep. Giovanni pulled the hoodie snug and dropped his head. It wasn't hard to pretend.

They drove all night, this time taking the shorter inland route, across the desert and past the Salton Sea, back to the Antelope Valley. Reyna paid for Giovanni and Mayra to stay in a Motel 6. It wouldn't be safe at home. The next day they would have to make decisions. "At that point I didn't have a plan," Giovanni says. "I was not thinking clear. I was not accepting reality for what it was." Whatever lay ahead, Mayra vowed to be at his side. "At the time, I didn't know what to really do," she says. "But, I mean, I tried to be there for him." Mayra's mom gave her a balm to rub into the gashes around Giovanni's neck.

Giovanni remembered his old friend Dennis Molina. The one who'd urged him to get out—who'd practically begged him to get on a plane—back when there was still time. Wherever North Carolina was, it sounded pretty good at the moment. "When he was on the run, I spoke to both him and his mom, and they both asked me if I can let him move in with me here," says Dennis, who was living with extended family, including a newborn nephew. He didn't know that Giovanni was a fugitive, only that his own gang had double-crossed him, but there was an infant in the house now, "and they are not gonna be OK with me bringing Giovanni in here."

Dennis wished that Giovanni had joined him earlier. He hated to let him down. "I remember telling his mom, like, 'Hey, I can't,'" says Dennis, who became an optician. "'It's just not gonna work, you know.'"

Giovanni turned next to his stepdad, Juan Monroy. At the moment, Juan was on probation for a DUI conviction, ordered by the Los Angeles Superior Court to attend AA meetings twice a week, but he'd left for New Mexico to take a construction job and had been living in Albuquerque for nearly a year. "He was saying, 'Send for me, send me over there,'" Juan says, "'to Guatemala, send me there.'" Juan, too, wanted to lend Giovanni whatever support he could, but he'd begun living with a new girlfriend and running a small handyman crew. It also dawned on Juan that Giovanni's phone might be tapped, that saying the wrong thing could implicate him as an accomplice—and just when his life was looking up.

"Turn yourself in, mijo," Juan told him.

A parent with the wherewithal, or at least a basic understanding of the rights Giovanni would be forfeiting, might have prioritized a lawyer for his son. Juan was goading him into surrendering to police without comprehending what Giovanni was up against—and without ensuring he'd have some leverage once he opened his mouth. The instruction emanated from a place of love; Juan wanted Giovanni to do the right thing. As a strategic matter, he was guiding his boy down a dead end.

"I want you to turn yourself in," Juan said. "It's for your own good."

"But I didn't do anything."

"If you didn't do it, you didn't do it," Juan said. All the more reason for Giovanni to turn himself in.

Giovanni chose a fresh start.

22

The Right Way

Six weeks after Luis Angel's murder, the FBI and LAPD fanned out across Los Angeles, the sky thick with smoke from wind-churned wildfires. That year, 2007, had been the driest in LA history, barely three inches of rain in more than twelve months. The whole city felt combustible. The FBI hit Tricky and Morena's house. Keenan had searched it eight months earlier, hoping to walk out with a prize informant. This time, he wouldn't be leaving empty-handed. Keenan called Tricky's cell.

"I'm back," he said.

The feds cuffed Tricky and guided him to a government car. Then Morena came out, and they handcuffed her too. Their kids cried. The eldest, a daughter, ran to Tricky.

"Daddy, what's going on?" she asked. "Why is Mommy under arrest?"

What could he tell her? A family that had extracted a solidly middle-class existence from the crack economy, that had applied their talent and ambition to the management of a predatory regime, was coming undone. All his daughter saw was dissolution, the forced removal of Mom and Dad. "I mean, that's a game changer," Tricky says. "You're talking about my kids. You're talking about my blood."

"Why?" the daughter sobbed.

Tricky decided right there to do what the FBI had thought all along he could be coaxed into doing. "Aside from all the crazy, violent drug dealing and everything else that was going on, they had a nice nuclear family—he and his wife, with his parents living in the back—and they seemed to take very good care of their kids," Keenan says. "It was different in their home versus, obviously, on the streets, where he was a maniac." The shotcaller of the Columbia Lil Cycos, the Mexican Mafia carnal-in-waiting, would turn his back on all he purported to believe in and aspire to. Before, 18th Street meant everything. Now it meant nothing. "I went from being a gangster," Tricky says, "to being a rat."

When they reached FBI headquarters in Westwood, Tricky asked for paper and pen. "Baby," he began. It was a plea to Morena, in Spanglish, urging her to speak to the cops and tell them everything. "Habla con los juras." He was doing the same. "Please do it for the kids. We will be OK, I promise."

Without a lawyer present, Tricky admitted to his leadership of the Columbia Lil Cycos, confessed to heading a drug-trafficking organization from his tattoo shop in the International Mall. He explained the traquetero and mayorista system, described the streets the gang ran and the rents they imposed. But when the FBI asked about the shooting on Sixth Street—his relationship with Face, the role of Giovanni—Tricky went silent. It was one thing to snitch about cocaine, another to own up to killing a baby. Or to admit to disposing of the killer. "I mean, I'm scared," Tricky says. "I don't know what's going on. I don't know what this is going to lead to. When it came down to being asked about certain things about this murder, I lied."

The LAPD grabbed Face that same afternoon, October 24. He was riding through South-Central in a gray Dodge pickup, the same truck that had been used to drive him and Giovanni to MacArthur Park the night of the attack. Officers found crack, packaged in plastic bindles stamped with a smirking devil's face, stashed inside the door handle. A black ski mask was on the seat. Face had $852 in his right-front pocket. At Parker Center, Holmes placed Face in a cell next to Grumpy, the gangster who'd menaced Shorty in the days after the shooting. It was an old trick: hidden microphones picked up their conversation.

Face and Grumpy went "back and forth as to who is being the rat, who is the one saying the names," Holmes says. Grumpy insisted that he'd delivered a proper warning to Shorty, reassured Face that he'd shut her up. But Face was worried that "the little girl was the rat." To Holmes's alarm, he heard Grumpy vowing to take care of it, "to send someone out again and tell her again and make sure she doesn't come to court and make sure she keeps her mouth quiet."

The LAPD moved fast. Holmes had convinced Shorty's family to relocate, but even with all his warnings about the peril she faced, the Matiases hadn't stopped vending. They had planted roots in the sidewalks of MacArthur Park, constructed their American lives from what could be harvested from LA's shadow economy. And that is where their daughter was still, witness to a gang murder or not. "We scrambled and scooped her up," says Holmes, who found Shorty in front of the International Mall and called a meeting with her parents. With the help of Spanish-speaking detectives, he "read them the riot act."

Shorty cried. She tried to explain her family's way of thinking to the police: the urgency, the obstinance, the worlds they'd bridged. "We just told her that she's going to have to start listening to us, or she's not going to be around to help her parents or anything else," Holmes says. "I don't think I would have forgiven myself if anything ever happened to her." Shorty agreed to join the LAPD's Explorer Program, which prepared several hundred young people every year for "future careers in law enforcement by offering a positive relationship between police and the youth of our community."

On October 24, the same morning of the takedown, the LAPD raided Reyna Flores's place in Palmdale, unit C81 of a subsidized apartment complex called Longhorn Pavilion. Officers had scoped it out before, watching as Reyna came and went. Guns drawn, flashlights blazing, the cops hollered for Giovanni to come out. Reyna opened the door in a nightgown.

"My son's not here," Reyna told the police. Then she lied. Reyna knew what it was to turn Giovanni in, to leave him in custody, to report him missing—to plead with anyone in authority to intervene. Covering for him now was all she had left to offer, the one remaining defense for a child who'd nearly been conned into his own death. "I don't know where he is," she said.

With nobody willing to hide him, Reyna a month earlier had put Giovanni and Mayra on a Greyhound bus bound for Ogden, Utah, a fifteen-hour slog across the Mojave, through Vegas, and around Zion National Park to the foot of the Wasatch Mountains. Mayra, who traveled with her Tasmanian Devil pillow, had a friend there who, like Giovanni's friend Dennis, had bailed on LA and hit refresh in an unlikely outpost. The friend lived with her parents in a beige 1950s home within a 1.5-mile radius of nine Mormon churches. Mayra told her only that Giovanni was trying to turn the page on some kind of trouble. Her friend had given birth to a baby boy just weeks earlier; the child's father, an 18th Streeter, was locked up in California. Recognizing Mayra's need, the friend convinced her folks to offer them a spare bedroom in the basement. "They greeted me with respect and love," Giovanni says. "I never felt awkward or like they were uncomfortable having me around. They treated me like a son."

The friend's stepdad worked for Swift & Co., one of the world's largest fresh beef and pork processors, which had a plant about forty miles to the north, past the Great Salt Lake, in the Cache Valley. He told Giovanni they were hiring: $10.50 an hour—double the state's minimum wage—plus a $1,500 signing bonus. It was a matter of supply and demand. Giovanni's arrival in Utah coincided with an ICE investigation that had swept up 1,300 Swift employees in six states, including 147 undocumented workers at its Utah facility. The raids separated families and spread fear, exposing all the contradictions of an economy that offers few legal opportunities to foreign-born people seeking to work in this country yet still welcomes and benefits from their labor, especially when the job is grueling and dangerous.

The probe of Swift originated in 2006 when ICE agents discovered that an unusual number of immigrants in an Iowa jail had worked at the company's local plant. ICE subpoenaed I-9 Employment Eligibility Verification forms for everyone at that facility, and when those documents revealed evidence of identity theft, the agency demanded I-9s for Swift's entire fifteen thousand–employee US workforce. Based on those records, ICE accused Swift of a companywide pattern of illegal hiring and raised the specter of visiting all six Swift plants. Swift sued to stop ICE, insisting that it was already participating in the Department of Homeland Security's E-Verify program and that the government's own measures had failed to detect false documents. Swift also argued that ICE's mass removal of undocumented laborers would cause irreparable economic harm and "cripple our company."

In court papers, ICE pointed out the "ironic twist" of a company complaining about the "deprivation in earnings it will suffer if it is not allowed to continue to profit through the use of illegal and unauthorized employees."

Armed with warrants, ICE raided the Swift plants at the end of 2006, initiating multistate deportations but declining to prosecute any corporate officials. Swift was shaken, estimating that the disruption cost it as much as $50 million in lost production, and within months, the century-old company was purchased by a Brazilian meat-packer.

Giovanni didn't realize that he was the beneficiary of all this—that the same government seeking to dismantle the Columbia Lil Cycos in MacArthur Park was also triggering a labor shortage in rural Utah. His neck was still shredded. His eyes remained blotchy. He had *18s* he was trying to hide. But Giovanni was just what Swift (renamed JBS Swift) needed: a US citizen willing to work in a slaughterhouse. "They kind of looked at me up and down," he says, "but they never asked any questions."

Giovanni awoke at two-thirty in the morning to catch a 3 A.M. shuttle: a middleman charged $75 every two weeks to drive workers from Ogden to the plant in Hyrum. The van had three rows of seats, "all of them full of paisas," Giovanni says. "I was the only pocho. They asked me all the time if I spoke Spanish." He wore blue hospital scrubs to work. Swift issued him protective gear—helmet, boots, earplugs, gloves, a metal-plated apron, a metal sleeve that strapped to his left arm, and a knife sharpener tied to his waist—a *Mad Max* ensemble that made Giovanni feel like a "professional, grade-A carnicero." HR taught him to stretch his hands, warm-up exercises for avoiding repetitive stress injury. Seeing that he was young and strong and unlikely to be squeamish, the company assigned him to the "pet shop," a cold, damp, grease-slickened room where a procession of cow carcasses, hanging from their hooves, inched his way. Giovanni wielded a knife, slashing from maw to tail, excising organs and other detritus to be turned into animal feed. With each swing of the blade, he felt the meaty warmth of the freshly slaughtered beast. The bovine vapors burned his nostrils. "It was vicious," Giovanni says. "In a way, death was around me all the time. I couldn't get away from it."

One day, in the cafeteria, a coworker noticed his neck. She asked Giovanni if he'd tried to kill himself. He told her he'd been in an accident. "She looked at me like she didn't believe me," Giovanni says. On October 28, four days after the LAPD searched his house in Palmdale, Giovanni received a Swift paycheck: $903.29.

"It felt good to make money the right way," he says. "I always had money out on the streets, and I would spend it as soon as it came into my pocket. But this felt—this felt different."

Giovanni and Mayra settled into a suburban routine that felt strangely comfortable, at once calm and unconstrained. They'd left behind the jostle of the LA barrio, the relentless maneuvering for economic turf, and found a life that seemed far removed, even proper. From the start of their relationship, Mayra had been on Giovanni to change, to put her—them—before the gang. Now, on the lam, she got her wish. He was attentive, responsible, focused on the possibility that he just might have it in him to be a reliable partner. They took walks together, tickled by the friendly greetings of neighbors, and ventured off on picnics, eating Mayra's favorite butter and sugar sandwiches at the foot of snow-topped peaks. They bowled, went to the movies, and fished at a farm stocked with rainbow trout. "I never did that at MacArthur Park," Giovanni says. "Over there, you'd probably get a fish with three eyes."

Relishing the quiet, the fresh mountain air, they imagined what their lives could have been, if they'd chosen this path earlier.

As far as the Columbia Lil Cycos were aware, Giovanni was still in La Rumorosa, his bones pecked clean. Their miscalculation gave him a rush of superiority—he'd never even seen a doctor. So great was his head start on the cops, Giovanni figured, he wasn't hiding out as much as finding himself. "I just started working towards, like, a change," he says. "Yeah, working for a change and a new me."

To stay in touch, his mom would drive to a pay phone in Palmdale and call Giovanni's prepaid cell. She told him that she missed him. Giovanni told her not to worry; they would get through this together. After the LAPD's search of Longhorn Pavilion, though, Reyna grew more anxious. Giovanni still hadn't summoned the courage to explain to her why the Columbia Lil Cycos had wanted him dead, and now the police had burst into her home—she'd protected him out of instinct but also out of ignorance.

Reyna's nerves mixed with Giovanni's guilt. He tried hard to pretend that what's done was done. Nothing he could do would bring back Luis Angel, no matter how much he might wish there were a way to give the baby another chance. But then reality would poke through Giovanni's avoidance: An infant was dead. Erased. Because of him. Nothing could reverse that fact, but nothing could relieve him of it either; he'd be the human being who did it for as long as he lived. Even if he hadn't meant to kill a child, he'd surely meant to kill the vendor standing next to the child—a man causing no harm, Giovanni could now see, "just trying to make a living." At least he alone bore the weight of that horror. The possibility that his mom might somehow be complicit in his crimes—that he'd left her with the task of misdirecting the police—was too much to bear. "I didn't want to be dragging other people into this," Giovanni says. "I'm not gonna let them go down for my bullshit."

He thought once more of splitting, of distancing himself from everything and everyone. He'd take his Swift & Co. money and go stealth; his mom wouldn't have to lie for him then. Mayra hated the idea. She begged him not to leave. Giovanni snapped at her: "If this is too hard for you, go home." Nighttime became intolerable. Giovanni would wake up in the dark, limbs twitching, lungs gasping. Mayra would press her thumb between his eyebrows and rub, back and forth, hushing and cooing, until sleep overtook him again.

Just to Set an Example

From the first days of the FBI's investigation, Paul Keenan eyed an elusive prize: the link between the Columbia Lil Cycos and the Mexican Mafia. He saw no point in pursuing Puppet. There was nothing the government could do to punish the Eme godfather beyond a slow death in the most demoralizing prison in the land, and there was nothing the government could dangle to entice his cooperation. But by the end of 2007, with two dozen Columbia Lil Cycos indicted and Tricky offering tepid cooperation, Keenan set his sights on Puppet's money man—the kind of board-level figure the RICO laws were designed to take down.

During the months that the FBI was up on the wire, Keenan noticed that Tricky was placing weekly calls to someone named Coach.

"I'm going to send my boy to practice," Tricky would say. He'd often mention something about bringing the gloves.

Then Tricky—or Baby or another high-status Columbia Lil Cyco—would head east, out the San Bernardino Freeway. They'd exit in El Monte, on Peck Road, and drive past Longo Toyota, the world's largest car dealership. Sometimes they'd pull up to the Denny's at the front of the block. If not, they'd continue a bit further to Chuck E. Cheese. In the parking lot, the Columbia Lil Cycos would align their car with Coach's or one of Coach's assistants and pass a bag from driver's window to driver's window. Coach's team would then transport the bundle another ten miles east, to the edge of the Eastland Plaza shopping center in West Covina. Tucked behind a towering jacaranda was a six-story smoked-glass building anchored by a Washington Mutual savings and loan. Up in suite 620, Coach had an office—and a safe. It's where he stored Puppet's cash.

Coach was not just a money launderer; he was a member in good standing of the California State Bar. A UCLA Law grad. Isaac Estrada Guillen made mid–six figures as a criminal defense lawyer, and still it wasn't enough. At the very moment that the FBI had him under surveillance, Isaac was pitching an autobiographical TV series to Fox, a drama tentatively titled *Brethren*. It would feature a defense attorney trying to outrun his past while law enforcement and his own clients worked to trip him up. The premise captured the imagination of Jennifer Lopez, who signed on to produce. "What interested me was the fine line the character must constantly walk in terms of both his professional and personal life," J.Lo said in a 2006 press release. "The fact that it comes from a true-life story makes it all the more compelling." *Variety* reported the story under the headline "Lopez Going Gangbusters."

Half of it was true: Isaac had a genuine redemption story to tell. Raised by a single mom, a house cleaner, in the Orange County colonia of Santa Anita, Isaac grew up believing that "machismo ran in our blood." Determined to never show weakness or bow to authority, he started shoplifting and stealing cars as a kid, then expanded into armed robbery, pills, and assault with a deadly weapon. At thirteen, after joining a gang in Riverside's Casa Blanca barrio, Isaac was sent to Rancho Potrero, a boys detention camp. Two escapes later, he graduated to the now-dismantled California Youth Authority, where his temper kept him locked up almost until his eighteenth birthday.

A million different things could have doomed Isaac, but he was brighter than he'd let on, analytical and organized when he didn't sabotage himself. He also had three kids by his early twenties; they motivated him to get sober and be a better dad than the one he'd had. With his juvenile record shielded from employers, Isaac found work as a materials inspector at the San Onofre nuclear power plant. He later became a warehouse manager at a 3M quarry, then a shipping dispatcher for a lighting manufacturer.

In the early 1990s, while earning straight *A*'s at East Los Angeles College, he helped found a student advocacy group called CHE: Chicanos for Higher Education. The goal was to build a pipeline to the four-year University of

California system. At a UC orientation in tidy, affluent Irvine, he fumed when
one of the presenters mistook him for a custodian; she'd asked if Isaac could
empty her trash can. When he visited UC Berkeley, though, nobody looked
twice at him—"they didn't care that I was tatted up"—convincing Isaac that
a nontraditional student, already in his thirties, could thrive there. A full
scholarship made the decision easier.

Isaac studied with sociologist Martín Sánchez-Jankowski, author of the
gang treatise *Islands in the Street*. "He was excited about ideas," the professor
would later say. "He wasn't a one-dimensional person." For his honors thesis,
Isaac wrote about the phenomenon of prison gangs: how rivals on the streets
formed racial alliances behind bars.

With all his years in and out of the criminal justice system, Isaac figured
that law was the logical next step. During one of his teenage court appearances, he'd been assigned a "very sharp" public defender, a UCLA Law alum,
so that became Isaac's top choice. He was accepted in 1994, though not
before security guards profiled him on a campus visit and stopped him for
questioning. During his 2L year at UCLA, Isaac sought an externship with
the Los Angeles district attorney's office but lost out—his criminal past was
a dealbreaker. He had better luck with the federal public defender's office,
which adhered to the credo that nobody should be defined by their worst
mistake. The office was also ramping up for a sensational trial that seemed
tailor-made for Isaac's life experience. In 1995, five years before the first RICO
case against the Columbia Lil Cycos, the government indicted twenty-two
Mexican Mafia members and associates on RICO charges, one of the first
public airings of the prison gang's financial grip on Southern California
street gangs. The case featured three murders tied to the Edward James
Olmos movie *American Me*, whose harsh portrayal of the Mexican Mafia
had triggered deadly reprisals.

As counsel for one of the lead defendants, deputy public defender Ellen
Barry put Isaac to work. Under his rough edges, she saw someone "on the
brink of fundamental change," a rejoinder to all the "rich white kids who

excluded and underestimated him." Although the Eme viewed Barry as an ally—"Mafia friendly," as ex-mobster Rene Enriquez has put it—she was still an outsider, a government-funded lawyer. Her protégé, on the other hand, could have passed for one of them. Fluent in barrio slang and built like a brawler, Isaac had coarse black hair slicked with Tres Flores styling oil, deep-set eyes, a heavy brow, and tats poking out everywhere. The Eme ran his name through the prison grapevine, an alternative background check. Isaac's troubled youth proved good for something. "It came back: 'Yeah, he's cool, he's not undercover,'" Isaac says. "So they began to open up."

By putting him in proximity to some of the most fearsome prison gang figures in America, tasking him with earning their trust and aiding their defense, the federal public defender's office laid the groundwork for Isaac's fall. The Mexican Mafia recognized something in him: a vulnerability his mentor had discounted, a character flaw not even Isaac may have sensed. "It's like asking an alcoholic to work at a bar," he says.

On the warm May afternoon in 1997 that Isaac donned the purple velvet hood of a Juris Doctor, graduating as a Phi Beta Kappa, the Mexican Mafia sent its own congratulations—a hand-drawn card signed by the RICO defendants.

Puppet dodged the big Mexican Mafia prosecution. But after the government indicted him in 2000, making him the headliner of his own RICO case, Puppet's needs grew more complex. Not only would he be spending the rest of his life in prison, but he'd lost his girl on the outside, Janie Garcia, who ended up with a twenty-year term of her own. Puppet had to groom a new fixer.

In 2003, he hired Isaac, by then in private practice, to handle the appeal for one of his RICO codefendants. It was a pretext to see how far the lawyer would bend. Puppet asked Isaac to pass along simple messages—*How you doing? Everything OK? Puppet sends his regards*—and Isaac convinced himself he could facilitate their communications while remaining insulated from their business. For the job, Puppet paid Isaac $30,000 cash. Puppet also had $15,000 of his money delivered to Isaac, just to hold.

Then Puppet upped the ante. He knew that Isaac was handling a 2004 drug case for a Mexican Mafia associate in Riverside. Between pretrial hearings, a federal judge summoned Isaac to the courthouse, explaining she'd received word from a confidential informant that the Eme wanted Isaac dead and that his own client was going to carry it out. Shaken, Isaac made a pilgrimage to Puppet, visiting him at the federal prison in Marion; he'd yet to be transferred to Supermax. Puppet told Isaac not to worry—he'd iron it out.

"After that, he would use it at times, you know, like actually, 'I saved your life,'" says Isaac, who never learned if the threat—or Puppet's intervention—was real. "There were times when I would tell him, 'I'm done. I don't want to be involved with this.' And he would be, like, 'You know I ain't got nobody else. I saved your life. You could help me. I'm doing life. I got nothing else. I need you.' And it made me feel bad—put it over my head. If it were true and he did save my life, then I felt like I owed him something."

From then on, Isaac was Puppet's medium to the outside world, their communications protected by something even better than Janie Garcia could offer: attorney-client privilege. Or at least the illusion of it; Puppet didn't have any open cases that called for a lawyer. Once a month, Puppet would direct Isaac to put $500 or $1,000 on his prison books, initially by check drawn from Isaac's attorney trust account and later by US Postal Service money order. To avoid raising suspicions, Isaac's office manager would alter the handwriting or switch post offices. At Puppet's instruction, Isaac would also make deposits to the inmate accounts of other Mexican Mafia carnales. Money couldn't buy many pleasures in a federal prison, but strategically dispensed, it could solidify power and preserve loyalty.

"He keeps a running tally of how much money should have come in, and if it doesn't come in, he wants to know why," says Isaac, who was paid $3,000 a week for his trouble. To satisfy Puppet's demands for accurate bookkeeping, Isaac would prepare an accounting of MacArthur Park revenue streams—the streets the Columbia Lil Cycos controlled, the corresponding rents they were collecting—and slip that document into a stack of legal papers. At Supermax, where security cameras monitored their visits, Isaac would hand Puppet the papers, "so it's not just one document that maybe they could zoom in on," and Puppet would fan through them, feigning interest until he reached the sheet he wanted, study it, then hand the whole bunch back.

Isaac's devotion to Puppet helped support a comfortable suburban life-style: a four-bedroom, three-bath house at the foot of a San Gabriel Valley country club, a pair of new Lexuses for him and his second wife (a UC Berkeley–educated probation officer unaware of his illicit work), and a live-in housekeeper for their two, soon to be three, young children. In his double-breasted sharkskin suits, Isaac continued to tell himself that he was drawing a line, that as long as he stuck to Puppet's finances, he was shielded from whatever havoc the Columbia Lil Cycos wreaked on the streets.

Puppet kept demanding more, prodding Isaac to jump-start ventures and oversee investments. They went in on a custom car shop, chopping Chrysler 300s in half and extending them into full-length limos. When the business flopped, Puppet blamed Isaac for rejecting his advice to assemble the limos from Hummers. Isaac sank $50,000 into a tequila brand, Tres Reales, that bombed. Puppet also used Isaac to deliver cash to his family in Tijuana, where a sister and brother-in-law were buying and managing apartments. Isaac would strap tens of thousands of dollars to his waist, wrap himself in a big jacket, and stroll across the border. But whenever Puppet demanded a better return on his investments, insisting that his lawyer go out and make things right, Isaac tended to drag his feet, not wanting to compromise him-self any more than he already had.

Puppet thought he should be sitting on at least a million or two—and that's "being nice." He'd begun running out of patience for Isaac's "it looks promising crap." He had eighteen grand on his prison books, an astronomical sum for a place as denuded as Supermax. But without Isaac's eyes and ears, without constant proof of the empire being built in his name, Puppet had no way to experience it. "I want to be set for life," Puppet groused.

When writing to Tricky, Puppet sometimes referred to Isaac as Huero—White Boy—a gibe meant to suggest the opposite, that his chief money launderer was darker complected than he was. As Puppet's distrust grew, he adopted a new, emasculating slur: Isaac became Tía Huera. "I really hope she gets right," Puppet wrote to Tricky. "Otherwise, I will find another hyna," a new chick. Puppet added: "I ain't got time for games. 'Cuz she ain't all that."

The FBI compiled a dossier on Isaac. His JD would be hard to overcome. As Keenan saw it, the Justice Department was understandably "sensitive" about going after another attorney, especially one who regularly squared off against federal prosecutors in his day job. Supermax staff recognized that the lawyer had an unusual relationship with Puppet, but they also hesitated to interfere. "To restrict attorney access," says Joe Guadian, the chief Mexican Mafia investigator at Supermax in those days, "would have been a big issue."

Keenan needed to get something else on Isaac, to unearth information that would force his hand. An FBI intelligence analyst named Candice Holcomb showed him the way. Young, tiny, blue-eyed, and blond, Holcomb was underestimated by men on both sides of the law. She used it to her advantage. Whether they wore a badge or prison blues, they'd read her one way, make gendered assumptions about her pink outfits and stiletto heels, then discover they were tangling with a millennial Clarice Starling—Holcomb's inspiration—a psych major who was already two steps ahead. "My preparation, my knowledge, my mindset had to be 200 percent," Holcomb says. "As a female in law enforcement, that's the only way you can operate."

Holcomb started off with data, extracting its latent secrets. Working through the FBI's National Gang Intelligence Center, she took lifeless gigabytes of government records and transformed them into graphic renderings—spoke-and-wheel visualizations—that mapped the contours of the Mexican Mafia. "Who's sending money to who, who's writing who, who's calling who, who controlled what, who put out the hit, who's doing this, and who's doing that—I just created a spiderweb of all the connections," she says. Holcomb then used that knowledge to conduct debriefings with Eme dropouts, to learn about their lives and their loyalties, "their moms, their girlfriends, their past girlfriends," she says. "The human side of things."

As her reputation as an Eme tracker grew, Holcomb traveled to cities where federal gang prosecutions were under way, which is how she found herself in downtown Los Angeles in 2006, listening to a tall FBI agent update officials on the Columbia Lil Cycos investigation. Holcomb left the presentation without giving Keenan a second thought, until she received a call from an associate who mentioned that a bunch of feds were gathering that night at Q's, a Westside sports bar down the street from FBI headquarters. Holcomb agreed it might be a good networking opportunity, so she freshened up and caught a ride to the pub—except there was no network to tap, just a couple of dudes and the tall FBI agent, whose bare ring finger caught her eye. "It was a total setup," she says. At the end of the night, when Keenan gave her his number, she saved it in her phone as "Prince Charming."

From then on, Holcomb found a reason to travel to LA every other week or so, planning her official duties to align with Keenan's schedule. She liked that he was strong and capable—"not necessarily a man of a lot of words," she says, "but when he speaks, you kind of had to listen." Best of all, he indulged her obsessions, understood her fascination with the Eme's ability to create a society out of deprivation. Holcomb wanted to know everyone's story, not just the criminal or legal aspects but "the whole process that got them there, the why, the how," she says. "In the back of my mind, it's the thought of, like, if they were just loved more, or had more of this or that, would their life have been different?" After a year and a half of long-distance dating, Holcomb and Keenan moved into a cramped apartment together near the water, in Marina del Rey.

It was around that time that Holcomb received a tip. Her work on the Eme had earned her the confidence of Supermax's Joe Guadian, who told her about a carnal ready to burn a bridge. After nearly two decades in federal custody, the guy was preparing to parole, and his cellblock mate there in the Rockies—Puppet—wanted him to launch a meth lab upon his release. Puppet had already set aside a hundred grand in seed money to get him back in business. But the defector was done.

After alerting their bosses that they'd be traveling as a couple—"work always came first," Holcomb insists—she and Keenan flew to Colorado together, sharing a hotel room about an hour outside Florence. The inmate they'd come to see had long black hair slicked back and flipped up at the collar, a mustache as thick as a shoeshine brush, and a deep crease between his dense eyebrows. In his fifties, he'd remained chiseled at Supermax, his abs tatted with the name of the San Diego barrio that generations of his family had ruled—Posole, as in the Mexican hominy stew. Holcomb could see the exhaustion carved in his face. "You could tell he was just tired," she says. "He was done with it. He wanted to just live."

From the bond Holcomb built in that first conversation, the FBI emerged with a document Keenan could have only dreamed of: a six-page letter from Puppet, lamenting his money situation, blaming Isaac, and cataloging everything he needed the carnal to do after his release. It was as blunt as anything Puppet had ever written.

"We need to be real on all issues because this is something I worked for," Puppet began, "and don't want to end up without shit." He vented about Isaac—whom he was back to calling Huero—griping that he'd been "greedy and running around using my $ for himself." Puppet wanted it known: "He is not my bitch for me to support." The carnal's first task was to visit the lawyer and conduct a full audit of Puppet's investments. Puppet wanted at least a $500,000 payout from Isaac right "off the top."

"Bro," Puppet wrote, "don't let me down."

Then in a PS, as if some half-formed thought had at that moment come into focus, Puppet added: "At the end of all this, I want Huero taken out . . . just to set an example." It was a darkly poetic repudiation. The mob boss who had once conjured a gang hit to cement his leverage over a UCLA Law grad was now setting him up for a real one.

24

The Kid Doesn't Know
What's Coming

News of Giovanni's death continued to spread. "That's what everyone said: 'He's dead, he's dead, he's dead,'" says LAPD gang cop Edgar Hernandez. In Shorty's follow-up interviews with detectives throughout October 2007, she repeated it: "I heard he's dead." Face—who thought he knew better than anyone that Giovanni was dead—wielded the fact of his disappearance as a defense. "Face was like, 'You guys got nothing on me—I'm not the shooter,'" Hernandez says, "and he kept saying, 'You're never gonna find the guy.'"

It chafed detectives that Face might be right. They knew he hadn't fired the gun on Sixth Street. The kid who had was gone. None of the surviving victims—Francisco, Jessica, Daniela—had placed Face at the scene. The two rent collectors, Atlas and Barrios, appeared to have fled the country. At the first mention of the baby, Tricky had clammed up. A murder charge would be a tough sell if it came down to Shorty's eyewitness account, her word against Face's. No matter how bravely she might testify, there were too many missing pieces.

Maybe the police had given up too soon on Giovanni. "I told the detectives, 'Hey, listen, he was always with his girlfriend,'" Hernandez says. "They were teenagers. They were in love. And they both had, like, hickeys everywhere—from here to here, both sides." He recalled his own adolescence, ensconced at his girlfriend's house "twenty-four seven," to the point that her parents had to show him the door. The homicide detectives may have been masters of persuasion, but they didn't know MacArthur Park the way Hernandez did, and they didn't know about Mayra. "So I go: 'I'm pretty sure she knows where he's at.'"

Hernandez already knew where Mayra lived. He'd helped investigate the 2003 case that put her brother away. It didn't bother Hernandez that they'd be winging it. He told the detectives: "Let's just go and talk to her."

On November 6, 2007—thirteen days after the big takedown, forty-four days after Giovanni and Mayra left for Utah, fifty-two days after the shooting—Hernandez headed for the little house at the side of the freeway, so close to downtown that from Mayra's front steps he could see the blue glass of the new fifty-four-story Ritz-Carlton beginning to rise. He knocked on the door. He was greeted by Mayra's mother, who was cooking breakfast for Mayra's dad. "She starts talking in Spanish and goes, 'I'm not sure if you remember, but my son's locked up already—remember, you locked him up?'" Hernandez says. "I go, 'Oh, I'm not here for your son. I want to talk to your daughter.'"

Mayra wasn't there. Giovanni wasn't there. But Mayra's older sister, the one who'd made the trip to Mexicali, was sleeping on the couch. Hernandez nudged her awake.

"Hey, where's your sister at?" he asked.

"She's been looking for you."

"Not hard enough."

The sister might have still been groggy. She might have figured that Giovanni and Mayra were running from 18th Street, not the police. Or she might just have wanted Mayra back safely at home. Whatever the case, her next words changed everything:

"They tried to kill Rusty."

It was the LAPD's first indication that they'd all been wrong: Giovanni might actually be alive. Hernandez now had an opening. He asked for Mayra's number. The sister said she didn't have it. If he wanted to speak to her, he'd have to leave his number and wait for Mayra to make contact.

Hernandez's house call set off alarms in Utah. The sister alerted Mayra, and Mayra texted Giovanni, adding "911" to her message. Giovanni was at the slaughterhouse. He called her at once. Mayra sounded panicked. Giovanni felt defeated. "Do you know what's about to happen?" he told her. "It's a wrap." He didn't realize that he was still off the LAPD's radar. The police had no idea where he was. But he understood that he'd lost the presumption of death. Now that the cops knew he was alive, he could see the end coming into focus. Giovanni had made some spectacularly bad decisions; he figured it was time to make a good one, the only one still available to him. Better to man up. *I'd rather get this shit over with*, Giovanni told himself. *While I'm still young.* Hernandez would understand, maybe even respect it. Square jawed, soon to become a brown belt in Brazilian jiujitsu, he resembled the commando that Giovanni once wished to become.

Giovanni dialed the number that Mayra had been given.

"Hey, big dog."

"Who's this?" Hernandez asked.

"C'mon, big dog," Giovanni said. "It's me."

Hernandez's eyes grew wide. He pointed to the phone, mouthing to the detectives at Parker Center that it was Giovanni. They put him on speaker.

"Listen, all this stuff going on: they're trying to say you did something," Hernandez told him. "I know you didn't, but I need to talk to you in person."

"They tried to kill me, man."

"Listen, what's your number?"

Giovanni didn't know. Hernandez told him to look it up and call him back. The detectives prepared to trace it. Soon the gang cop and the gangster he'd watched grow up were on the line again, talking like old friends. Born in the Mexican state of Guanajuato, Hernandez had come to the US at age nine—with papers—thanks to his dad's job manning the grill at the Original Pantry, an all-night diner owned by a former LA mayor. He recognized the challenges he might have faced if not for a solid male figure in his life, one with the security of legal status, and he'd glimpsed the deficits in Giovanni's home that had left him so susceptible to 18th Street's allure. "He starts telling me, 'I got a job now. Like, killing cows. I'm making good money. The first thing I bought was a big-screen TV and a PlayStation,'" Hernandez says. "And I'm, like, aw, dude. He doesn't know what I know. This kid doesn't know what's coming." It was hard for Hernandez to take. He knew that some of his colleagues were saying "horrible things" about Giovanni, that "the baby stuff" had poisoned their view. "I get it, it *is* a horrible thing," he says. "But I didn't see him like that. I still saw him as a kid."

The number came back: Ogden, Utah. Giovanni agreed to divulge the address, but on one condition. There was a newborn—the child of Mayra's homegirl—and he wanted an assurance that the police wouldn't break down the door and endanger the baby.

"Please don't raid this house," Giovanni said. "I'll come out on my own."

These were the moments Dave Holmes lived for. The kind of police work that drew on wits and persistence, that hinged on his ability to read a suspect's triggers, another human being's response to fear and self-interest and contrition. Holmes listened closely to Giovanni's voice while they had him on the phone—the way he spoke of the rope, his neck, the cliff down in Mexico, his improbable survival—on alert for a lie or a trap. "It's a wild story, a beyond-belief story," Holmes says. "You sit down in your chair and you shake your head. But the way he was saying it and telling us, you know there was truth to it."

Holmes didn't go home. He didn't pack. He left Parker Center and, with several other officers, went straight to LAX. "We knew we had a small window," Holmes says. "I thought maybe 75 percent, when we got there, he was going to be gone. He would wise up and run, or somebody would tell him to take off or whatever."

At the slaughterhouse, Giovanni felt weak: empty, queasy. There was no point in returning to the evisceration room, but he was stuck; the afternoon shuttle to Ogden didn't leave for several more hours. A supervisor told him to get back to work. "Don't worry," Giovanni muttered. "I won't be here tomorrow."

He tried to think through his next steps, racking his brain for what he might say once the police arrived. Giovanni was badly outmatched—he knew nothing about Holmes, the detective who was dropping everything to fly to Utah—but he'd at least show the LAPD he wasn't a monster. Surely, they'd understand that the baby was an accident. Giovanni didn't have as good an explanation for the vendor. He was just glad the chilango didn't die.

Once again, it would have been in Giovanni's interest to negotiate his surrender through a lawyer. Or to keep his trap shut until one arrived. He'd watched enough TV to know that's how it was supposed to be done. But he couldn't afford an attorney, and he didn't understand that a government-appointed one would be sworn to defend him, ethically bound to keep his confidences. "I thought if I told my attorney the truth, he'd end up telling the DA whatever I said," Giovanni says. "That's how messed up my mind was. I didn't know how the system worked."

When he finally made it back from the plant, Giovanni was disappointed to discover that Mayra had gone to work: her friend had helped her land a job as a telemarketer at a call center. Giovanni thought that Mayra should have recognized the heaviness that was descending on them, that she would have allowed for a proper farewell. They had only a few more hours together, and then—it was hard to say. Her sister's unexpected disclosure had compressed the timeline, hastened their last embrace. "We didn't get a chance for anything," Giovanni says. He showered. Put on some sweats. Apologized to his hosts for what was about to happen. The friend's mom made empanadas for dinner. "That was, like, my last meal," Giovanni says. He kept looking out the window, wondering which set of headlights would be the ones to stop there on Fifth Street, at the house with the crimson maple tree.

Holmes landed in Salt Lake City that evening. He wore a charcoal suit and crisp white shirt, his silvery tie still knotted. It wasn't enough for the autumn chill of the Mountain West; Ogden was already dipping into the thirties.

Holmes would later wander the aisles of a Walmart in search of warmer clothes and toiletries. But his first order of business: marshal an Ogden tactical team. Even though Giovanni had volunteered to come out on his own, Holmes needed backup; he couldn't take any chances, especially in a jurisdiction outside his own. From the red-brick Ogden police headquarters, he called Giovanni a couple of times—no answer. A wasted trip, he worried.

Holmes hated to drag the local cops down a dead end, but he still had an obligation to check out the address Giovanni had provided. He'd cross it off his list, then revert to "manhunt mode." The house was just a few miles up Washington Boulevard, anyway, around the Daughters of Utah Pioneers Museum, past the gravesite of gunsmith John Moses Browning, the father of modern firearms, and under the "It Pays to Live in . . . OGDEN" arch. At Doug's Trading Post, they turned onto Fifth, and Holmes tried Giovanni again. It was near 11 P.M. This time he answered. Holmes told him they were outside.

"You can't come out here doing anything stupid," he said.

"Yes, sir," Giovanni said.

"You need to keep your hands up in the air," Holmes warned.

"Yes, sir," Giovanni said.

Holmes, who had an FBI surveillance photo of Giovanni to go by, paced the foot of the driveway, service revolver strapped to his right hip and handcuffs tucked in the small of his back. The Ogden police trained their guns on the door. At least Mayra had clocked out and reached the house before the cops. Giovanni gave her a goodbye kiss. Whatever awaited him, he just wanted to avoid a life sentence. He needed to know that he'd have a chance again with her. Then he puffed his chest and flexed his arms. It was not so different from that night seven weeks earlier on Sixth Street, at Video Mania, when Giovanni had to ask himself if he had it in him—if he *dared*—and there was only one answer he could live with. He again stood at the portal to a new life, a new future, one that was no less irrevocable.

"To be honest," Holmes says, "when he opened the door, I was shocked."

Giovanni looked pale and painfully thin. His neck was still scarred; twin strips of discolored flesh ringed his throat, splotchy pink in the center of the bands and dark olive at the edges. Even with the temperature close to freezing, he seemed damp.

Holmes went to pat Giovanni down. He told him to lift his shirt, to give everyone a good view of his waistband, then to turn around and face away. Holmes had one hand on Giovanni's back, the other poised to feel for weapons. It was then that Giovanni pivoted, slipping an arm over the detective's shoulder. "I thought, 'Oh, shit, here we go,'" Holmes says. "I almost took him down. I didn't know what he was trying to do."

By the time Holmes figured it out, Giovanni had completed his pirouette. He swung around his other arm. Tears glistened in Giovanni's eyes. He squeezed Holmes tightly, stealing a hug, as he pressed his face into his captor's chest.

Part Three

2007–2013

Photo by Miguel Rodriguez

25

I Want to Go Home

Your job's cool, huh—being a detective?"

"Yeah, it's a good job."

"There's lots of adventures, huh?"

"You know what, everything's kind of—everything's a little different. Every case is different, you know. There's always, uh—there's always different things to it. But it's good."

"How much an hour is it?"

Giovanni was doing his best to sound ingratiating, curious about the passions of the man across the bare desk from him, as if this were just a polite chat between strangers seated next to each other on a plane. Holmes slipped off his suit jacket and draped it over a chair, then unzipped a portfolio stuffed with papers and realigned the stack with a tap on the tabletop. He'd already removed Giovanni's cuffs and asked if he'd like water. The slamming of jail-cell doors in the Ogden police station echoed beyond the interview room. It was near midnight, November 6, 2007.

"The bottom line is," Holmes said, "I just want to get to the bottom of everything."

He asked Giovanni to spell his name and confirm his birth date.

"You have the right to remain silent, do you understand? Anything you say may be used against you in court, do you understand? You have the right to the presence of an attorney before and during questioning, do you understand? If you cannot afford an attorney, one will be appointed for you free of charge, do you understand?"

"Yes, sir," said Giovanni, nodding to each question.

"Do you understand what I want to talk to you about?"

"Yes."

Giovanni seemed eager to talk about himself; better some biography than whatever else the cop wanted to know. He explained that he'd lived on Burlington Avenue, in the middle of Columbia Lil Cycos turf, and before that in South-Central, which is where his parents' marriage imploded. He told Holmes that his mom plunged immediately into another relationship, only to have the new guy run out on her. "You know, what goes around comes around," Giovanni said. "She ended up taking some pills. She OD'd."

It was a sorrowful detail to volunteer just minutes into a murder interrogation. In narrating his short life—in reaching for the milestones that made him who he was—Giovanni had fixated on the moment when he'd witnessed his mom nearly drift away. He hoped it would soften the detective.

"Oh, goodness," said Holmes, rocking back in his chair, arms folded.

They talked about the Columbia Lil Cycos' control over the 500 Building, Giovanni's jumping in, the rejection he suffered at the hand of Tricky. "We had issues," Giovanni said. He explained that Tricky judged him too harshly, always demanding displays of bravado and enterprise that Giovanni could never manage to satisfy. After he was spotted talking to Officer Hernandez, the pressure seemed to increase. "It got out there that I was a fuckin' snitch," Giovanni said.

Holmes asked who was under Tricky. That would be Face, Giovanni said, "the fool who did this to me." He then described how Face picked him up from Mayra's house and took him to Mexico, an account that featured two names new to Holmes: Midget and Ranger. Giovanni told him about the terror of his asphyxiation, the miracle of his awakening on the side of a cliff. Holmes kept shifting in his chair, rubbing his forehead, scratching his collar.

"You're lucky to be alive, man," he said. "Lucky to be alive."

"That's right," said Giovanni, pleased that the detective was seeing events his way.

Holmes allowed Giovanni to guide the conversation for a good forty minutes, interrupting mainly to clarify a pronoun or unpack a bit of vernacular.

He was a practiced listener, skilled at allowing a cornered young man to feel himself heard. Finally, Holmes leaned in, his voice serious. The LAPD, along with the FBI, had a trove of evidence: surveillance, wiretaps, informants, "and so on and so forth," Holmes said.

Giovanni's hands were tucked between his thighs. His knees bounced side to side. He took a sip of water and swallowed hard.

"You are eighteen years old," Holmes said.

Giovanni nodded.

"These guys are much older than you."

Giovanni nodded again.

"And I understand that they were putting a lot of pressure on you, OK? You have got to be honest with me about everything."

"Yes, sir."

"We already know the answers. You understand what I'm saying?"

"Yes, sir."

"And I know it's going to be tough for you."

Giovanni folded his right leg over his left knee. An untied shoelace dangled. He'd lost control of the story.

"Listen to me," Holmes said. "I can't give you everything. Do you understand what I'm telling you? Not gonna work that way. You have to be the one that's gonna be forthcoming. You have to be the one that shows that you're being honest and truthful. I know that makes you awfully nervous. But you know who we're after—we're after the big fish."

Another drink of water, then a plea. "You gotta help me, sir," Giovanni said.

Holmes had the edge now. He wanted details on the vendor tax, on Face's enforcement techniques, on Giovanni's role in the scheme.

"When the vendors didn't pay, what happened?"

"He'd just tell 'em, 'You know what, you better have the money.' That's the rule."

"Who is 'he'?"

"Face."

And if they still didn't pay?

"I guess he'd beat them up."

"You *guess*?" Holmes said. He was losing patience with Giovanni's equivocation, the dancing around. "Listen to me, you gotta take a deep breath," said Holmes, pointing a finger at Giovanni's chest. "We already know everything. I see what these guys did to you. I'm being sincere to you when I try to tell you these guys are obviously much bigger, and that's who we want."

"Yes, sir."

"You, a youngster—these guys put a lot of influence on you. Sometimes you get to a point where you don't know how to say no. Especially when you're dealing with assholes who do stuff like this to you." Holmes had found his groove, a mix of authentic indignation and shrewd coercion. He jabbed his finger again. "Do you understand what I'm telling you? You've got to start thinking about yourself."

"You know why they did that to me?" Giovanni said. "Because I know too much."

"That's what I want to get at," said Holmes, dropping a fist onto the table. "Once you get out of that hood, you're a different person."

"You're gonna help me, right?"

"You're a different person."

"Yes, sir."

"You're out there busting your ass, trying to make a living, trying to do the right thing with your girl. And when you're in that other environment, these guys have control of you."

"They were peer pressuring me, you know what I mean?"

"You know what, unfortunately, it is sad—I know *exactly* what you mean."

His defenses eroding, Giovanni offered a more precise description of a dollar's path up from the sidewalk, from the vendors to the paisas to Face and then Tricky.

"Alright, there was one time that there was a vendor that wasn't paying, and you and Face went out," said Holmes, guiding Giovanni's attention to Francisco Clemente. "And there was an altercation, remember that?"

"Yeah, I know. I'm not gonna lie."

"Good, thank you. Tell me what happened with that."

"They just didn't want him right there—Tricky and Face."

"OK, kinda see what I'm getting at?"

"I was right there," said Giovanni, knees bouncing again, faster and more reflexively than before. "When the shit happened."

"When what happened?"

"The shooting."

"I know, I know," Holmes said. "You've come a long way, brother."

"I want to be honest with you," Giovanni said.

"I know this is tough for you," said Holmes, placing his right hand on Giovanni's left knee, steadying it with his palm. It was both paternal and strategic, a gesture of intimacy that caught Giovanni off guard. His heart pounded so fast he feared that the detective could see it right through his black sweatshirt. He pleaded again.

"I want to go home."

"Are you gonna be truthful with me?"

So began the starts and fits of Giovanni's confession. He admitted that he understood the purpose of the mission: to take down a vendor who "got an attitude and didn't want to pay rent." He named the 18th Street participants: Face, Big Guy, Lil Primo. He recalled the two paisas—a skinnier one who brought the gun, a heavier one who pointed out the vendor—neither of whom he'd ever met.

But Giovanni was still dodging, hoping against all odds he could outwit Holmes. To minimize his role, Giovanni described himself as only a lookout, a passive observer. When Holmes asked who the shooter was, Giovanni grasped for a name. Lil Primo—a quiet nineteen-year-old from Mexico who spoke little English and wasn't in custody yet—popped into his head. It was a shameful lie to introduce, one that Giovanni instantly regretted. Holmes knew to ignore it. He was determined to steer Giovanni to the truth, to free him from the awful secret that had taken them both far from home on a cold November night.

"What happened to the gun?"

"They throwed that shit in the water."

"In the lake? The MacArthur Park lake?"

Giovanni didn't know. He clasped his hands, spinning his thumbs like raffle drums. "Once that shit happened, I said, 'Man, fuck this shit, they took it too fuckin' far.' 'Cuz they did take it far, sir. Even though—I know the bullet wasn't meant for that baby. It's fucked up. 'Cuz if I had a baby . . ."

"I know," said Holmes, inching closer. "It's kind of an unfortunate thing that happened, but it kind of goes back to who these guys are and the influence they have on people."

"Motherfuckers, man. I want you to—could you fuck 'em up for me, sir?"

"Well, I don't fuck 'em up probably in the same way you think fuck 'em up. But these guys are gonna go away."

Holmes opened a thick binder of mug shots arrayed in six-packs and asked Giovanni to ID the people he knew. First up was Clever, the original suspect. His booking photo predated the gouge on his face. Giovanni said that Clever had no role in the attack.

"I know he's gone out there and kinda been muscle," said Holmes, hoping to elicit any detail that might place Clever at the scene. "Has he ever been muscle with you?"

"Like, what do you mean?"

"Like, going out there, making sure people pay up."

"I never knew, no—not like that, sir."

"Alright, now's gonna come the hard part for you," said Holmes, scooching his chair forward. "But it's all part of being honest, telling the truth. And

I know these guys put a lot of pressure on you. And you kinda got yourself in a predicament you couldn't get out of."

Giovanni nodded. Holmes leaned in closer.

"But we know what happened that night, and we know who the shooter was. And that's OK."

Giovanni reached for a sip of water.

"They put you in a spot," said Holmes, shaking his head. "I dunno, I dunno, if I was in your same position . . ."

"My position?"

"If I was in your position, it would have been tough that night. You know, they're the big homies. It's OK. You gotta get it off your chest."

Giovanni took another sip.

"Tricky, Face—it just came down to some bullshit that you got yourself wrapped up into," Holmes said. "Some *bullshit*. And, and, and, I call you today, and I find out you're working." Holmes paused to rub his face. "I mean, if you had grown up out here, it would have been a totally different thing for you." He waved his arm, as if to wipe away the whole putrid ecosystem Giovanni had belatedly broken free of. "You got sucked in down there."

The choice of words drew a giggle from Giovanni.

"You did."

More water.

"And you need to pull yourself out."

Holmes had been verbally circling Giovanni for two hours by then. He'd indulged his evasions, shrugged off his untruths. He'd expressed empathy for Giovanni—in service of his own interests, of course, and those of the People of California—but he'd done so in an undeniably genuine, even benevolent manner, the way the fakery of the best actors is also fundamentally honest. Now Holmes turned blunt.

"What happened that night?"

Giovanni's legs bounced faster than ever.

"I know you shot," Holmes said. "I know." He placed his hand on Giovanni's knee again. "You gotta tell me what was going through your head. Tell me what happened. Tell me what these guys said to you."

"Basically," Giovanni said, "that I was gonna die either way."

There it was, the acknowledgment Holmes had been working toward. He had his triggerman.

"They still thought you were snitching?" he asked.

"I was put in a fucked-up predicament."

"I know."

"You think I want to go shoot somebody?"

"I don't think you did, to be honest, sitting here talking to you."

"That wasn't me, sir."

"I know, I know that's not in here," said Holmes, touching his fingertips to Giovanni's chest. "I know."

"You're gonna help me, right?" Giovanni asked.

"What are we doing here?" Holmes said.

"Thank you, sir," said Giovanni. He extended his right hand, inviting his questioner to join him in a soul-brother shake. Holmes accepted, and then Giovanni added his left palm to their grip, so that he was sandwiching the detective's hand between both of his.

"I'm a changed man," Giovanni said.

"You've probably been having nightmares about this," Holmes said.

He grabbed a small camera and told Giovanni to take off his shirt. Giovanni stood up, wiry and exposed, ribs protruding, fists tight. Holmes aimed the lens at Giovanni's neck, rotating him counterclockwise to capture the full circumference of the wound. The flash ricocheted off the walls of the windowless room.

"Sir, do I get to go home?" Giovanni asked. He'd cooperated. He'd confessed. Having been unfairly labeled a snitch, Giovanni had now fulfilled the prophecy—ratted out his gang. He'd done everything that had been asked of him. "I want to go home already."

Holmes seemed confused. He told Giovanni that there was a warrant out for his arrest, a nationwide warrant for murder. "I've got a three-week-old baby that's dead," Holmes said. "Because of these assholes."

"But why do I got that warrant then, sir?" asked Giovanni. It was a hopelessly naive question. Giovanni was so thoroughly invested in Holmes's framing of the crime—that he was the victim, preyed on by the real culprits here—that he'd practically erased his own role. For the moment, that version of the truth served them both.

"Because you took off—I never heard from you," Holmes said. "We now know what was going on and what kind of pressure you were under. I understand why you took off."

He explained extradition to Giovanni, how as a fugitive he'd first have to face a Utah judge, and then wait while the authorities processed the paperwork formally transferring him to the custody of California. Once it was complete, Holmes vowed to personally return for Giovanni and escort him back to Los Angeles.

"Then I'm gonna be out—of, like, the jail?" Giovanni asked.

"You'll be out of jail when I take you over there, but you're gonna be handcuffed—you're in custody," Holmes said. "You got a no-bail warrant. No bail."

"What do you think's gonna happen then?"

"What do I think's gonna happen? I believe that Tricky and Face and that whole operation, um—I think we've seen the end of Tricky and Face, I'll put it that way."

"What about me?"

"That's something that, that—we're gonna have to sit down and sort through."

"I can't go home then?"

"Go home where?"

It became clear that they'd been talking past each other, home meaning one thing to Giovanni—a place that included Mayra in Ogden or Reyna in

Palmdale—and another to Holmes, who was already strategizing about where in LA to house his star witness without anyone discovering he was alive.

"Unfortunately, no," Holmes said.

"You gave me your word," Giovanni said. He leaned back and folded his arms. His chin sunk to his chest.

"What'd I tell ya?" Holmes said. "I said we're gonna come out here and we're gonna sit down and talk. I treated you fair from the beginning, and I'm gonna continue. You're just gonna have to sit tight for a bit."

"How much time am I looking at?" Giovanni asked.

"How much time?" Holmes finally realized that Giovanni wasn't understanding how abruptly his freedom had ended, couldn't fathom the brutal, shrunken world he'd just bought for himself. "How much—?" Holmes repeated, then stretched his arms wide, as if to suggest an interminable path. "Just based on what I have right now, life in prison. You know that."

Giovanni stared at the floor.

"Let me just tell you," Holmes said, "the best thing that could've happened to you was that we came out here." It was a fair statement; cooperation was Giovanni's only hope. But he'd offered it rashly, without a lawyer, freestyling against a professional inquisitor.

"So, if everything works out," asked Giovanni, still bargaining for a break, "how much am I looking at?"

"I-I-I-I don't know," Holmes said. "I don't know. Don't know."

Giovanni's head drooped.

"But usually," Holmes said, offering a kernel of reassurance, "with the truth comes good things."

"Is this gonna help me, though?" Giovanni asked. "All I say?"

The interview was over. Holmes ordered Giovanni to stand up and turn around, placing him in handcuffs once again.

26

Stained

Midget wanted to forget that final night in Mexico, the travesty she'd allowed herself to be lured into. A self-help adage she'd later post on Facebook captured the life she longed for: "Be kind but not weak. Be humble but not timid." It was so hard, though, especially as a young mother in the hood, a woman who was belittled every time someone spoke her name. Midget's whole life she'd felt the pressure to give in, to take it. Face had insisted on borrowing her truck. Giovanni had insisted on having his way.

Midget's complaisance in La Rumorosa now entangled her in a crime she'd never set out to commit. She hadn't wanted to know anything; she now knew too much. She'd witnessed Ranger—the uncle to one of her children, a babysitter to the others—squeeze out the life of another 18th Streeter in her car, at her side, inches from where she sat. Ranger's malevolence wasn't theoretical. It hung over Midget's head. To protect herself, to ensure her kids' safety, she compartmentalized the murder. Tucked it away. "I was vulnerable," she says, "because I had nobody." Their pocket of South-Central was Ranger's world. Ranger's sister lived upstairs from Midget in the same apartment house on Eighty-Third Street. Over the years, Ranger had lived on Eightieth, Eighty-First, and Eighty-Fourth. After the trip to Mexico, Ranger started staying on Eighty-Second with his nephew, also an 18th Streeter. Midget had been due in court that October, to resolve a DUI charge from the summer, but never showed. She didn't want to imagine what could happen to her kids if she had to do time in jail.

As much as she hated to admit it, Midget still needed Ranger's help. The back seat of the Chevy Tahoe had a brownish patch, about the size of a rib eye, permanently soaked into the gray herringbone cloth. "We tried cleaning it," she says, "but it was just stained."

Face had promised to take care of it. Then Face got arrested. Midget told Ranger they really needed to get the upholstery changed. Ranger gave her $30. "I told him that wasn't going to be enough," Midget says. "He said he was going to give me some more later."

Instead of erasing the evidence, Midget drove her truck back down to Mexico at the end of November and spent another night on the town with Ranger. Midget's son wanted to visit his dad, Ranger's brother, who lived in Tijuana. Ranger wanted to celebrate his thirtieth birthday on Avenida Revolución. Two months after Giovanni's farewell, they were once again on the strip, partying at El Torito, the kind of club that engulfs the dance floor in soapy foam on Saturday nights. They ordered a bucket of Coronas and posed for a photo. Ranger grins in a crisp white dress shirt, his left arm draped around Midget; she wears an abstracted floral print, eyes narrow and mouth pinched.

Had Giovanni not mentioned their names during his interrogation three weeks earlier, Ranger and Midget might never have entered the equation. They didn't fit into any of the existing cases. They were not from the Columbia Lil Cycos clique of 18th Street. They didn't participate in the Sixth Street shooting or any MacArthur Park rent collections. Giovanni knew only their monikers. He couldn't even supply an address, only vaguely remembering a car wash outside Midget's place the night they left for Mexico. It took the cops several weeks to trace her and her Chevy Tahoe to the apartment on Eighty-Third Street, but even after ID'ing her, Holmes and Evens had little to work with—only Giovanni's extraordinary tale of a flubbed execution on a mountain road in Mexico.

Midget's failure to appear on the DUI gave them an excuse to detain her. Early on the morning of December 6, 2007, a week after she'd returned from the birthday bash in Tijuana, the LAPD surrounded Midget's apartment. Ranger was there, as he often was; he still helped Midget get her kids to school. She was surprised to find him dressed up: button-down shirt, slacks, leather shoes. Ranger explained that he was waiting on a visit from his parole officer. He told Midget "that's the way he was going to start dressing from now on," she says, "because Face told him that he had to be low-pro."

As soon as Midget left the apartment, police swarmed her truck and arrested her on a bench warrant. Ranger followed her out, but spotted the cops and sped off in a Toyota Corolla. The LAPD gave chase. Ranger bailed from the car and sprinted down an alley. The police lost him.

Holmes and Evens advised Midget of her rights. "You know, I cannot talk to you," Midget told the detectives. "I can't. I just can't." They told her to think of her kids. Had it not been for them, she felt certain she would have kept quiet—taken one more for the team—and paid whatever price the government demanded. That's the way the homies had raised her. But the prospect of her sons repeating her life, instruments of 18th Street, melted Midget's defiance. Without a lawyer present, she made the tactical decision to divulge only Face's name, describing him as the instigator, the one who proclaimed Giovanni "a good homie" while wrenching his neck. When it came to Ranger, Midget obfuscated. She told police that "I didn't know who he was, that it was just, you know, somebody that I didn't know." It was Face and the "other guy" who yanked Giovanni so hard that his head ended up in the back seat. It was Face and the "other guy" who returned to the truck, without Giovanni, causing Midget to fear that she might be next. "I told them that I didn't know who was the other guy," she says.

Midget was arraigned the next morning at the Inglewood courthouse, where she pleaded to the drunk-driving charge. A judge ordered her to pay $390. Midget didn't have the money. Although she'd fretted about being separated from her children, Midget asked a friend who "nobody from the hood knew" to look after the kids, and instead of the fine, she chose thirteen days in jail. "If I had to go to jail or had to leave," she says, "I knew they were safe." Then she called Detective Evens and said she needed help. She was scared. She couldn't stay on Eighty-Third anymore.

"In that short period of time, she was able to go: 'I'm fucked,'" says Evens, who hadn't realized until their conversation that Ranger was the uncle to one of Midget's boys. "She realized right then and there that if she did not cooperate with us, she'd be in prison."

Each time Midget retold the story, now placing Ranger alongside Face in the middle of La Rumorosa, Evens began to empathize with her just a little more—not something she'd ever felt for a participant in a murder plot. "When you look at her life story, not from a cop perspective, but: Why'd you get into a gang? Why'd you do this? Why'd you do that? It's just very, very unfortunate," Evens says. "With her family situation, her kids, and just, you know, the whole thing, it's very sad. Considering her role, it's hard. I've never had a case like that. But it's almost like she's one of my good friends now."

Midget's confession matched Giovanni's version of events, giving the detectives a solid case not just against Face but also Ranger, if and when he could be found. But there was still another link to confirm, one last piece of physical evidence. The LAPD impounded Midget's truck, and a criminalist went to work swabbing for blood. The dark stain on the upholstery came back positive. The criminalist cut out a swath of the fabric, photographed it, preserved it, and booked it into evidence. A forensic analyst tested Giovanni's DNA and compared it to the sample from the truck.

The night they left Tijuana for La Rumorosa, Midget had feared that her DNA would be found on Giovanni's corpse, but it was his DNA that 18th Street had failed to erase. For all of Midget's pleading, Face and Ranger had allowed her to drive around with traces of their victim for seventy-six days.

27

Not Part of Nothing No More

The Ogden jail was all steel and concrete. A bunk bolted into the wall. A stool bolted into the ground. Giovanni's cell had a narrow window, a slit in the bulwark, that afforded him a glimpse of the junkyards on the other side of the railroad tracks. One crisp November day he pressed his nose to the glass and for the first time in his life saw snowflakes twirling in the gray sky. "It reminded me of, like, a Christmas movie," Giovanni says. The peacefulness of the scene magnified his sadness. Doing the right thing didn't feel as good as he'd hoped.

Giovanni had never been one for solitude or stillness. He'd do almost anything to avoid being alone with his own thoughts. Giovanni's adolescence had revolved around a series of hasty decisions, his fitfulness an antidote to the melancholy that hung over his home. Twice he'd busted out of juvenile placement facilities, the urge to escape greater than the fear of getting caught. Even the trip to Mexico had the benefit of movement—a phony getaway that precipitated a real one. Now he'd gone the opposite direction, volunteering for confinement, and for the first time in his life doing it as an adult.

He called his mom, collect, from a pay phone. He lied. "Don't worry, it's all a mistake," Giovanni told her. "I'll be out of here soon."

He awaited his weekly visit from Mayra, who'd been questioned by the detectives but cleared. Through the glass partition, Giovanni asked if she'd stick with him, if they'd be able to get through this mess together. Mayra made promises she couldn't keep. Giovanni pretended to believe her, but he knew: "It was just a matter of time." He'd eventually be required to take the witness stand and publicly condemn the gang that had left him for dead. Once word of his cooperation spread, he assumed that 18th Street would pressure Mayra into dumping him, that her brother in Pelican Bay would forbid her to stand by a rat. "I knew," he says, "they were going to get into her head."

One Sunday morning toward the end of November, Dave Holmes boarded the lone plane in the LAPD's fleet, an eight-seat 1976 military-surplus Beechcraft twin-prop—rickety enough to stir dark thoughts, he says, "like the Buddy Holly story." He left the Van Nuys Airport, better known for its private jets, and flew to Ogden. Giovanni was happy to be reunited.

Edgar Hernandez also rode the Beechcraft. He hadn't been present for Giovanni's interrogation, but he felt a paternal tug to help get him back to LA. They had history. Giovanni appreciated having another familiar face as his escort, and after boarding the cramped plane, he turned to the officer for reassurance. "I'm talking to him, and I'm like, man, I feel bad again," Hernandez says. "Like, he goes, 'Hey, Hernandez, how much time you think I'm gonna do?' I go, 'I don't know, dude.' And he goes, 'Yeah, I'm willing to do eleven years,' something like that. 'Can you talk to the judge or the district attorney, you know, tell them I'm a nice guy, I'm cooperating?' I go, 'Uhhh, listen, that's up to your attorney. I don't want to lie to you.' He was talking to me like a kid. I felt so bad."

As the plane chugged over forest and canyon, it was buffeted by angry jolts of turbulence. The Beechcraft pitched and rolled, at times seeming to fly sideways. Giovanni, who hadn't flown since he'd traveled to his father's deathbed in Guadalajara as an infant, couldn't believe that the LAPD had faith in a plane that "looked like it had been recycled from a junkyard." It became a running joke. "He's thinking, 'Shit, I survived falling off a cliff,'" Holmes says, "'and we're all going to go down in the airplane.'"

Holmes needed somewhere safe and out of the way to stash Giovanni. Men's Central—where Clever's face had been cut open—would likely be a death sentence. He settled on the sheriff's substation in San Dimas, an equestrian-friendly bedroom community in the San Gabriel Mountain foothills thirty miles east of LAPD headquarters. The town had a wood-plank promenade and old-timey

Western facades; its high school provided the backdrop for *Bill & Ted's Excellent Adventure*. Holmes booked Giovanni under the name John Elway. Giovanni got no pleasure from his temporary identity as the Denver Broncos quarterback—he had no idea who that was.

The Los Angeles County Bar Association's Indigent Defense Panel selected an attorney for Giovanni, an alternately gracious and mordant University of North Carolina graduate named Richard Lasting who'd been practicing law in California since 1972. With his shock of white hair, bushy eyebrows, and even whiter Mark Twain mustache, he could play the Southern gentleman, his speech courteous and measured before judges and juries, yet still carp about the arrogant prosecutors who held all the cards and knew it.

Lasting's most famous case had involved an LAPD officer—the "most corrupt policeman in the city of Los Angeles in its history," the DA had thundered. A mild-mannered traffic cop charged with orchestrating a pair of contract murders in the late 1970s and early '80s, William Leasure was everything Giovanni was not: calm, reasonable, secretive, and insistent that he'd been framed. Lasting took it to trial, poking holes in most of the damning evidence, and emerged with a hung jury, deadlocked ten to two in favor of guilt. Although his client vowed to keep fighting, Lasting warned him of the likelihood of a conviction, and on the eve of retrial, Leasure hedged his bets, pleading to two terms of fifteen years to life.

With Giovanni, Lasting inherited a scared kid who'd already spilled the beans. "It was, sadly, an all too familiar experience," he says. "He was young. He wasn't a sophisticated criminal. The gang had tried to kill him. So he didn't really have anybody that he could turn to, except for his family, and his family was not going to be of any help. He was alone, essentially." There was nothing Lasting could do about Giovanni's confession: it was on tape. It had also been extracted by an expert interrogator—a "good detective" and a "decent guy," Lasting says—who had not made any procedural errors during the interview. Lasting still owed it to Giovanni to examine the evidence and see if he could construct a defense, but he had nothing to work with. "I quickly came to the realization," he says, "that that was a lost cause."

Giovanni's mood darkened. He acted out in the San Dimas jail, erupting in anger and screaming that he wanted to be left alone. He clogged the toilet and flooded his cell. He told Lasting that he was "mad with the world." Lasting told Giovanni to pause and think. "Ask yourself if you're about to do something fucked up," the lawyer counseled him. "And if the answer is yes, don't do it." Giovanni didn't have anyone like that in his life, a grandfatherly adviser who spoke to him straight. He hadn't expected an attorney to care. It still wasn't enough to ease Giovanni's foreboding, though, his sense that he'd painted himself into a corner. While he'd never looked forward to prison, Giovanni had always taken comfort in knowing that 18th Street would at least have his back—that if he ended up doing hard time, it'd be because he'd stood up for the hood. Now he was facing an eternity in prison and excommunication from the brotherhood that had put him up to his crime. Giovanni cursed his fate: *I'm not part of nothing no more.*

His mom had her own security to consider. Fearing that she'd become a target once news of Giovanni's survival leaked out, Reyna Flores left her job at the mall and packed up the apartment in Palmdale. Her boyfriend at the time had family up north, on the industrial side of the San Francisco Bay, so she and her daughter took shelter in his parents' place. It was a miserable escape. Reyna worried incessantly about Giovanni—was he safe? was he eating?—but she hadn't seen him since September, when she put him on the bus to Utah, and she wasn't around to visit now that he'd been returned to LA. She found work as a cleaning lady. Her boyfriend, who'd been hired to paint houses, drank on the job and, when she complained, beat her.

In moments of despair, Reyna called her younger son, Israel, who at seventeen had tried to insulate himself from his mom's "crying spells," as he once put it, by moving into a musty hotel near LAX. When she could no longer bear it, Reyna pleaded with Israel to drive up and rescue her and his sister.

After several months, he brought them back to LA, and they all camped out together at the Four Points on Aviation Boulevard.

Giovanni's stepdad wasn't in a position to offer anyone help either. Not long after Giovanni was taken into custody, Juan Monroy was heading home from work in New Mexico when he drove his new Tacoma pickup, with his new set of tools in the back, right into a sobriety checkpoint. At booking, the Albuquerque police ran his name and discovered that he'd been deported twenty-two years earlier, nabbed by la migra as a young man in Texas, before he'd ever made it to LA. "Why are you telling me this? You're not immigration," Juan protested. The police in New Mexico weren't like the LAPD. They told Juan: "We help one another out."

Juan was moved to federal custody and charged with "Reentry of a Removed Alien." It didn't take the government long to place the only dad Giovanni had ever known on a one-way flight to Guatemala.

In time, Giovanni earned an eviction from the San Dimas jail and a new cell in the Twin Towers Correctional Facility, a pair of conjoined twelve-story behemoths wedged between Union Station and the Los Angeles River. It housed some four thousand inmates, the majority of them mentally ill. Despite being rebooked as John Doe and segregated from the general population, Giovanni now found himself back in LA proper, under the same roof with 18th Streeters who might recognize him and Mexican Mafia carnales who'd have authority to reinstate the green light. Giovanni's paranoia spiraled. He heard voices behind his back, choruses of "baby killer" ringing in his ears. He caught himself talking to the walls, yelling "shut up" at people who weren't there. He stopped eating. Nights were the worst, a descent into shame and self-pity. Giovanni cried over the baby, cried over the rope that he could still feel branding his neck. He dreamt he was suffocating.

The Sheriff's Department gave him Benadryl to help him sleep and Remeron, an antidepressant, to stabilize his mood swings. Giovanni didn't think the meds helped. His lawyer retained a psychologist to assess Giovanni's condition. She found him "cooperative" and "unimpaired," his eye contact "appropriate." Giovanni grew emotional when discussing his crime with her, even more so when reflecting on the dysfunction of his home: "It should be noted that recollections of his family history and family dynamics consistently elicited the most tearful reactions." The twelve-page report concluded that Giovanni was suffering from post-traumatic stress disorder and the early onset of persistent depressive disorder.

With no hope of putting on a defense, Lasting focused on saving Giovanni's life. The charges against him included a "special circumstances" allegation—a crime committed for the benefit of a street gang—making Giovanni eligible for the death penalty. The district attorney's office had yet to signal whether it intended to pursue a capital case, which in California was largely theoretical; the state carried out so few executions, condemned prisoners were more likely to expire from natural causes or suicide. Still, if he could get death off the table, Lasting at least had a shot at negotiating a plea that might someday give Giovanni a second chance.

He hired a social worker to develop mitigating evidence, to piece together the fragments of Giovanni's childhood into a portrait of a boy hobbled by generational trauma. She interviewed family members, reconstructed his educational and criminal histories, and compiled medical records, both Giovanni's and his mom's. Despite the danger it posed, Lasting also endorsed Giovanni's continued cooperation with law enforcement, counseling him to answer questions truthfully as he submitted to interviews with not just LA detectives and prosecutors but also the FBI and the US attorney's office. To have any hope of leniency, Giovanni would need to take the witness stand in two trials—state and federal—and face the men who'd tried to kill him, the big homies who would now have yet another reason for wanting him dead.

The prospect of seeing them again both intimidated and intrigued Giovanni. As long as the Columbia Lil Cycos believed that they'd succeeded in disappearing him, Giovanni had a kind of superpower—the gift of invisibility. Turning himself in had stripped him of that safeguard, bringing him back into the world of the living. Once his killers learned of their blunder, as soon as they realized that their betrayal of him had brought about his betrayal of them, Giovanni would be returned to that one ugly week in September. His nightmares wouldn't be just in his head.

At least Giovanni wouldn't be confronting his tormentors alone. He had an ally in Holmes, an authority figure who'd told him that good things would come from accepting responsibility. Testifying against the Columbia Lil Cycos would be agonizing but maybe also purifying. It was the only way forward for Giovanni, the only possibility he'd ever be able to live with himself. "My victims deserved it," he says. He couldn't handle the thought of failing them a second time.

Giovanni first had to be arraigned at the Clara Shortridge Foltz Criminal Justice Center, the downtown courthouse that since the 1970s has served as the stage for LA's most notorious trials. On the fifth floor, in Department 30, bailiffs shuffle an all-day procession of defendants in cuffs and scrubs from a holding tank into a rectangular wooden enclosure along the right side of the courtroom wall, roughly where a jury would sit. The box is sealed off with iron bars and smudged plexiglass, a corral for the newly charged on their way to entering a plea. On December 12, 2007, the Robbery-Homicide detectives brought Giovanni through the courtroom's public doors—their John Doe couldn't mix with other detainees—guiding him past the gallery benches and into the dull fluorescent glow of the oak-paneled chamber. Giovanni stiffened. He clenched his jaw and tightened his brow. The judge asked him to state his true name.

Giovanni's voice struck the defendants' box like a thunderbolt. His accused crime partners had been summoned that same day, at least the ones the LAPD had apprehended. Shackled, clad in orange jumpers, and awaiting scheduling orders, Giovanni's former homies all turned to see the dead man standing before them. None was more horrified than Face, who until that moment was certain he'd redeemed the gang by killing Giovanni with his own hands.

"They look one way and—boom—they look at Face," Holmes says. "And Face was like, 'Oh, my God.'"

"The look on Face's face," Evens says. "There was nothing better."

Now the Columbia Lil Cycos knew: Giovanni, the ghost of La Rumorosa, had come back to haunt them.

28

Sideways from There

Shorty's family disregarded the warnings. They dismissed the threats. They discounted the vulnerability of a teenage girl who, like Giovanni, would be called on to testify for the prosecution in at least two trials. Once again, the Matiases were out on Sixth Street, right where they'd been for more than two decades, flouting the law that stood in the way of their livelihood. If Shorty saw a conflict between the values the LAPD's Explorer Program sought to inculcate and her family's daily act of civil disobedience, it didn't deter her. "What I used to do for a living," she says, "it was illegal vending."

In 2008, on the last day of February, officers from the Rampart Division cruised down Sixth Street, prowling for bootleg DVDs. Working with investigators from the Motion Picture Association of America, the police often prioritized antipiracy enforcement, raiding clandestine burner operations and rousting curbside vendors—a crackdown in defense of the company town. The LAPD would serve twenty-nine search warrants that year, make forty-seven arrests, and seize nearly $23 million in counterfeit intellectual property. On that Friday afternoon, five months after the shooting, Shorty's parents had laid out an assortment of movies on the Sixth Street pavement, enough to catch the antipiracy squad's eye.

"The movie companies or whatever would pay for overtime shifts, and they would have a task force go down to, you know, scoop up the illegal DVDs," Holmes says. "Mom and Dad got wrapped up in that."

The officers moved to impound the Matiases' discs. Andres and Juana blocked them. The standoff turned into a tug-of-war. A lawyer for the Matiases would claim that police "roughed up or mistreated" both parents, a scene their daughter couldn't ignore. In an instinctive burst, Shorty "basically jumps on the back of a police officer," Holmes says. "And it kind of goes sideways from there." It was an absurd fracas: a five-foot-one girl wrestling a cop over some janky DVDs that the city was confiscating at the behest of Disney, Fox, Sony, Universal, and Warner Bros.

The LAPD booked Shorty's parents on charges of battery and resisting arrest, which required them each to post a $20,000 bond. Shorty was charged as a juvenile. Arguing that the Matiases were victims of police abuse, their lawyer filed a Pitchess motion—a procedure for accessing police personnel records when misconduct is alleged. In a deal with the city attorney's office, the Matiases pleaded to a reduced charge of disturbing the peace, earning them each a two-day jail sentence, a year's probation, and $264 in fees and fines. Shorty—witness to murder, victim of gang intimidation, candidate for a taxpayer-funded reward—was suspended from the Explorer Program and ordered into counseling. She later took a "long trip" out of the country.

"I don't know, like at fifteen, who has to deal with that," says Victor Avila, the deputy district attorney who would be relying on Shorty to help prove the state's murder case.

Several months after the scuffle in 2008, the LAPD cited Andres again for illegal vending (suspended fine of $50). The next year, the police cited Juana ($775 in fines and assessments). And a few years later, Andres was cited yet again for illegal vending ($269 in fines and assessments).

Getting ticketed by the cops became the cost of doing business, another line item on the family ledger, a temporary setback in the low-grade forever war the city waged against its vendors. As Shorty puts it: "Money comes and money goes." Each time prosecutors would summon her to the courthouse— every time Shorty testified about her experience vending on Columbia Lil Cycos turf—either Andres or Juana also had a court date hanging over their head. Even when the Los Angeles city council issued Shorty the largest share of the reward money, $50,000, her family still had outstanding fines to pay. They might have dodged the gang's tax but not the city's cut.

29

He Let Me Live

Like Giovanni Macedo, Francisco Clemente was supposed to die. He felt like he had. "My life, for me, it was lost," he says. "More than anything, I was already dead." He became overwhelmed whenever he talked about what he'd endured, even more so when he spoke of the baby, "an angel who God had just barely sent here to live."

In those moments, grief would get the better of Francisco's pride. His face would dissolve. He'd wipe his eyes with the chapped, ferrous hands of a mechanic and shake his head. "Excuse me," he'd say, "but when you have a sensitive heart, you double over with feelings more than some cabrón out on the street." Francisco was so distraught, the detectives initially suspected he was Luis Angel's father. He kept explaining that no, he was with Jessica, but he understood too well the challenges Daniela would face raising a newborn alone.

"I know what it is," he says, "to live without a dad."

For weeks after leaving the hospital, Francisco was too weak to walk without a cane. He moved gingerly, afraid that the bullet in his back would migrate if he tried to exert himself. The one in his jaw jutted from the bone and bulged through his skin—he'd sometimes crane his neck and rub a finger over the lead slug, still cylindrical and intact. It felt strange to have the thing that was designed to kill him lodged right there, within reach, and to know that it would stay there as long as he lived. His mother cooked him soup and blended him licuados. He couldn't even chew a piece of bread.

The police wanted to relocate Francisco, to house him somewhere away from 18th Street's influence. The way Francisco saw it, 18th Street was everywhere: "They're wherever they want to be, in all states, in all countries; you can't hide." If the gang really wanted to find him again, he figured they could, and he refused to give them the satisfaction of driving him away. Under the masculine codes Francisco subscribed to, his would-be killers were unworthy of his fear. "Why did they do this to me if they're so manly?" he says. "Because they're not men. Or supposedly they think they're such badasses, but in the moment they're not. They're cowardly men."

Only one explanation made sense to him: God didn't want him dead. "He is the only one who can take my life, nobody else," Francisco says. "Nobody, not even those guys, can do it—not gunshots or slashes or whatever. If God doesn't want me to die, I'm not going to die."

Rather than accept the LAPD's offer of protection, Francisco asked Jessica to join him at his mother's house. He had a room of his own there—"a small room, super, super small," says Jessica, who did her best to ingratiate herself with Francisco's family, both as his nurse and partner. "The accident definitely brought us closer together, especially because I learned she was pregnant," Francisco says. "When this happened to me, I told her, 'Don't go, I don't want you to leave.'"

Although they'd stopped vending on MacArthur Park's streets, Jessica had begun prenatal visits at a clinic in the neighborhood, driving right past Sixth Street for her care. Neither she nor Francisco had insurance, and because of their immigration status, they didn't qualify for full Medi-Cal benefits, but the state covered pregnancy-related services. Returning to the scene of the crime rattled and disoriented Francisco. "I don't know, but I see myself as if I were dead and yet passing through there as a living being," he says, "as if you were alive, looking at where you'd died. It's something— something incredible."

Whenever Francisco seemed to waver, daunted by the prospect of taking the witness stand and reliving the worst day of his life, the detectives reminded him that he and Jessica had an indispensable role to play—that their courage could deliver justice for Luis Angel. The sad truth was that the baby's mother wasn't capable of doing it. A jury would never get a chance to meet Daniela, whose time in and out of jail and treatment centers made her a problematic narrator, exposed to attacks from defense lawyers. The state needed someone to speak for the child, and Francisco and Jessica were "just outstanding people," Holmes says. "True righteous victims."

The first gauge of their resolve came at the preliminary hearing, in May 2008, eight months after the shooting. Before proceeding to trial, prosecutors typically must make an abbreviated presentation to a judge, an initial test of the evidence. It was a low bar to clear but still more adversarial than the federal system, which allowed the government to take most cases to a grand jury in secret. Francisco and Jessica would have to enter LA's criminal courts building, just two miles from the crime scene, and confront the gang that targeted them. Five members of the Columbia Lil Cycos made appearances: Face, Big Guy, Lil Primo, Silly, and Clever. Missing were Barrios and Atlas, both fugitives. Giovanni wasn't there either; as a cooperator, he would have a separate, more perfunctory hearing.

Jessica went first, taking her oath through a Spanish interpreter. Nine months pregnant—"literally ready to pop," Evens says—she was the steelier half of the couple, pragmatic and assured. When the prosecutor asked how she felt about being on the witness stand, Jessica gave a clipped reply: "Fine."

Much of the questioning focused on Clever, the lone defendant who maintained he was the victim of mistaken identity. From a photo lineup, Jessica identified Clever as a regular at Video Mania, where she'd often seen him playing the machines. Jessica testified that she'd also seen Clever the night of the shooting—as she'd told Holmes, he was the one who'd shouted at the gunman to hurry. But when Jessica was asked if she saw Clever in the courtroom, she said no. Asked again, she said she was certain. Later, after the lunch break, Jessica reversed herself, insisting she'd misunderstood the question: Clever was right there, in the orange jail scrubs. It was just that he looked different than she remembered him. He now had a scar across his cheek.

Francisco took the stand next, revealing himself to be as fragile as Jessica was composed. Within minutes, he had to pause, grimacing as he covered his belly with his hand. The prosecutor asked if he was OK. "Sometimes I just have some pain," Francisco said. "A bit of pain. And I just hold it, but I think I can tolerate it."

Unlike Jessica, Francisco did not think Clever had egged on the shooter—he thought Clever was the shooter. And yet, like Jessica, Francisco struggled to reconcile his memory with what was before his eyes. He looked at a picture of Clever. He looked around the courtroom. For a moment, he couldn't speak.

"Are you OK, Francisco?" the prosecutor asked. "Why do you have your head down and you're rubbing your eyebrows and your forehead area?"

"I feel somewhat confused," Francisco said. He explained that Clever "looks like the guy" who opened fire. Except something about his appearance had changed. Francisco stared at the left side of Clever's face. "The scar, is that something—I don't know whether the scar is something new, something more recent," Francisco said. "That's what is so confusing."

Francisco was more certain about his assailant after studying a picture of Giovanni. Compared to Clever, he said, "this one looked more like the person that was there that shot me."

Holmes recognized that the evidence against Clever was at best inconsistent. He'd located another street vendor in MacArthur Park who'd been assaulted for not paying rent; that victim was said to have identified Clever as the enforcer who'd beaten him. But besides Francisco and Jessica, Holmes didn't have another witness who could place Clever on Sixth Street the night of the shooting. Giovanni—who would presumably know better than anyone—denied that Clever was there. So did every other defendant who'd agreed to speak to the police. Daniela had seen Clever before, but not that night. And Shorty continued to insist that Clever was not among the six people she saw hatching the plot outside USA Donuts.

Clever's lawyer made an impassioned plea to have the murder charges against him dismissed. He cataloged every witness and every defendant who'd been specifically asked whether Clever was at the scene and who'd specifically said he wasn't. The lawyer acknowledged that Francisco thought Clever resembled the shooter, but that wasn't the prosecution's theory—everyone agreed that Giovanni had pulled the trigger. That left Jessica as the only one who'd plausibly suggested that Clever participated in the murder, and her testimony was "overwhelmed by all the evidence that he was not present."

The prosecutor refused to concede. Clever was a member of 18th Street, a gang that perpetrated a taxation scheme against street vendors, and he was a regular on the block where that scheme had turned murderous. It made no difference that Clever didn't appear to have a particular assignment at the time of the attack—if he was there, he was in on it. "This is an individual who obviously knew what was going on," the prosecutor argued. "So the fact that he's out there on the day of the shooting makes pretty good sense."

Pretty good was good enough. The judge ordered all the defendants, Clever included, to stand trial for murder.

Two days after Francisco and Jessica testified, their daughter was born. She had a crop of ink-black hair like her father—"the spitting image of Francisco," says Evens, who celebrated the birth along with Holmes. They cradled the infant, marveling at the blessing that was now visiting these new parents after so much torment. "There was goodness to it," Evens says. "In the tragic loss of a little one, we were there for, you know, a new life."

For Francisco, the sight of his daughter filled his heart with something inexplicable. She was it, the sign he'd awaited. Since the moment he'd opened his eyes in the hospital, Francisco had wrestled with the randomness of his survival, cursed the unfairness of the one errant bullet that found its way to Daniela's baby. Now it was so much clearer. Francisco still would have traded places with Luis Angel. Here in his arms, a warm, squirming bundle of innocence and possibility, was the reason he hadn't been asked to.

"You know what, Mami?" he whispered to his daughter. "For you, God has me here. Believe me. Because if it wasn't for you, I think maybe He wouldn't have done it. He wanted me here so that I could watch over you in your life and help you get ahead. For you, He let me live."

Francisco believed it in the most literal sense: His daughter had brought him back from the dead.

30

Everybody Else's Fault

On a June morning in 2009, nearly two years after the Columbia Lil Cycos went gunning for Francisco, the FBI surrounded Isaac Guillen's house. Keenan had agents posted up and down Calle Francesca, a stretch of suburban dream homes that dead-ended in the hills of San Dimas's Via Verde Ridge neighborhood.

After securing an indictment against the Columbia Lil Cycos in 2007, the federal government had continued to amass and present evidence, and now a grand jury had handed up a 114-page superseding indictment that captured the full scope of the gang's racketeering activity. The number of defendants had surged to thirty-nine, and at the top of the list, sandwiched between Tricky's and Morena's names, was Isaac's. Even with all the arrests—no matter the likelihood that someone in the Columbia Lil Cycos' ranks would see the advantage in flipping—the lawyer hadn't stopped working for Puppet.

"He knew the risk he was taking," Keenan says, "but he thought he was a pretty smart guy."

The FBI's pounding woke up Norma Guillen. She walked down the stairs from their second-story bedroom and opened the door. "Your brain takes you to what makes the most sense," she says, "and I thought, 'They have the wrong house.'" The feds told her to get her husband, who was still asleep. So were their three kids, the youngest of them barely a year old. Norma had never lived in a place so grand: 3,100 square feet.

Isaac and Norma were marched into the driveway. Both were cuffed. "They thought I had something to do with whatever they were arresting him for," says Norma, who'd spent a decade as a Los Angeles County deputy probation officer. She knew about Isaac's past, of course: his record, his sobriety.

She understood that as a criminal defense attorney, he handled gang and drug cases, a line of work that appeared to pay for whatever they desired. But she'd never suspected the kind of relapse he was concealing, the history he was repeating. "The brain takes you to denial," she says, "just for safety or just to keep you from fragmenting or whatever." The FBI asked if she owned a gun. Agents wanted to know if she'd ever used a police computer to feed information to Isaac. "I was like, 'I don't even know what's going on,'" she says. Their next-door neighbor was a lawyer. Across the street lived a police sergeant. Around the corner, there was a retired Superior Court judge. "We lived in a really nice neighborhood," she says. "It was humiliating."

When she first met Isaac, on the East Los Angeles College campus, Norma was practically a kid, just eighteen and living at home in Compton. Her dad, a construction worker from the Mexican state of Zacatecas, held stubbornly machista views on raising daughters. "He didn't want me to go to school," she says. "He wanted me to get married and have babies." Her mom's life revolved around domestic chores. "I was like, I want to have a life where if I don't like how I'm treated, I can leave because I have skills and can support myself."

Norma had exuberant eyes, wide and welcoming. Isaac wanted to date her. She shot him down. He was divorced and thirteen years older. His firstborn was just six years younger than she was. "I was like, no way," Norma says. "My dad would kill me." But several years later, as she was completing her sociology degree at Berkeley and Isaac was entering UCLA Law, their paths crossed again. "We started talking, and I don't know, he just seemed like he knew what he wanted in life," Norma says. The age difference—his kids—didn't faze her either. "I figured, well, he already knows how to behave. I guess he's an adult."

The year Isaac passed the California bar, they married in Laughlin, the Nevada resort town. They had a daughter two years later and a son two years after that. In 2005, just about the time that Keenan was launching his investigation into the Columbia Lil Cycos, the Guillens bought the house on Calle

Francesca, with a curvaceous, free-form swimming pool and adjoining spa, for $998,000. Isaac reported income of over $683,000 on his taxes the year after that. It was all picture-perfect on the outside—a socioeconomic transformation jump-started by education and public service—but "Isaac was never really home," says Norma, who'd become a full-time homemaker. His destination was always the same: Colorado or Mexico. "He never told me why," she says, "and I never asked."

Even with Isaac's illicit income, they were overspending, racking up debt and drowning in interest. They took out a $200,000 second mortgage. They owed more than $150,000 on eleven different credit cards. When they filed for bankruptcy in 2008, their liabilities exceeded their assets by almost $800,000. "I couldn't breathe in that house," Norma says. Instead of insulating them from insecurity, allowing them to sequester themselves from the struggles of the working poor, money was destabilizing the Guillens. Isaac, according to Norma, blamed her for pressuring him to provide more extravagances than they could afford; she accused him of using material trappings to make up for his absences.

Keenan transported Isaac to FBI headquarters in Westwood. It wasn't a chatty drive. Isaac had spent his career telling clients to shut their trap; nothing good ever came from trying to talk your way out of trouble. When Keenan explained the charges to him—RICO conspiracy, including ten counts of money laundering, which carried a sentence of up to twenty years—Isaac remained defiant. "I wasn't worried about the indictment," he says. As long as he kept quiet, Isaac figured he could ride it out: do a couple of years, retain the Eme's respect, "end of story." Even when Keenan alerted Isaac that he was in danger, that Puppet had marked him for death, Isaac treated it as a ploy. Puppet had told him to expect some trickery—a false suggestion of betrayal— if he ever found himself in the government's sights. "Hey, the feds work like that," Isaac recalls him saying. "So if you hear that, don't believe them." That the FBI was now warning him of a hit only confirmed Puppet's prescience. "I thought, 'Yeah, OK,'" Isaac says. "Whatever."

Keenan was struck by the lawyer's arrogance, but not surprised. In an FBI interview room, he whipped out the Eme kite he'd extracted from Supermax with Holcomb's help—the dispatch from Puppet with the "I want Huero taken out" postscript—and waved it in Isaac's face.

"Do you recognize the handwriting?" Keenan asked. Isaac did. Puppet wielded his pen like a rapier, scoring and slicing the letters. "I want you to read this," said Keenan, handing him the final page. Isaac stared at the words.

"He was shocked," Keenan says. "You could tell on his face. Shocked. I took the letter back from him, and he was just shaking his head."

Isaac asked to see the letter again. "I read it actually a couple of times," Isaac says. "I asked to see it again and again."

After everything Isaac had done for Puppet, risking his license, his career, his liberty to manage the Columbia Lil Cycos' tax revenues, it was hard to accept that he'd become expendable. "It told me, this dude don't even care about you, even though you're trying to do something for him," Isaac says. If Puppet wanted him dead, "there's no going back," he figured. "For him to do that . . . sh—, nah," Isaac says. "That's it. Game over."

On the spot, Isaac Guillen flipped. The FBI placed him in protective custody and gave Norma $9,000 to help her and the kids safely relocate. The implosion of Isaac's redemption story was especially infuriating for his mentor, the former public defender Ellen Barry. She'd not only vouched for his integrity when California's legal gatekeepers held up his bar membership, risking her own reputation to ensure that Isaac had an opportunity to transcend his past. She was now rewarded with the news that he had pivoted to a third identity: neither gangster nor attorney but fink. Cooperating witnesses were the shapeshifters of the criminal justice system—sometimes courageous, sometimes conniving—and the bane of defense attorneys. The government viewed informants as a necessary evil, especially in RICO cases, the only way to pull back the curtain on enterprises with strict codes of silence. If you wanted to present a jury with a firsthand account of a gang's internal workings, as the old saw went, it probably wasn't going to come from a saint or an angel. So prosecutors dangled leniency or other benefits to unsavory conspirators, hoping to extract testimony that could be wielded against the rest of the organization.

"Isn't it ironic that the day they busted him, they welcomed him into their fond embrace, all sins forgiven in return for information?" Barry says. "When they were working up the case, he was something they wouldn't scrape off the soles of their shoes. When he assessed his situation and found it dire, he rolled right over and began acting again, only changing the character he was playing."

The version of Isaac that found himself behind bars, the beginning of what would be a seven-year sentence, didn't sit well with Norma either. When he suggested that they assume new identities and live out their lives under government protection, she refused to give up her name or freedom. "I'm not doing that to the kids or to myself," Norma says she told him. "You fucked it up. You can deal with it." She settled in Idaho and filed for divorce, remaking her life as a family therapist and addiction counselor. The more she treated clients caught in the cycle of substance abuse, the more she saw "how they manipulate and how they brainwash and how they justify and how they charm you into believing things," Norma says, "and I realized, like, oh, my God, Isaac's just like that! He'll minimize—it's everybody else's fault."

With Isaac now on the government's side, Keenan at last had the key pieces of his RICO case in place. There was still more work to do before anything would be ready for trial, but Keenan, who'd invested four years in the investigation by then, used that summer of 2009 to carve out a moment for himself—and for the intelligence analyst who'd helped him reel in Isaac. "It did give us an opportunity to slow down, take a breath," he says. Three months after the raid on Calle Francesca, Paul and Candice Keenan exchanged vows at the water's edge in Westlake Village, the Westlake of his youth. The one far from MacArthur Park.

31

Tell the Truth

The hood had only itself to blame. That's what Giovanni kept telling himself as he waited for the first trial, the state's case, to begin in 2010. If the Columbia Lil Cycos seethed at the idea of him taking the stand for the prosecution, they'd had every chance to avoid it. Maybe by not trying to kill him. Maybe by trying harder to kill him. "Motherfuckers forced my hand," Giovanni says. Gangsters weren't supposed to flip, but they also weren't supposed to carry out half-assed strangulations against their own. Now Giovanni would guarantee that his assailants were "lying awake at night, like I do, wondering how they could be so fucking stupid."

By agreeing to cooperate, Giovanni ensured that he'd be entering the courtroom as a victim as much as a victimizer, a casualty of the mayhem he'd helped unleash. When a jury was finally impaneled to hear case BA329116, at the Clara Shortridge Foltz courthouse, Giovanni wouldn't be on trial. When Francisco and Jessica testified, Giovanni wouldn't be at the defense table, forced to endure their gaze or relive their agony. When Giovanni testified, they also wouldn't be in the courtroom, searching his eyes for hints of humanity or remorse. And Daniela wouldn't be around for any of it. Criminal trials tended to be plodding, technical exercises, a series of obligatory boxes for the government to check, not morality plays with satisfying denouements. As a cooperating witness, Giovanni would never have to—or get to—face his victims again. It deprived them all of something vital, maybe necessary, as they tried to piece their lives back together.

Someone else wouldn't be around for the trial: Clever. In the two years since the preliminary hearing, the district attorney's office had interviewed several other 18th Streeters, including some ensnared in the FBI's case, and had come to the conclusion that the evidence to try Clever for murder was insufficient. The lead prosecutor, Victor Avila, acknowledged it was unusual to argue at a prelim that the evidence justified a murder charge—and receive a favorable ruling—only to turn around and drop the charge. "But, you know, we're constantly evaluating the case," he says, "and if there's something that shows us that, hey, maybe he wasn't there, or maybe you have mixed evidence of people saying he was there, but you also have other people, including code-fendants, telling you he may not have been there, you got to make a decision." Avila thought the evidence was stronger that Clever may have been involved in the larger conspiracy to commit extortion, a charge that the detectives maintained he should have faced if nothing else. Even then, "I didn't feel comfortable with that," Avila says. "We just didn't think a jury would be convinced beyond a reasonable doubt."

The state filed its motion to release Clever in January 2009, which meant he spent sixteen months in jail for crimes prosecutors ultimately didn't think they could prove. He couldn't make a case for compensation; there was no evidence that testimony had been coerced or manufactured. But he would have appreciated a word somewhere, by somebody, about his exoneration. After Luis "Clever" Silva was arrested and charged with the murder of a new-born infant on Sixth Street in 2007—after it was reported he could face the death penalty—the news lost interest in him. "I still have that in the back of my head," says Clever, whose scar remains etched in his cheek. "I still live through this, you know, this fuckin' trauma."

By the time Giovanni was called to testify, the trial had been reduced to just three defendants, each of whom was looking at life without the possibility of parole: Face, Big Guy, and the newly apprehended Barrios, who'd been taken in by border agents while attempting to return from Mexico. Lil Primo and Silly had both agreed to enter pleas for their respective roles: handling the murder weapon (eleven years) and driving the getaway car (thirteen years). Atlas continued to remain a mystery—no sightings, no clues.

To work up the courage he'd need, Giovanni tried to narrow his focus to Face, to channel the bitter residue of his betrayal. Giovanni no longer had visible scars; his neck had scabbed over and the pigment had returned to pale wheat. The rejection had stayed with him, though, the sudden violence that supplanted the hoped-for love. Giovanni had already sacrificed his soul once for Face. *You think I'm going to throw my life away for you again?* It was easier to relive that hurt than to think that his testimony would help condemn Face's codefendants. They'd done nothing to him. He wished them no harm.

But he didn't get to pick and choose. If he wanted to begin his penance, to someday prove himself worthy of a second chance, Giovanni had to answer whatever question was asked of him. His attorney, Richard Lasting, didn't waste a lot of breath on coaching. "I offered advice: tell the truth," he says. "Listen to the question and answer it, and once you've answered it, stop talking."

In anticipation of the trial, the LAPD had moved Giovanni out of town again, to the relative safety of the Santa Ana Jail, a state-of-the-art detention center built across the Orange County line during the lock-'em-up '90s. The $82 million investment in municipal incarceration almost immediately proved shortsighted—as crime rates plummeted in the early 2000s, the jail became an albatross. Santa Ana tried to make up the shortfall by marketing the beds to pay-to-stay convicts, typically short-timers willing to pony up $82 a day to avoid the grim, overcrowded conditions of a county jail. It also rented out modules to ICE, to house undocumented detainees, an arrangement that would prove politically toxic in the majority Latino city.

For Giovanni the dorm-style rooms—appointed with green bunk beds, blue tables, and carpeted floors—made for a welcome upgrade but also an awkward reunion. Because his pod would come to house other Columbia Lil

Cycos who had flipped and were waiting to testify for the prosecution, there would be no reason to segregate Giovanni. He would now have a cellie. It turned out to be Lil Primo, the homie Giovanni had falsely implicated as the shooter during his interrogation, and there were only so many apologies you could make for a blow that low. "I told him I wasn't thinking clearly," Giovanni says. "I just panicked and said the first name to pop in my head."

Lil Primo was two years older than Giovanni but less entangled in gang life, a late arrival to both the US and the Columbia Lil Cycos. Everything about him was humbler, more temperate, including his reaction to Giovanni's mea culpa. "The past is the past," says Lil Primo, who received an additional seventeen years of federal time in the RICO case. "I learned to live without grudges." If anything, Lil Primo empathized with Giovanni's distress and isolation, sharing with him whatever food or toiletries his family supplied. Giovanni had little to no money on his books. His visits from Mayra, as he'd suspected, had reached an end. His mom, who'd returned to Palmdale and her job at the mall, struggled to make the hundred-mile drive down to Santa Ana, leaving the future of their relationship in doubt.

"What I noticed about Giovanni is he was still a kid," says Baby, who had also landed in the Santa Ana Jail, swept up in the federal racketeering indictment. Despite the advantages of being lodged there, Baby worried that Giovanni was slow to grasp the fragile etiquette of jailhouse coexistence. As an elder statesman of sorts, he cautioned Giovanni about being loud, complaining too much, walking in front of the TV while others were watching—"little things that were not cool," says Baby, especially for a youngster with a notorious crime to live down. "I used to tell him all the time, 'Hey, sharpen up, man. You're gonna go to a place where they're not going to tolerate this kind of stuff.'"

Giovanni's turn to testify came on the fifth day of trial, a Thursday afternoon in May, almost three years after the shooting. Holmes picked him up in Santa Ana—no sheriff's bus for a vulnerable witness—escorting Giovanni the thirty-plus miles up the 5 to the courthouse in downtown LA. Giovanni wore brown jailhouse scrubs. He'd begun letting his hair grow into a tight fade, covering the helmet of scalp tattoos he'd acquired as a teenager. He'd be twenty-one in a month.

"Do you solemnly state that the testimony you may give in the cause now pending before this court shall be the truth, the whole truth, and nothing but the truth, so help you God?" the clerk asked him.

"Yes, ma'am," Giovanni said.

Victor Avila guided him through the basic plot points, from Giovanni's entry into 18th Street to his short-lived tutelage under Face to the catastrophic events on Sixth Street to his near-death experience in La Rumorosa. As a performance, it was terse yet respectful; Giovanni neither rambled nor bristled. Because Avila already knew the answers to his own questions, Giovanni mostly had to confirm the narrative being unpacked for him. "Yes, sir," he said, again and again. "Yes, sir."

The defense took an antagonistic tack, probing for Giovanni's weak spots. The lawyers needled him about being a snitch. ("That's not new for you, is it?") They accused him of going rogue out on Sixth Street, bent on redeeming his own reputation regardless of the harm it caused the gang or the community. ("Now, this shooting of this vendor, that was a good thing for you, right?") They noted that Giovanni had been willing to sacrifice Lil Primo during his interrogation in Utah, implying he would lie about anything if it meant evading the consequences. ("You were saying whatever you could to go home that night.") And they reminded him that his mother had tried to save him by moving to Palmdale, distancing him from the tumult of MacArthur Park, only to have Giovanni shun her efforts.

"Because you wanted the gang more—you wanted the love of the gang more than the love of your mother," one of the lawyers insisted. "Isn't that correct?"

Giovanni bowed his head. "Yes," he said.

When it was done, he'd spent parts of two days and some five hours on the stand. It was painful and embarrassing, but Giovanni had weathered the cross-examination without losing his temper or credibility. "I thought he did what he was supposed to do," Lasting says. "He swore to tell the truth, and it appeared to me, from what I knew about the case, that he was truthful."

As measured and authentic as Giovanni proved to be, Face was all dark theater. Accused murderers don't have to testify, of course; it's the state's burden to prove the case, not the defendant's to disprove it. Given the risk of blurting out more than they should, most never put (or are allowed to put) themselves in that position, but Face had a reckless ego to satisfy and his own security to consider. The Mexican Mafia wasn't going to offer a warm welcome to the 18th Streeter who'd bungled Giovanni's death. So Face—his name was Juan Pablo Murillo—invented a wild tale, using his access to the witness stand to put an alternative history on the record.

Face claimed that he'd known nothing about the Sixth Street plot, supposedly learning only after the fact that Giovanni had tried to take out a vendor and made a mess of it. In his telling, the trip to Mexico just days later was purely coincidental; he planned to visit family, and Giovanni, knowing that Face liked to party down there, "wanted to tag along." All was well until the night they traversed La Rumorosa. With wind and rain pelting the SUV, Face thought it too dangerous to continue driving and pulled to the side of the road. Hoping to rest, he instead grew agitated by Giovanni's chatter—bragging about different shootings, Face said, "how he is putting it down in the hood."

As he understood it, Giovanni had been branded a snitch, "a piece of shit." Face supposedly couldn't tolerate the false bluster. "I said, 'What the fuck you say, motherfucker?'" Face recounted. "I just went off on him." Face took pains to portray himself as volatile and pugnacious, a bruiser who'd once won silver in a Baja California boxing tournament.

"Can I show you?" he asked the judge.

There on the witness stand, Face started throwing punches into the air, pretending to pummel Giovanni in an imaginary car. "I continued beating him down," Face said, fists flying. "Anything that came across my hand, I'm hitting him with." Midget's truck had all kinds of equipment in the back, and somehow "a rope pops up," according to Face. "I just happen to grab it." He continued to whale on Giovanni while holding him in place with the rope, slugging and cinching at the same time. "I mean, this dude, I'm just beating him down," Face said.

With the rope around Giovanni's neck, Face dragged him from the SUV. He asked the judge again if he could demonstrate. This time Face exited the witness stand and pantomimed pulling Giovanni to the ground. "I started stomping him out," Face said. "Kicking him, punching him, everything that was in my power until I finally broke my hand." He held up his right hand for the jury to see, as if he were a wounded warrior and not a killer on trial. Face claimed that Giovanni then suffered a seizure. "It looked like a knockout," he said.

He described both Ranger and Midget as alarmed by his brutish temper. "I'm not a politician," he insisted, denying any involvement with the Eme's business affairs. They tried unsuccessfully to calm him. Face kicked Giovanni one last time and spit on his limp body. Face's final words to him: "Dude, you're walking home."

Nobody in the courtroom could believe what they'd witnessed. It was gross, fantastical, and incriminating. "If you could see the jury's faces, they were floored," Holmes says. The judge, Larry Paul Fidler, was a strict, unflinching jurist who'd presided over all manner of infamous cases, including the undoing of the LAPD's tainted Rampart convictions. "He's like one of the most stoic judges up there," Holmes says, "and even he looked like his jaw was on the ground."

A few months later, after the jury found Face guilty of first-degree murder, the same disbelief spilled into his sentencing. Judge Fidler singled out

Face as "the instigator, the controller, and the primary reason that this—these crimes took place." He described the Columbia Lil Cycos as "parasites on this community," a gang that had "helped ruin and make life in this county lesser than it ever was," and he reflected on Face's disregard for anyone unlucky enough to get in the way. Thanks to Face, "an innocent baby has no life, will never have a life, and will never have a chance to succeed at anything because you had to be the tough guy."

Face no longer had anything to lose. He interrupted: "I'm an innocent man."

The judge shot back: "You are not only not innocent, sir—"

"I am innocent. I am innocent."

"You deserve to spend the rest of your life in a cage, which is exactly what is going to happen to you."

"That is your opinion."

"It is my opinion," Judge Fidler said, "and it is borne out by the facts. You are a sad, sad excuse for what we call human beings. Your behavior is abhorrent, and you will be punished for your behavior with the maximum that the law can give you. I usually say that sentencing is not a very enjoyable thing for any judge to do. We do it because it is what we do when someone is convicted of a crime. We have an obligation to do it. In your case, this is enjoyable, knowing that you are off the street and knowing that you will not hurt anyone again for the rest of your life, however long that is."

The eruption was still on Judge Fidler's mind two weeks later, when it was Giovanni's turn to be sentenced. Having used "some real—people might say—strong language" in addressing Face, the judge didn't intend to comment on Giovanni. Plus, given what he had read about him in presentencing reports, he concluded that Giovanni merited his restraint. No need to pile on.

From Avila's perspective, this was a case "where I could see many people wanting the death penalty," a punishment his office had declined to seek. If there was going to be a plea bargain, life without parole had to be the starting point. Although Holmes didn't have a formal say, he let it be known that he favored thirty to thirty-five years, an appropriate balance between the crime and Giovanni's efforts to make up for it. "I looked at what he did for us," Holmes says. "It was substantial, extremely substantial." Lasting pushed for twenty years, a sentence that would account for Giovanni's age, the pressure he'd faced, and his courage as a witness. But because the prosecution knew it had all the leverage, Lasting says, "my efforts were continually banging my head against a stone wall."

In the end, the best deal he could negotiate for Giovanni was not much of one: fifty-one years and four months. "I thought," Lasting says, "it was fucked."

Giovanni didn't know how to wrap his head around five decades. He'd been alive for only two. He knew that he'd been spared—he was guaranteed of getting out one day—but he felt lost at sea, too far from the shore to know which way to paddle. His mom wasn't even fifty-one.

When he first turned himself in, Giovanni thought he'd be content with anything less than life. Mayra would wait for him. Their love, tested by separation, would grow stronger—proof that they were meant for each other. *Yeah, right.* It didn't take Giovanni long to snap out of it. The last time he'd called her, a year earlier, maybe two, she'd just cried into the phone, unable to talk. He'd understood what she was up against—he was an 18th Street pariah—but his sentencing was a coda of sorts, society's verdict on his debt, and the thought of seeing her once more put a lump in his throat.

Giovanni asked Holmes if he could make a call. To his surprise, Mayra answered. Giovanni told her he'd be in Department 106 of the criminal courts building on August 31, if she wanted to say goodbye. Mayra didn't know how to respond.

That morning, Judge Fidler cataloged Giovanni's offenses: the voluntary manslaughter of Luis Angel Garcia, the attempted murders of Francisco Clemente, Jessica Guzman, and Daniela Garcia, and all the gang and gun enhancements that could be applied. Giovanni owed $7,500 to the state victim compensation fund, plus $2,760 to Daniela for her burial expenses. He was to pay $120 in conviction assessments and a court security fee of $20.

It was a lot to take in, too much to digest. Giovanni swiveled in his seat and looked back toward the gallery. He hesitated to get his hopes up, but, damn—there she was. Mayra had come. Against her better judgment, she was seeing him off. Giovanni mouthed "I love you" before the detectives led him away.

It Took Getting Shot

I n 2011, Francisco and Jessica had a second child, a boy. The detectives visited again, bearing gifts. "We're like, wow, they keep having kids," Evens says. "I mean, that's good. It's like they weren't afraid. They kind of settled into, you know, a life."

Francisco's wounds had healed enough that he could return to Transformer Auto Repair. He wasn't a hundred percent—he suspected he never would be—but he was skilled and stubborn. "I'm a worker," Francisco says. The California Auto Body Association recorded his rates: $65 an hour for refinishing, $95 for frame work, $135 for mechanical repairs. To anyone who might doubt his industriousness, Francisco would offer his hands, tempered by decades of manual labor: "Look at my fingers."

After the shooting, Holmes had asked Francisco about his work history, and Francisco had surprised him by saying he owned a business. "Do you have records?" the detective asked. A jury might appreciate that the victim of a horrific gang shooting was also a by-the-book proprietor, not a fly-by-night reseller of knockoff accessories. Francisco had receipts. The city had issued a tax registration certificate to Transformer Auto Repair, and he'd been charged a rate of $5.07 per $1,000 in gross revenue. Holmes seemed perplexed: "How'd you do that if you don't have papers?"

"Well," Francisco told him, relishing the question, "here, if there's a will, there's a way. We're in a place of possibility. It's just that people don't want to, or are afraid, or don't have the intelligence to say, 'I can, I can, we all can.'"

It was a hard dichotomy to explain: to be legally unrecognized yet economically productive, at once politically stigmatized and culturally ubiquitous. So many immigrants made do without papers, it was quite possible to invent an

American life while sidestepping the immigration system altogether. Especially in LA, where so many family narratives and traditions spanned the border—where so much art and food and slang and music and fashion flowed from Francisco's homeland—one could be, in a statutory sense, an alien and still be at home. "It's not about having papers," he says. "It's your mentality."

California had tried once to make life inhospitable for the undocumented. In 1994, not long before Francisco came to LA, Governor Pete Wilson bombarded voters with grainy black-and-white videos of migrants sprinting across the border as a grave voice intoned: "They keep coming." The scare tactics helped win approval for Proposition 187, promoted as the "Save Our State" referendum, which denied a host of public services, including education and healthcare, to those without proof of legal residence. It also deputized teachers and doctors, requiring them to report anyone suspected of being undocumented—an exercise in racial profiling that would have turned California into an immigration police state. Struck down on constitutional grounds, Proposition 187 backfired spectacularly. It galvanized a new generation of Latino leaders and reconfigured the state's political landscape. A top Democrat in Los Angeles famously celebrated the measure's demise as "the last gasp of white America in California."

If the more than two million people living without papers in California had earned a modicum of recognition, assured of access to the most basic functions of the public sector, they still felt the constrictions of the immigration laws. The summer that Francisco stood his ground against the Columbia Lil Cycos, Congress came as close as it had in decades to hammering out a deal that could have offered him legal residency. Pairing enhanced border security with a path to citizenship for undocumented immigrants already here, the 2007 "Grand Bargain" appeared to have broad bipartisan support. President George W. Bush pushed hard for it, explaining that the government couldn't and wouldn't deport millions of folks who'd put down US roots. "I know there are some people out there hollering and saying, 'Kick them out,'" he told an audience of federal law enforcement trainees. "That is simply unrealistic. It won't work." But as with other congressional attempts at reform, members of his own party denounced the legalization of undocumented immigrants as amnesty—a reward for disrespecting US borders. Six weeks before Francisco was shot, the bill died.

Without papers, Francisco couldn't obtain a driver's license (California was still a few years away from making those available to undocumented applicants), he didn't have health insurance (the state would need even longer to expand Medi-Cal to all), he wouldn't be accruing Social Security benefits, and he hadn't found a way to obtain a line of credit that would allow him to grow his business. Then there were his daughter and son—and the two more soon to follow—full-fledged US-born citizens whose lives in this country would be upended if ICE ever had occasion to scrutinize their parents. As much as Francisco rejected obstacles, he couldn't deny: "Without papers, it's like you live only half here, and the other half, you have a foot over there."

His immigration status hadn't deterred him from testifying in the state trial, but the prospect of doing it again at a federal proceeding was beginning to weigh on Francisco. The US attorney's office wanted him on the stand for the RICO case: the face of bravery, the voice of agony. He was continuing to insist that nothing could scare him, that the bullets still buried in his flesh and bone were proof that God wasn't done with him yet, but federal court was the domain of the US government, the lair of the immigration enforcers. To enter that arena: "Oh, Dios mío," he says. It would be something "much heavier—la máxima."

By then, Holmes had spent several years as Francisco and Jessica's advocate and protector. He'd come to admire them in ways that went beyond the needs of the case. He recognized a grit, especially in Francisco, a no-matter-what provider instinct that registered with his own ready-or-not plunge into fatherhood. "Francisco was trying to take care of what he had to take care of, you know, as a man," Holmes says. Even though street vending remained a violation of the city's municipal code, "it went a long way with me that they weren't doing anything illegal," he says. "I felt that they were doing the right thing."

Holmes wasn't in the habit of rationalizing misdemeanors. He wasn't inclined to take sides, either, on an issue that touched a nerve the way immigration did. But he had to admit: Francisco and Jessica, their refusal to be counted out, had altered his perspective in unexpected ways. "I just felt that they needed to be given a chance and, you know, their voice needs to be heard," he says. "It was the first time I really got a sense of what was going on out there from a vendor point of view as opposed to the police side, you know, that it was a nuisance and so on and so forth."

He knew there was only so much a cop could do, or should do, but he'd come to the conclusion that Francisco and Jessica were "the kind of people that if anybody's going to come over to this country, those are the kind of people, you know, that should be given a chance." Holmes saw that they were anxious about the federal phase of the case, and even though he reassured them that nobody was going to use their presence in the courthouse against them, he believed they deserved better than to be burdened by that doubt. He'd never done it before, and he wouldn't do it for anyone else, but he wanted to help fix Francisco's and Jessica's papers.

Had the Columbia Lil Cycos not targeted them, Francisco and Jessica wouldn't have qualified. The immigration system didn't award papers to undocumented people for being hardworking members of society. It didn't care if they had businesses or paid taxes. It didn't make exceptions for parents of American-born children, at least not until their kids turned twenty-one. Other than possibly marrying a US citizen or permanent resident, there was no "right way" for Francisco and Jessica to become eligible for a green card. But as crime victims, they could apply for a U visa, a humanitarian benefit created to encourage assistance to police. Holmes would sponsor them. "Unfortunately," he says, "it took Francisco getting shot."

Created in 2000, the U visa program made up to ten thousand visas available annually to undocumented victims who suffer harm and help the authorities. Immigration restrictionists detested the idea, describing it as a bribe that rewarded noncitizens for doing what they should do anyway. The newly formed US Citizenship and Immigration Services, a product of 9/11, didn't appear eager to implement it either, taking eight years to develop guidelines before issuing the first visas in 2009. But police and prosecutors, especially in immigrant-rich communities, understood how the U visa aided public safety. Applications almost immediately began exceeding the annual quota, creating a backlog that subjected would-be recipients to years-long waits.

The application, an I-918 petition, ran eight pages and read like a House Un-American Activities Committee interrogation: Are you a Communist? Do you plan to engage in espionage? Have you ever served in a paramilitary unit, rebel group, or insurgent organization? Then came the I-918 supplement, the police portion. It asked Holmes to "briefly describe" the criminal activity he'd investigated, as if he hadn't spent years by then assembling a case spanning state lines and international borders against a dozen suspects, and to detail the injuries inflicted on the applicants. There were police reports and hospital records to attach, birth certificates and personal statements to translate. The I-192 inadmissibility waiver required a confession that Francisco and Jessica had each entered the US illegally, while the I-193 fee waiver required a catalog of monthly expenses, evidence of income, and an inventory of assets.

"The paperwork is insane," Holmes says. "It was a nightmare. I mean, you lose patience."

It continued to amaze Francisco that a representative of the same LAPD that had once shooed him from the streets of downtown's apparel district and into the clutches of MacArthur Park's rent collectors would invest so much care in him. Nothing about Francisco's experience in the US had prepared him for this gift. He'd never asked for help; nobody had ever offered it so freely. "How is it possible that the police would treat me like this?" Francisco says. "How is it possible that the police would worry about me?"

U visas offer only temporary relief, not permanent residency. With the federal case not headed for trial until 2012—five years after the shooting— Holmes turned his attention to the next phase of the immigration process: converting visas into green cards. That meant another confounding round of paperwork, plus photos, fingerprints, background checks, medical exams, and vaccination records. He took Francisco and Jessica downtown for more submissions. To renew his affidavit of support, Holmes had to swear to its veracity before an immigration judge.

Francisco didn't know how to thank Holmes. So he prayed. "The truth is, I love him as a friend," Francisco says. "I ask God to look out for him. He has such a dangerous job. And one never knows—it can be your turn at any time."

The arrival of their green cards spelled a new chapter for Francisco and Jessica. He wasted no time applying for a license: "I did everything—the driving test, the written test—and had my license in three days." It allowed him to clear a ticket that had lingered for years. "My life changed a lot," Francisco says. "I started to resolve everything." Papers gave Jessica the ability to return to Mexico to care for her ailing mother. Later, she found work doing kitchen prep at a Cheesecake Factory in Beverly Hills.

The way Francisco saw it, there was an even greater benefit to what Holmes had done for them, a gift beyond the green card he carried in his wallet. "David taught me a lesson," Francisco says. It was one that defied easy explanation, a lesson tangled up in the superficial racial categories and economic classifications that box people in, that reduce individuals to types. Looking back at the day that upended his life, Francisco wouldn't have been surprised if nobody had listened to him or believed him, if the case had collected dust or slipped through the cracks, if his assailants had evaded capture or wriggled out of the consequences, if someone, somewhere along the way, had dropped the ball out of inattention or overwork or disdain—because, well, who was Francisco Clemente to expect that a government agency or a legal system would ever value what he'd lost?

33

The Rogues

O ne by one, they pleaded out. A dozen. Then two dozen. Those with more to spill—like Tricky, who finally owned up to both botched murders—bartered for better deals. But few 18th Streeters saw the point of fighting their cases, not against the feds.

Trials in federal criminal cases had been declining for decades, from a rate of more than 20 percent in the 1980s to barely 3 percent in the 2010s. In 2012, the year that Paul Keenan's case against the Columbia Lil Cycos went to trial, more than 80,000 criminal defendants were charged in US district courts. Fewer than 2,500 tested the sufficiency of the government's case at trial. And, of those, only 355 emerged with not-guilty verdicts.

A conviction rate that bordered on 100 percent was a point of pride for the feds, proof that the government wielded its superior tools and boundless resources to noble ends. If practically every criminal defendant folded, that could mean only one thing: the right people were being brought to justice. Where prosecutors saw virtue, defense lawyers spotted a stacked deck. Between draconian drug laws, mandatory minimums, and the possibility of leniency only if the defendant provides substantial assistance, the government had an arsenal of weapons for coercing guilty pleas and turning offenders into cooperators. The result is that a defendant who fights his case faces a substantially longer sentence—a roll of the dice known as the "trial penalty."

The US district court judge in the RICO case, Dean D. Pregerson, admitted at one hearing that the prospect of disparate punishments between defendants who cooperate and those who go to trial "is something that concerns me." He thought "it does seem unfair" that some senior 18th Streeters would end up with lighter sentences, and would avoid having their worst deeds aired in court, based only on their willingness to finger their coconspirators. It was "part of the problem of going to trial, and it shouldn't be," Judge Pregerson said, "but it's a reality."

In the end, the federal trial featured more cooperators than defendants. Over the course of two months in 2012, a parade of shotcallers and lieutenants, representing different eras of the Columbia Lil Cycos, agreed to take the stand—to offer a window into the gang's uncanny ability to adapt, regroup, and persevere. Members might come and go, factions could rise and fall, treachery and turnover forever reshuffling the ranks, and yet the structure always seemed to hold. Even though only four 18th Streeters sat at the defense table, the government kept reminding the jury that the case was bigger than any one individual or any single crime. It was about an organization whose operations continued "day to day, week to week, month to month, year to year—a systematic manner of operation such that should anything happen, there's always somebody else to step up, to step in," the lead prosecutor, assistant US attorney Kevin Lally, told the jury. So enduring were the Columbia Lil Cycos, he added, they "might as well be the AT&T of criminal enterprises."

Of the four defendants on trial, only one meant something to Giovanni. The FBI had finally captured the second strangler, Javier "Ranger" Perez. He'd spent three years hiding in Tijuana. When Ranger's nephew got arrested on an unrelated charge in 2008, Ranger's girlfriend brokered three-way calls for them—the nephew dialing out from LA County lockup, then the girlfriend looping in Ranger from Mexico. The jail's pay phone system was supposed to terminate calls if it detected a third line, but if you blew into the receiver or kept talking during the transition, you could override the security feature. During one call, Ranger asked his nephew about the status of the green light. The nephew told him that it had been canceled but could be reinstated—word was out by then that Giovanni had survived. "That's why I don't want them to catch you, dude," the nephew said, "because you are going to have it."

Alert to the jail's practice of recording calls, Ranger tried to redirect the conversation. "Never mind, never mind, never mind, fool," he said. "Forget about it. Never mind. Hey, just forget about it."

Two more years went by. Ranger stayed on the run until someone called the FBI to ask if he was still wanted. Tib Aguilar received the tip. The caller revealed that Ranger was in a Tijuana jail, busted possibly for driving a stolen car. Aguilar obtained a copy of Ranger's birth certificate—he was a US citizen—and shared it with the Mexican immigration authorities. They arranged for a hand-off at the border. "A reverse deportation," Aguilar says. "He wasn't in the country legally."

Aguilar took Ranger into custody at the San Ysidro port of entry. He told Ranger that he was charged with racketeering and kidnapping. Ranger gave a fake name. He insisted he was from Mexico and had never set foot in the United States. Aguilar showed him a booking photo from one of his Los Angeles arrests. Ranger admitted "there was a resemblance," but swore it wasn't him. Then Aguilar showed him a booking photo of Giovanni, a face Ranger hadn't seen since he'd heaved him off the cliff in La Rumorosa. "He became a little emotional—watery eyed," Aguilar says. "I'm not a psychologist, but just the way he looked at it, you knew something hit him."

Ranger was an odd addition to the RICO case. He hadn't been part of the FBI's original investigation. There was no evidence he'd involved himself in the MacArthur Park drug and tax business. He'd certainly played no role in the plot to shoot Francisco Clemente. But the racketeering laws transcended those distinctions. What mattered was that Ranger was homies with Face, who had elbowed his way into MacArthur Park from South-Central, and that Face had then enlisted Ranger to help resolve a dire threat to the Columbia Lil Cycos' ability to do business. It made no difference if Ranger hadn't formally joined the enterprise—prosecutors needed to show only that by participating in Giovanni's disposal, he'd agreed to advance the Columbia Lil Cycos' interests.

On an April day in 2012, more than four years after he rose from La Rumorosa, Giovanni made the trip again from the Santa Ana Jail, this time to the old Spring Street federal courthouse, a seventeen-story Art Moderne slab. The building was poised to become a National Historic Landmark for its most famous trial, a Mexican American desegregation lawsuit from the 1940s that showcased the work of a young civil rights lawyer named Thurgood Marshall. Judge Pregerson's second-floor courtroom had towering plaster ceilings and walls blanketed in walnut wainscotting. Despite already testifying once and receiving his sentence, Giovanni struggled to get comfortable, swallowing his words and rushing his answers. More than once, the judge had to caution him to slow down and enunciate.

"Do you have any concern for your safety going forward?" the prosecutor asked him.

"Yes."

"Why are you concerned about your safety?"

"Because I'm telling."

"Because you're telling?"

"I'm a rat."

"You're a rat? Why is it that you would be concerned about your safety if you're telling and you're a rat?"

"You don't supposed to do that when you're a gang member, period."

"And you've broken that rule?"

"Yes."

Giovanni spent at least an hour on the stand—recounting his entry into the Columbia Lil Cycos and his role in the Sixth Street shooting—before even uttering Ranger's name, a reminder of how late an arrival Ranger was to the conspiracy. When Giovanni finally described their first meeting, the prosecutor asked him to identify Ranger in the courtroom. Ranger, dressed in a white shirt and white and gray tie, looked away.

"Is there any doubt in your mind that one of the individuals who threw that rope around your neck is sitting in this courtroom?" the prosecutor asked again.

"No," Giovanni said.

"And who is that person?"

Giovanni looked at Ranger. "White shirt with a white and gray tie," Giovanni said.

Ranger's lawyer tried his best to trip up Giovanni, to catch him second-guessing his own memory. Giovanni, after all, had spent less than thirty-six hours in Ranger's presence.

"You mentioned that you met a man named Ranger. And you believe that to be my client Mr. Perez?"

"I don't—I know it's him," Giovanni replied. "I don't believe. It's him."

"Pardon me?"

"I don't believe. I know it's him."

"Oh, you don't believe it's him? You know it's him?"

"I know it's him," Giovanni repeated. "I don't believe."

"OK. So you're saying that you know that Mr. Perez is Ranger?"

"Yes."

The lawyer kept poking, fishing for inconsistencies.

"How is it that you remember from five years ago or thereabouts that this person is—is that person sitting right there?"

The question did Ranger no favors. "You don't forget the face of a person who tried to kill you," Giovanni said.

The lawyer focused the bulk of Ranger's defense on the theory that the conspiracy to kidnap and murder Giovanni did not originate in Los Angeles, within the reach of US laws, or that if it had, Ranger wasn't in on it. If it was so urgent to get rid of Giovanni, "why even wait twenty-four hours?" he asked the jury. And why take on the risks and hassles of a cross-border plot, he added, when "there's plenty of desert in the state of California?" Even after they arrived in Tijuana, there was no apparent coercion, no rush to finish him off. Until they left for La Rumorosa, Ranger's lawyer added in a court filing, Giovanni "literally enjoyed wine, women, and song."

Nobody bought it. The jury found Ranger guilty of multiple "violent crime in aid of racketeering" counts, and the judge sentenced him to life.

The case against the other three defendants relied almost entirely on informants. It might have been the only way to bring down Oso—Eddie Hernandez—the gangster whose raw energy had thrilled the director of *Domino*. Despite his status as a Columbia Lil Cyco ringleader, one of the elders whose blessing Baby had sought before instituting the vendor tax, Oso had managed to elude the feds for more than a decade. In the late 1990s, during the internecine war that culminated in Puppet's order to "fumigate" Termite, it was Oso's crew that carried out the hit. That earned Oso a death threat from the breakaway faction, credible enough that FBI agents working the first RICO case felt duty bound to warn him. They spoke to Oso's mother, his girlfriend, his lawyer—hoping that Oso might return the favor by cooperating. He didn't. He wasn't indicted either. During the ensuing power struggle to find a new shotcaller, Oso took his payday from the Rampart scandal and treated himself to a vacation in Cancun.

Keenan came face-to-face with Oso for the first time on an October morning in 2005, the day before *Domino*'s US release. Keenan was assisting a separate task force on the hunt for a trigger-happy 18th Street fugitive, a mission that took him to the 500 Building. Knocking on the door of a fourth-floor unit, the FBI was greeted by Oso, who tried to block their way. The agents found their man on the other side of a window, clinging to the ledge, which allowed them to also detain Oso. Keenan saw a chance to flip him. "You could tell he was a smart guy—very, very nice, cordial—a little more educated, less into the gangster lifestyle," Keenan says. "Like a guy you'd want to have beers with." Once again, Oso refused. Even after investigating the Columbia Lil Cycos for the next two years, Keenan still didn't have enough to include Oso in the 2007 narcotics indictment. It would take another two years—and the cooperation of a half dozen Columbia Lil Cyco street bosses, chief among them Tricky—to connect Oso to the RICO conspiracy.

After arresting him in 2009, Keenan sat Oso down at the FBI's office in Westwood, giving him yet another chance to cooperate. Oso wouldn't budge. Keenan reminded him of the jeopardy he faced.

"I wish I could tell you stuff," Oso replied, "but that's not me."

Keenan asked Oso if "this was real" for him—if he understood that talking might be his only hope.

"I don't want to be remembered like that," Oso said.

His lawyer, and the lawyers for the two other defendants—identical twins who'd served as Oso's muscle and worked as extras alongside him in the movie—tried to save their clients by attacking the character of the cooperating witnesses: liars, manipulators, con artists, and most of all Tricky, "a completely amoral sociopath."

"Those are the rogues," Oso's lawyer told the jury, "the characters that you've been treated to."

The jibes didn't alter the outcome: life, life, life. The government waited for the guilty to be sentenced, then made good on its promises.

34

Sensitive Needs

The old bus barreled through the San Gorgonio Pass and into the desert, past Palm Springs, across the Coachella Valley, and around the festering Salton Sea, the landlocked resort turned toxic stew. Giovanni stared out the tinted windows that September day in 2012. The mysterious body of water, the pallid moonscape: he felt like he'd dreamt it before. He tried to summon the image, to bring the memory into focus. Middle of the night, shredded and sapped, back of a minivan. *Oh, hell no.* He laughed at the symmetry—the cosmic prank of returning this way. It was the same highway his mom had taken on the trip home from Mexicali, the road of his rescue. Five years later and Giovanni hadn't made it very far.

As the bus continued down State Route 111 and into California's south-easternmost corner, where Riverside County yields to Imperial County, it rolled alongside the orange cones and blinking cameras of a Border Patrol checkpoint. It skirted the squatter's paradise of Slab City and the psychedelic folk monument to biblical love known as Salvation Mountain. Algae ponds, growing nutrient-rich spirulina, simmered under the metallic sky. A gridiron of solar panels cast a purplish glow across the scorched earth. Legs shackled, hands cuffed at his waist, Giovanni at last reached Calipatria, a mole of a town, where half of the 7,500 residents lived behind bars. At 184 feet below sea level, the prison was said to be the lowest in the western hemisphere.

The temperature that month topped out at 108. The air burned Giovanni's throat. It smelled like a feedlot.

Built for $204 million on a sandy octagon about forty miles north of the Mexican border, Calipatria State Prison opened in 1992 amid a historic tough-on-crime construction boom. By the time Giovanni arrived, it was one of fourteen prisons that California had built since the year of his birth—a period in which the state opened just four new public universities. Three fences enclosed the grounds: two twelve-footers topped with razor wire and, sandwiched between them, a thirteen-foot, four thousand–volt "death fence," the first to be installed at a California correctional facility. The fence initially electrocuted so many birds—a seagull, two burrowing owls, a finch, and a scissor-tailed flycatcher—the state had to hire an ornithologist to design a layer of protective netting.

Strange as he knew it sounded, Giovanni was almost looking forward to prison. From the moment of his surrender, he'd been a managed risk, bounced from jail to jail. He'd been interrogated and prepped and cross-examined by investigators and prosecutors and defense attorneys, asked to relive his ignominy who knew how many times. He wanted to believe that Calipatria represented the end of those formalities, the start of his true debt. He deserved prison. There was no point in pretending otherwise. "I felt like I was going home," Giovanni says. "Get comfortable. Get on with my life."

Given that Giovanni's cooperation spanned both the state and federal cases, his lawyer had argued that he should be allowed to serve his five-decade sentence in a federal prison. There would be fewer violent offenders—fewer 18th Streeters, for sure—in the US penitentiary system, where more than half the population was serving time for a drug, sex, or immigration crime. The judge at Giovanni's sentencing agreed, and made that note on the record, but nobody in the government saw fit to carry it out. The disregard for Giovanni's well-being infuriated Richard Lasting. It galled him even more when the US attorney's office started issuing sentencing recommendations for the other cooperators, offering lenient terms for a slew of older, savvier 18th Street players.

No sentence illustrated the gulf between expedience and justice more than Tricky's. If he'd been charged in the state case, which was all about accountability for the Sixth Street shooting, he'd more than likely be doing life without the possibility of parole. But the federal government had a different agenda—the disruption of the Columbia Lil Cycos organization—which made Tricky, as the shotcaller, particularly useful. His reward for testifying: twenty-four years. Giovanni's tormentor, the architect of his execution, received less than half the time Giovanni did. "A skewed view of punishment," Lasting says.

The best the state could offer Giovanni was a Sensitive Needs Yard, the prison system's equivalent of protective custody. It was an incongruously delicate term—as if the wish to avoid getting shanked in a general-population facility made a man "sensitive"—but that didn't stop inmates from clamoring for SNY placement. When the state first began carving out SNYs in the late 1990s, about a thousand inmates, mostly sex offenders, signed up for the opportunity to self-segregate. Within a dozen years, forty thousand inmates—nearly a third of the state's prison population—were doing time in an SNY, making it the largest such program in the nation. Its ranks included Mexican Mafia defectors, ex-cops, the old and frail, those who identified as queer and gender-nonconforming, and virtually every high-notoriety inmate, from Manson acolyte Tex Watson to one of the parent-slaying Menendez brothers.

As the SNYs swelled, they began to take on the threats and temptations of the active yards: drugs, gambling, even SNY gangs. After a spate of homicides in the SNYs, an inspector general found that staff had too liberally approved applicants, allowing inmates to vouch for their own security concerns without corroboration. Still, the SNYs offered a relatively steadier environment, insulated from a facility's heaviest rackets and rivalries. A gang dropout like Giovanni would be able to sidestep an immediate crisis even if he'd have to navigate the everyday affronts of prison life.

On his arrival at Calipatria, Giovanni submitted to an Institutional Staff Recommendation Summary, which described him as "cooperative" throughout his initial screening and noted that he'd so far had "no adjustment problems." The staff assigned him a placement score of seventy-one based on his offense, sentence length, the degree of violence, and his criminal history; anything over sixty meant Level Four housing, the most secure environment, with armed guards inside and outside the unit. Giovanni had to disclaim any ties to a security threat group—a term that encompassed both street and prison gangs—formalizing his severance on a Renunciation of Security Threat Group Affiliation, Association, and Illicit Behavior statement. Another form, Advisement of Expectations, explained that it is "your responsibility to abstain from activities that assist, promote, or endorse" any gang within or without the institution.

Giovanni scribbled his name. It didn't matter how many times. Whatever he had to do to clear his slate or at least blur his past. Calipat's SNY was the D yard, which had a 270-degree layout, giving guards in a central command booth a sweeping view of the three cellblocks within the facility. The door to Giovanni's six-by-nine cell was a sheet of perforated steel—a cheese door—which allowed someone on the outside to peer in without being pelted or sprayed by something thrown out. One of the first skills Giovanni learned was to hang a towel from the cheese holes, so he could sit on the crapper without the indignity of putting on a show.

Giovanni's cellie, a man with a couple of children Giovanni's age, had already made his home in the bottom bunk, a springless slab bolted into the concrete. He'd also blanketed the walls with pictures of women from the pages of *Lowrider* magazine. Giovanni accepted the top bunk. He didn't have any decorations to add and didn't want to upset the status quo. "When he first got here, I know he was traumatized—sleeping with one eye open," says the cellmate, George Ruiz, who'd spent fifteen of the previous sixteen years locked up for robbery and had at least that much more time to go. "After a while he started opening up and telling me why he was here, and I was like, 'What the heck? All this happened to you?' That was the first time I had had a cellie in that type of predicament, you know."

Ruiz took it on himself to mentor Giovanni, teaching him to avoid conflict and resist oversharing: "Don't be going out there talking about anything you shouldn't be talking about." He supplied him with snacks and hygiene products, to make sure Giovanni didn't become beholden to anyone. He also tried to instill discipline, directing Giovanni to polish their stainless-steel sink and toilet with sandpaper and rags; he liked seeing his reflection in the shine. "He turned out to be a good cellie," Ruiz says.

Not long after his arrival, Giovanni received a letter from Richard Lasting: Was there anything he needed? It didn't seem right to take a handout, especially since Giovanni had given the lawyer so little to work with, but his mom had more struggles than she could manage. Giovanni didn't know when the opportunity would come his way again, so he requested a small TV. It arrived in a clear plastic shell, its guts exposed to eliminate a hiding place for contraband, and with the speakers removed, to prevent a nightly cacophony. Giovanni plugged in a pair of headphones. To his surprise, the antenna picked up some soft-core shows beamed after-hours from Mexicali.

An inmate whose mop of uncombable hair reminded Giovanni of Einstein lent him *The Alchemist*, a fixture of prison libraries. Giovanni had never been much of a reader—his first assessment as a state inmate placed him at the sixth-grade level—but he enjoyed the tale of a wandering shepherd boy. He understood that the book had something to do with overcoming fear and pursuing a dream: the secret of life, its author, Paulo Coelho, counseled, was falling seven times and getting up eight. "I knew it was about everyone having a purpose," Giovanni says. He liked the sound of that, the idea of a journey, but as best Giovanni could tell, he'd reached the end of his. "I was like, 'How does this apply to me?'"

The inmate with the mad-scientist hair had more to offer. He'd cooked up a batch of ink by burning a grease-soaked cloth in a locker, then scraping the soot off the metal interior and mixing it with shampoo. Giovanni asked him to cover the *1* and *8* on his forearms. Wielding a tattoo gun jury-rigged from the motor of a CD player, Einstein poked Giovanni's skin with the tip of a guitar string. He drew feathers and an Aztec deity on one arm. On the other, he etched a collection of female faces—hands over eyes, hands cupped around mouth—as if they were denouncing the evil Giovanni had surrendered to. Or just tuning it out.

Days were dull, mostly aimless. Because he was so far behind in his schooling, Giovanni didn't qualify for a prison job. He attended Adult Basic Education
classes, but Giovanni kept failing his assessments, spinning his wheels. He
pushed himself only out on the rec yard. The prison system had banned
weights a dozen years earlier, reasoning that bulked-up inmates posed a menace to guards inside an institution and to society upon their release. But that
couldn't stop Giovanni from putting himself through a personal boot camp.
He ran across the dust until he was drenched. He played soccer and handball,
kicking and swatting, then repeated a pull-up and push-up routine until his
body gave out. In the blistering heat, wrapped in long sleeves, he told himself
he was bracing for combat. SNY was still prison: Giovanni had plenty of
neighbors who knew what it meant to take a life.

Three months into his Calipat stay, Giovanni faced his first challenge. An
18th Streeter from the south side of LA had figured out who Giovanni was,
heard that he'd snitched, and when they met out on the yard and Giovanni
offered his hand, the other dude refused to shake it.

"Do I know you?" Giovanni asked.

"I'm not in favor of what you did."

"It don't got nothin' to do with you," Giovanni said. "We all got our reasons."

"Well, keep Eighteen out of your mouth."

It was too late for Giovanni to follow his cellie's advice. Conflict had found
him. Worse, he'd been disrespected in public view. A failure to respond, even
if he'd renounced 18th Street and no longer cared what the gang thought of
him, could set him up for untold abuse. "If you degrade me as a man," Giovanni
says, "it's on."

The next morning, Christmas Eve 2012, Giovanni returned to the yard,
intent on striking first. His antagonist was a year younger but a head taller,
and despite coming at him hard and fast, Giovanni couldn't avoid his longer
reach. He felt the thud of a fist on his right eye, which bruised and swelled,
but he kept on swinging, making a statement. Guards sounded the alarm and
activated the PA, ordering everyone on the yard to prone out. Giovanni knew

that he'd be shunned if he stopped voluntarily, so he ignored the commands and damned the consequences, until a stream of MK-9 oleoresin capsicum dropped him to the ground. The pepper spray scalded his eyes. It choked his airways. He was handcuffed and dragged to an outdoor shower to decontaminate. A strip search added insult to injury.

Giovanni knew the drill, as did the 18th Streeter: to avoid a trip to the hole, you shrugged it off as a personal beef, not gang politics. They both signed a marriage chrono—slang for an agreement to put their quarrel to rest—"indicating they could remain on the yard without further incident."

The prison added ninety days to Giovanni's earliest possible release date. He hadn't been at Calipat much longer than that.

In reflective moments, usually at night, Giovanni tried to think through where he was headed, the work that needed to be done. If there was a journey for him to take, it would be "to become a better me, as a human, to learn from my mistakes to hopefully get a chance to give back to the community in a positive way," but he couldn't make out the path. He felt remorse but didn't know how to express it or to whom. He felt guilty for even feeling guilt. He believed that anything he might try to say about the life he hoped to construct would be badly received, an indulgence that would elevate his importance at the expense of his victims. "Like I was letting myself off the hook," Giovanni says. He didn't want to be seen as a hypocrite, "trying to do good after doing wrong."

Visiting days were Saturday and Sunday, a chance for inmates to see family and friends in a cafeteria-style room lined with fickle vending machines and scorched microwaves. A visitor could bring in up to $50 (singles and quarters only) in a clear plastic bag, enough to treat their loved one to a state-issue feast: frozen El Monterey burrito, Big Az burger, Flamin' Hot Cheetos, Starburst, Skittles, and a couple of Cactus Coolers. The first year, nobody came for Giovanni. Or the second. Or the third or the fourth.

He sent his mom a visiting questionnaire—you couldn't enter without being invited by the inmate and approved by the staff—but when Reyna mailed in her application, it was denied. No explanation. Giovanni sent her another one, urging her to read it carefully and provide all the information it asked for: name, birth date, relationship, address, ID number, history of arrests and convictions. Reyna tried again. Again she was rejected.

"I'm like, 'How hard can it be?'" Giovanni says. He wished that he could sit down next to her and fill out the form together instead of trying to explain things in fifteen-minute increments on a pay phone at $1.45 a call. Giovanni began to wonder if he would ever see her, if she had the capacity—if it really mattered to her—to figure it out. He needed her in ways he hadn't before, for both routine tasks and emotional sustenance, and her limitations magnified his solitude. He wanted to repair their relationship: to absolve himself for rejecting her, to absolve her for exposing him to so much rage and despair. "Her biggest sin was just trying to be happy," Giovanni says, "and not knowing how."

His soul longed for a hug. For human interaction that didn't require him to be on alert.

Every year, he had to submit another form—it was called Notification in Case of Inmate Death, Serious Injury, or Serious Illness—a reminder of the distance that stood between him and the outside world. Every year, Giovanni listed his mom as the responsible party.

35

Parables

The attendant at the twenty-four-hour Pemex station near Colima's bus terminal wore no disguises and used no aliases. He didn't lie about his birth date or his address or his CURP, the eighteen-character alphanumeric code that is Mexico's version of a Social Security number. Nobody asked about his work history or thought to run a background check. When he clocked in for his shift each day, he even placed his hand on a scanner that read his fingerprints and confirmed his identity.

"You know, it never occurred to me to use a fake name or get false documents," says Juvenal Cardenas Mejia, the rent collector who went by Atlas. "I wasn't hiding."

It was much like the other stories Atlas told about himself: a shell of truth, a core of self-delusion. He'd managed to fashion a new life in the lush, volcanic tropics of southwestern Mexico, working an honest job in a conspicuous green jumpsuit for the state-owned petroleum conglomerate. He traveled the countryside without hesitation, sailing through checkpoints on the one-hour drive between Colima and his native Jalisco. But if he wasn't hiding, Atlas surely was running. He'd taken off after the madness on Sixth Street—after Baby had pointed a gun at him, demanding to know who'd done the shooting—and he understood the risks of returning well enough to know he'd never be able to do it. "I was aware," Atlas says, "aware that something ugly had happened."

Still, he'd convinced himself that the police would never bother to come looking for him, a MacArthur Park paisa. He'd never sworn allegiance to the Columbia Lil Cycos, never committed any act of violence on their behalf. He was their pawn, a willing one, but not their muscle. Even when he learned from his Pemex coworkers that Mexican federal agents had paid an unexplained visit to the station on Boulevard Rodolfo Chávez Carrillo in 2011, four years after his escape, Atlas kept showing up for his shift, stubbornly committed to his theory of innocence. He had so misread the damage he'd done, he'd lost any instinct for self-preservation. "Because I didn't kill anybody," he says, "I didn't think I had anything to worry about."

In the days after the shooting, Detective Holmes had gone to Atlas's Westlake Avenue apartment several times, hoping to catch him. He set up surveillance teams in case Atlas returned. He tracked down Atlas's mom—she lived a few blocks away—warning her that her son was wanted. After a few weeks, though, Holmes asked the LAPD's Foreign Prosecution Liaison Unit to submit a request for assistance to the Mexican attorney general's legal attaché in Los Angeles, which meant that Atlas was more or less free until he screwed up.

He might have continued living tranquilly in Colima had a girlfriend not tipped off the Mexican authorities. On a September evening in 2011, federales showed up at the gas station again and arrested Atlas, the final suspect to be captured in any of the MacArthur Park investigations. The US embassy in Mexico City notified the LAPD, and at the beginning of 2012, a detective transported Atlas back to LA in the last row of a commercial flight. As Atlas understood it, he was being charged with extortion and possession of a firearm. "Extortion, yes, I accept it," he says. "But never did I use a gun. If I'm going to pay, it should be for something that I did." When he discovered that he was also facing murder and attempted murder charges as an aider and abettor of Luis Angel Garcia's death and Francisco Clemente's injuries, Atlas again offered an evasion wrapped in a truth.

"I'm no one to be ordering someone to be killed," he told Holmes.

If Atlas had wanted to come clean—to confess and cooperate, as so many others had—he was too late. There was nobody left to use his testimony against. The state trial was over. The federal trial was under way. Whatever Atlas might have to say, it no longer had any value to the government.

Victor Avila, having already won three life-without-parole verdicts at the first trial, insisted that the same sentence should be the starting point for any negotiations. Atlas's state-appointed attorney, Antonio Bestard, says his client received an offer of fifty years, adding that he was "disillusioned" with him for rejecting it. "I don't know about you, but I'm Catholic, and there's a lot of gospels and parables about tax collectors and how despised they were in the time of Jesus," says Bestard, who feared that Atlas would face a hostile jury even if he was just "one level above these poor vendors." For his part, Atlas claims that nobody offered him any deal, though it's likely that a forty-year-old man would have looked at a fifty-year sentence as the equivalent of life without parole.

In the summer of 2013, six years after the shooting, LA's criminal justice machinery ramped up for a third trial—one that featured the same witnesses whose testimony had already helped convict the other 18th Street defendants in Atlas's absence.

Francisco Clemente and Jessica Guzman, on the verge of having their third child, appeared again, and again Francisco grew so emotional that Avila had to pause and ask if he was OK, noting for the record that the witness "started to become upset or started crying." But that didn't stop Francisco from identifying Atlas as the conduit between the Columbia Lil Cycos and the street vendors, the rent collector who'd warned him a week or two before the shooting that he "should leave that place, because the gang will get there, and something would happen to me." The next time Francisco saw Atlas, he was escorting Giovanni down Sixth Street, walking to the corner, then circling back and "looking at us" before stepping into Video Mania.

Baby was called to testify, to recount the story of how he recruited Atlas and enlisted him as his proxy to collect from the vendors. In the days before the shooting, though they'd stopped working together, Atlas had visited Baby and told him that "something was going to happen to a vendor, because I guess that vendor had disrespected Tricky."

Shorty, who was twenty-one and had given birth to a daughter just the month before, made another trial appearance. She repeated the story of how she'd spotted the gang huddling on Sixth Street, by the International Mall, then followed them as they marched east toward Burlington Avenue. She knew both rent collectors—Atlas and Barrios—and watched as they "pointed out at the vendor that didn't pay," even if she couldn't be sure which of the two had done the pointing. "They said, 'That's the vendor there,'" Shorty testified.

Then the People of California called Giovanni. Although he'd fulfilled his obligation to testify twice already, Giovanni's plea agreement required his continued cooperation. He resented being yanked from Calipatria, barely a year into his new routine, and transported back to the LA County jail system for the duration of the trial, and he had little patience for Atlas, the straggler late to judgment day. Having already implicated Atlas, Giovanni couldn't see how he hoped to fight his case. "Atlas was the one that was going to point out the vendor to me," Giovanni told the jury, "because I didn't know the vendor."

Avila asked several times if Atlas appeared clueless or reluctant, if he'd said "anything to the effect of 'Don't do this'? 'Stop this'? Anything like that?"

"No."

"When you were in the video store with the defendant, does he tell you anything to the effect of 'Stop. Let's get away from here'?"

"No."

"'Let's don't do this?'"

"No."

"Nothing like that?"

"No, sir."

Avila asked again if any member of the crew had objected to any aspect of the plan that night. Giovanni flashed him a look of exasperation.

"You have this reaction as if: Why am I asking that?" Avila said.

"I mean, everybody knew what was going to be done before I shot the vendor," Giovanni replied. "They knew the vendor was going to get shot, you know. So, I mean, I—just coming into this courtroom and talking about it gets me mad, you know what I mean? I mean, I could man up to it and say what I did, right?"

Giovanni went on, practically demanding that Atlas confess. "I don't know why other people can't say, 'Fuck it. I did it. I'm going to man up to it and do my time,' which I'm doing. I'm putting my fucking life at risk, too, you know."

Atlas was sentenced to life without the possibility of parole for first-degree premeditated murder on behalf of a street gang, plus an enhancement of twenty-five years to life for a crime that involved a firearm. He was sentenced to another life term for attempted premeditated murder, plus another gun enhancement of twenty-five years to life, and then, for good measure, one more life term for conspiracy to commit extortion.

It was incomprehensible to Atlas that he, such a lowly member of the Columbia Lil Cycos' taxation scheme, would pay such a pitiless price. That the rent collector would fare worse than the shotcaller he handed the money to, worse than the lawyer who accepted the shotcaller's tributes on behalf of the prison godfather. Most confounding of all to Atlas, the killer who'd pulled the trigger would someday get a second chance while he, who'd pointed only his finger, was considered beyond redemption. The law didn't make those distinctions, couldn't be asked to account for every circumstance and contextualize every offense. It was a blunt instrument, and Atlas had missed the chance to spare himself by wielding it against someone else.

Part Four

2014–2023

Photo by Stephen Tourlentes

36

Deep Inconsistencies

In 2015, a few days after Giovanni's twenty-sixth birthday, an extravagantly coiffed TV star descended the golden escalator of a Manhattan high-rise and declared the American dream dead. He portrayed the United States as "a dumping ground for everybody else's problems," aiming his grievances at immigrants. "When Mexico sends its people, they're not sending their best," said Donald J. Trump.

Throughout his presidential campaign, Trump continued to play to xenophobic fears, pledging to build a "beautiful wall" to keep out unauthorized immigrants and to create a "deportation force" to purge the ones already here. "We have at least eleven million people in this country that came in illegally—they will go out," he vowed.

In blue-state America, especially in global centers like Los Angeles, Trump's rhetoric was more than performative hyperbole. The specter of mass deportations threatened to rip apart families, upend industries, and convulse civic life. Much like Proposition 187 two decades earlier, it also triggered a backlash—one that redounded to the benefit of LA's street vendors. Trump was the perfect bogeyman.

Just days after his election in 2016, two city council members issued an open letter, proposing the decriminalization of street vending given that "recent talks about changes to our nation's immigration policy, including threats to deport millions of undocumented immigrants," were sparking fear across Los Angeles. "Continuing to impose criminal misdemeanor penalties for vending disproportionately affects, and unfairly punishes, undocumented immigrants, and could potentially put them at risk for deportation," the letter continued. "Swiftly moving forward to adopt this policy gives us as a City the opportunity to stand up to the overt racism that has plagued our national discourse as of late."

LA's street vendors had of course endured decades of unfair punishment and overt racism. The city had shrugged off countless opportunities to protect immigrant entrepreneurs from criminal enforcement. And deportation? Under the Obama administration, some 3 million undocumented immigrants were expelled from the US, more than 1.2 million of them from the country's interior—numbers that four years of Trump wouldn't match.

But Trump's presidency allowed the Los Angeles city council to signal its virtue. Lawmakers promptly drafted an ordinance that stripped the municipal code of criminal penalties for vendors. The California legislature followed suit, passing the Safe Sidewalk Vending Act, which decriminalized vending statewide and required local jurisdictions to develop their own rules for regulating street vendors. In Los Angeles, the city council again wasted no time, unanimously approving the city's first legal vending ordinance in 2018—a historic turnaround that as one council member put it, "will lift this shroud of fear in our street vending communities."

Then reality set in. After working outside the law for so many years, LA's vendors had to make their way into a new bureaucratic labyrinth and decipher a new rulebook of fantastically precise regulations. To meet city standards, every vendor had to remain at least eighteen inches from the edge of the curb. Two feet from any utility boxes. Three feet from streetlights, parking meters, and tree wells—and three feet from other vendors. Five feet from fire hydrants. Twenty feet from the entrance to any building, store, theater, or house of worship. And five hundred feet from Dodger Stadium, Universal Studios, the Hollywood Walk of Fame, and other sports and entertainment venues that became de facto no-vending zones.

To obtain a license, a vendor had to apply for a business tax registration certificate from the city office of finance and a seller's permit from the state department of tax and fee administration, and then for the vending permit, pay the city bureau of street services $541 a year. A vendor of food had more hoops to jump through, including the construction of a pushcart that could pass county public health department inspection and a commissary for storing it. The fees for a public health permit—atop the vending permit—were $393 a year for a "low risk" food cart (packaged items) and $772 for a "high risk" operation (cooking and assembling non-packaged food). Although criminal penalties were gone, the city unveiled a schedule of civil fines that started at $100 for a violation of the vending rules and $250 for vending without a permit and went up from there.

"There's still a whole culture within the administrative and enforcement regime that views vending as something to be contained or regulated or stopped or prohibited," says Doug Smith, an economic justice advocate formerly at Public Counsel, which has sued the city to rescind the no-vending zones. "There are these deep inconsistencies between the public rhetoric and the actual practice on the ground."

Of each $541 vending fee, only $27 and change was actually needed to cover the expense of issuing the permit. City hall earmarked the other $513 or so for the salaries of nearly two dozen investigators—at an annual cost of more than $3 million. Even if vending was finally legal in LA, the vendors still had to pay to be policed.

37

A Second Chance

Under California prison guidelines, Giovanni would shave three days off his sentence for every twenty days he went without a write-up—a 15 percent good-conduct rate. If he stayed out of trouble for the next four decades, he could accelerate his release by about seven years. The incentive didn't inspire him. The difference between paroling in 2051 and completing his full term in 2058 was still too theoretical, a rounding error that would leave him an old man either way.

As the notoriety of his crime began to fade, so did Giovanni's need to prove himself. He managed to avoid more fights, or at least more fighting violations. But he still struggled to conform to the regimentation of prison, all the standards and boundaries and decrees that go into promoting the illusion of a controlled environment. In 2014, he was reprimanded for covering his cell's ceiling light at night. Over the next six months, he was spotted three times in the education building without a hall pass—the final violation, for "refusing to follow procedures," costing him thirty days of good-conduct credit.

Giovanni was written up again in 2015 after a guard searched his cell and discovered a cardboard box under the lower bunk that contained a plastic bag with several gallons of reddish and brown liquid. There were pieces of apple fermenting in the sickly sweet brew. Giovanni confessed to making pruno, prison moonshine, which he'd package in water bottles and sell for $6 a pop. "That's my hustle," he told a correctional officer. "My people don't send me money." Another 120 days of good-conduct credit lost. It got to where Giovanni failed to see any benefit in even trying to follow the rules. "I was like, 'Fuck it, I'll just enjoy myself,'" he says. "Max it out."

Giovanni might have continued down that path if not for an extraordinary rethinking of punishment and rehabilitation that was sweeping California in those years. Born into an era of throw-away-the-key policies—three-strikes laws, gang enhancements, adult prosecutions of kids—Giovanni was bumbling through prison just as the state's lawmakers were embracing a philosophy of second chances. The change had champions across the political spectrum: fiscal conservatives daunted by the runaway costs of mass incarceration, libertarians dismayed by the broad license that drug laws give the government to snoop and seize, evangelicals committed to the promise of personal transformation, activists whose communities bore the brunt of the zero-tolerance practices that fed the school-to-prison pipeline. But the crusader who would most alter Giovanni's view of the future was maybe the hardest to peg.

Before establishing himself as the leading force in California's criminal justice reform movement, Scott Budnick was the executive producer of the raunchy, uproarious *Hangover* movies, then the top-grossing R-rated comedy franchise in history. Just about the time that Giovanni arrived at Calipatria, Budnick stepped away from a salaried position on the Warner Bros. lot and pledged his life to unlocking the redemptive potential of California's incarcerated population. He'd already spent years as a volunteer teacher in LA's juvenile halls, encouraging young offenders to express themselves in writing, and he'd come to see just how far a little hope could go in a hopeless environment. "Hurt people hurt," Budnick liked to say. "And healed people heal."

He founded a nonprofit called the Anti-Recidivism Coalition and, using his Hollywood credentials to open doors, became a regular at the legislature. Often he'd show up in Sacramento with a cadre of ex-offenders—the "real experts"—and watch opposition melt as they articulated who they once were, and why, and how they came to no longer be that person. In 2015, Budnick's organization cosponsored Senate Bill 261, which expanded parole eligibility for inmates who were under the age of twenty-three at the time of their offense. (He'd already helped win passage of a bill that opened up early parole to convicts under eighteen at the time of their crime.) The proposed law drew on breakthroughs in neuroscience showing that the prefrontal cortex—home to risk assessment, impulse control, and emotional regulation—was one of the last regions of the brain to mature. Even well-known Republicans endorsed Budnick's cause, helping him promote the idea that young offenders were both less culpable and more rehabilitatable.

"People who commit offenses before their capacities are fully formed deserve a second chance," Newt Gingrich, the former US House Speaker, wrote in a pro-SB 261 column.

The new law, which took effect in 2016, changed life for sixteen thousand California inmates, Giovanni included. It entitled him to a youth offender parole hearing in his fifteenth year of incarceration, and it required that the parole board, when evaluating his suitability for release, consider Giovanni's diminished culpability—the "hallmarks of youth"—and any increased maturity. The new process didn't guarantee the outcome, only a chance to make his case. What was the story he'd tell? Giovanni wasn't convinced that he merited any special consideration. He surely hadn't done much during his time in prison to change any minds. But just like his awakening on a cliff in La Rumorosa, he'd been handed a gift—one that demanded a response. "It was the first time I felt like, damn, I might actually have a chance of getting out," he says.

He didn't change overnight, but Giovanni began making an effort. After Senate Bill 261's passage, he went more than a year without a serious rules violation. He raised his reading score to a twelfth-grade level. He completed a twenty-two-hour Alternatives to Violence workshop that taught communication, cooperation, and creative conflict resolution. He also qualified for a preliminary parole consultation, which led to a recommendation for more self-help programming, vocational training, and educational progress. Giovanni would have six years to prepare for his first hearing—"to explain and show how he's a changed person," a parole commissioner advised, "and why he no longer poses an unreasonable current risk of danger."

It was a lot to accomplish, especially without much family support, but Giovanni was starting to think he might have it in him. His optimism inspired him to reach out to his brother, Israel, to revive a bond that had frayed over the course of Giovanni's life on the streets and then in jail. Although just a year younger, Israel didn't grow up with the same disaffection—he'd avoided the worst of their stepfather's furies and castigations. Still, between Giovanni's incarceration and Juan's deportation, Israel had lost the two most important male figures in his life, and he'd struggled to find an identity that could fill the hollow they'd left. "I don't want to say he was soft, but he had a heart," Giovanni says. "I did, too. But he wasn't afraid to show it."

Israel became a regular at Snooky's, a down and dirty bikini bar in the Antelope Valley with $5 beers, tattooed girls, and Russian security guards. He worked for a time at a factory that manufactured ballistic panels for bulletproof vests, a job that left him caked in metallic fiber. Finally, as a merchandising associate at the Home Depot in Palmdale, Israel found a position that felt right, that rewarded him for being kind and helpful while still tackling rugged chores. Three times in 2016 he received a "Living Our Values" award for his teamwork and good cheer. His supervisors called him a payaso romantico—a romantic clown—buoyant, generous, sentimental.

After a bad breakup with a girlfriend, Israel moved back in with his mom—"my queen," he called her on Instagram—even taking her to the Home Depot holiday party that year as his date. Using the handle "Savage Izzy" online, he cataloged his best qualities: "unstoppable," "independent," "living life to the extreme every moment."

With Reyna still unable to visit, Giovanni sent an application to Israel. He couldn't get approved either. Israel had been arrested several years earlier, when he was twenty, for driving on a suspended license and placed on three years' probation. He was also deluged with penalties: a fine of $300, a state assessment of $840, a criminal fine surcharge of $60, a criminal conviction assessment of $30, an accounts receivable fee of $30, a court security assessment of $40, a warrant assessment of $15, a citation processing fee of $10, a court cost of $129, and a restitution fine of $100.

Instead of paying, Israel chose to serve ten days in jail—his freedom for a debt. Somehow it wasn't sufficient. Under the system of fees that required defendants to pay for their own punishment, Israel remained $269 in arrears to the State of California, and after finding him delinquent, the court added a civil assessment of $300 and referred the case to a collection agency. Israel was still making installment payments when he died.

It happened at Christmastime, 2016. Israel, by then twenty-six, had spent the holiday with family, drinking Modelos, feasting on Salvadoran pan con pavo at his Tía Dina's house. The next day, December 26, a bit before 9 P.M., he drove his four-door Toyota Camry into Palmdale on Avenue S, an arid stretch of road dotted with wind turbines and Joshua trees just a mile from home. The car had seen better days: the odometer topped 267,000 miles, and each of the four tires was a different brand, three of them undersize. It was not the kind of ride you'd want to test in a street race, but Israel apparently caught sight of a speeding blue car with tinted windows and yellow fog lights, and he punched the gas, pushing the poor Camry up to ninety.

Before reaching the intersection with Sierra Highway, Israel hit the brakes. They locked, sending him into a clockwise drift. He skipped the curb and slammed into a concrete light post, then started spinning counterclockwise and sheared a second light post. By the time his car collided with a railroad-crossing signal post, he'd left a trail of skid marks longer than a football field. Israel's seat belt held him in place. The car's airbags deployed. He had no alcohol or drugs in his body. But the impact crumpled the Camry's steel. A woman driving that direction stopped to help. She was a nurse. Just as Midget had felt for Giovanni's pulse as he lay unconscious in her car, this witness placed her fingers on Israel's wrist. He was alive but fading. Doctors pronounced him dead on arrival at Antelope Valley Hospital. The cause: blunt neck trauma.

Reyna worked that day. She'd landed a job in Beverly Hills, housekeeper for a music industry executive. It was a trek from Palmdale, sixty miles each way, but Reyna had earned her boss's trust and was free to work at her own pace. Plus he paid her in cash. On her drive home, Reyna called Israel to ask if he was hungry, then stopped at Del Taco to pick up dinner. She called him again when she got home, but he didn't answer. She tried to eat but couldn't. "I felt something in my heart," she says. With no sign of Israel, Reyna called his cell again. Still no response. When she finally got through, the hospital answered.

Reyna had to be nudged into viewing the body. Whoever was lying in that bed, battered and silent, wasn't her son anymore. She froze. Tears eluded her. "I'm—how do you say?—muy tímida," Reyna says. "I can't cry like other people. I hold it in."

There was no way to get word to Giovanni. He could call out, but Reyna couldn't call him. She didn't know what she would tell him anyway. Giovanni eventually phoned home to wish his mom a happy New Year. The news crushed him. "I went off the deep end," Giovanni says. "I didn't sleep for, like, five straight days." He berated himself—for having not been around to guide his brother, for not being free to properly mourn him—but his guilt ran deeper. Giovanni experienced Israel's death as karmic punishment, just deserts for his own survival. Because he was supposed to die and didn't, his brother had died instead.

"You know the saying: Hierba mala nunca muere?" Giovanni asks. It was a version of "Only the good die young." He was the bad weed, unkillable. Not Israel. "I was like, 'God, I see what you're doing,'" Giovanni says. "'You want me to feel the pain of losing someone.'"

Reyna went to Joshua Memorial Park in Lancaster to make burial arrangements. Home Depot helped with the costs. The cemetery offered Reyna a discount on a double plot with a double headstone. It was at the far southwestern corner of the grounds, where the grid of shaded grass gives way to barren dirt and the prospect of future gravesites. On the left half of the marble, she requested a heart with Israel's name and the date of his passing. "Beloved Son, Brother, and Friend to All," it says. On the right half, there was another heart, but it remained an empty outline.

38

What Do I Have to Offer?

Before the alarm could wake her, Reyna was up. It was a November morning in 2019, five days before Thanksgiving, and to give herself an extra hour of sleep, she'd spent the night in a guest bedroom of the Beverly Hills condo she cleaned three days a week. Reyna slipped on a loose black sweater and olive cargo pants. She added sandals that revealed a crescent of purple nail polish on each big toe. Her eyes were frosted, her bangs streaked. She was out the door by 5 A.M. "I couldn't sleep," Reyna said. "I was so nervous."

Reyna was at last going to close the distance—a dozen years, two hundred miles—that separated her from her only living son. She hadn't seen Giovanni since he'd been in prison, hadn't hugged him since he'd made his initial appearances in court, hadn't shared a meal with him since she'd brought him back from Mexicali. When Israel died, Reyna had inquired about a compassionate release for Giovanni to attend the funeral, a long shot given his security level, but she abandoned the idea after learning she'd have to foot the bill for a prison guard to accompany him. She wasn't sure, anyway, that she could handle two goodbyes in one day. "It would have been too hard to see him there," Reyna says, "and then watch him taken away."

A few months before the visit, Giovanni qualified for a transfer from the furnace of Calipatria. He'd earned enough credits to enter a Level Three facility, which meant more time out of his cell and less supervision. The state moved Giovanni to a prison near San Diego, where he settled into another, lower-security Sensitive Needs Yard. It was home to rap mogul Suge Knight and Kennedy assassin Sirhan Sirhan. When Giovanni made the move, he sent his mom a new visitor application, and by then, he'd pieced together the reason for her denial.

It was embarrassing—she'd tried to avoid telling him—but back in 2011, while making her janitorial rounds at the Antelope Valley Mall, Reyna had found a credit card on the ground. She knew that she wasn't entitled to it, that she should turn it in or try to find the owner, but life at the moment was so hard and sad, her poverty so unyielding, that the plastic rectangle glittered like a lottery ticket. Reyna treated herself to a lonely mom shopping spree: clothes, perfume, makeup. Security caught her in the parking lot.

Reyna was arrested, stripped of the merchandise, fired, and charged with petty theft. That earned her a fine of $150, a state penalty fund assessment of $448, a $40 court security assessment, a $32 criminal fine surcharge, a $10 crime prevention fine, a $30 criminal conviction surcharge, a $10 citation processing fee, a $30 installment plan fee, and a $100 restitution fine—a total of $850. Reyna was already struggling to pay off fines and assessments of $601 after getting cited for driving without insurance. She'd been poor; she became poorer. It took her three years to work off her debt and complete a hundred–plus hours of community service—to at last clear her record. She'd removed any barriers to visiting Giovanni, except for one detail: Reyna didn't think to include these misfortunes on the visitor application. The omission triggered an automatic denial. It robbed years from her and Giovanni.

With those unhappy facts disclosed, Reyna was on her way. The drive from LA took about two and a half hours, an almost straight shot down Interstate 5, past Knott's Berry Farm and Disneyland, along the stretch of Camp Pendleton beachfront where the Marines practice amphibious assaults, skirting the San Diego suburb of Detective Holmes's youth, and butting right up to the border, even closer to Mexico than Giovanni had been at Calipatria. The road bends east there, carving through an industrial park of fulfillment warehouses and shipping centers, until finally reaching the brown crags of the Otay Mountain Wilderness.

The prison was tucked between container yards and dirt bike trails, on a mesa that peered out over Tijuana. Reyna showed her driver's license at the guard shack and again at the reception center. Her color of pants caught a correctional officer's eye—too close to the staff's forest green uniforms. She was sent back to the car, where she changed into a pair of gray sweats she'd stashed in her overnight bag. Her hair clip, which scrunched and hoisted her amber streaks into a bun, came under scrutiny. An officer with black latex gloves made Reyna remove it, then studied it for points and edges that could function as a weapon. She had to show the nape of her neck and the straps of her bra. She was directed to take off her sandals, pivot, and kick back her legs, to confirm she had no contraband taped to the soles of her feet. The exercise, if justifiable as a security measure, was torturous for a mother who just longed to hold her son.

After Reyna cleared the metal detector, the same officer stamped the inside of her wrist with black-light ink—proof, in an emergency, that she'd passed all protocols. Reyna was in. She walked through a security door, into an interior plaza, where she zagged down a paved path with succulents along the bottom of the fence, electrified like Calipatria's, and coils of razor wire atop. She stopped at a sally port of remote-controlled gates, pausing for the guards in an octagonal tower to open one, then stepped through and waited, briefly captive, for it to close behind her before the second one parted. Reyna felt naked without her cellphone or pocketbook. She didn't have her house keys, her makeup, her Halls lozenges, her reading glasses. She tugged at her sweater and straightened her hair. "Oh, my God, I feel like I'm shaking," she said. "What if he doesn't recognize me?"

At the SNY visiting center, all dull concrete blocks, a guard buzzed her inside. Reyna showed her ID for a third time. Another guard perched on a podium, two steps above the linoleum floor, pointed her to a round cafeteria table topped in simulated wood grain. It was kiddie height, not even clearing her knees, a design meant to discourage lewd maneuvers underneath. Fans spun noisily overhead, breezy enough to induce a shiver. Fluorescent lights, some reduced by age to a muddy yellow, ran across the ceiling. Wide-angle mirrors and domed surveillance cameras captured every move. Reyna waited: five minutes, ten minutes. Where was he? She'd come all this way, solved the riddle of their separation, but still felt at the mercy of forces she couldn't see or comprehend. At last a door on the far side of the room, the kind that requires a jumbo jailer's key, swung open.

Giovanni was wearing pull-on pocketless dungarees and baby blue scrubs tucked into the elastic waist. His hair was buzzed short, maybe half an inch carpeting his scalp. It was enough to cover the EIGHTEEN on his forehead, to erase any evidence of the devil horns and demon watching his back. Giovanni was thirty years old. A smile burst through his taut face, stretching his cheeks and carving them with creases.

Reyna jumped at the sight of him. He looked skinny to her but handsome, a lot like his father when she'd first met him in MacArthur Park: taller than she by six inches, even a few specks of gray at his temple. Reyna threw her arms around Giovanni. He squeezed and spun her. Prison rules allow inmates and their visitors to "briefly kiss and/or hug" at the beginning and end of visits, but nobody looked to be policing this embrace. Reyna cradled Giovanni's head and showered him in kisses. He pressed his nose into her hair, breathing in.

"Do I look old?" Reyna asked when they finally pulled themselves apart.

She was forty-eight. All the darkness she'd endured, the deficits of security and stability, had depleted her. Stolen time. After AIDS claimed Giovanni's father, Reyna lived for years with the certainty that she would be next, or her two baby boys, or some horrible combination of the three. She didn't know how she'd dodged the disease—it seemed nothing short of miraculous. She'd felt blessed once she knew that her sons had also been spared, only to watch them seek out fresh risks, to subject themselves to age-old tests of manhood. She'd lost Israel. She'd come so close to losing Giovanni.

"I look old," Reyna said, "don't I?"

"No, ma," Giovanni said. "You look beautiful."

Life would have been easier for Reyna if she hadn't also lost contact with her parents. Maybe she'd never had their love, or maybe it was so conditional that her litany of disappointments sapped their capacity to keep making emotional room for her. Reyna had run from them early on; it wasn't hard to imagine them wishing to distance themselves from everything that later went wrong. Even as an adult, Reyna perceived the chasm between them the way a child would. It mystified her and tormented her. In a moment of sadness, she called a dear uncle, her father's brother, in El Salvador.

"I told her, 'Look, mi amor, do something for your good and for their good as well,'" says Tío Chepe, a publicist and radio personality. "I'm going to give you five words—keys—that are like a prayer, a mantra. You have no idea how mysteriously powerful those phrases are for bringing peace and tranquility." They were easy to remember—simple enough, he explained, to count on her fingers—but not easy to say:

I love you.

I forgive you.

I free you.

I bless you.

And I wish you the best.

"Oof, how difficult it is to free someone who's caused you so much harm!" Tío Chepe told Reyna. "But in freeing that person you're also freeing yourself."

Reyna couldn't do it. Wouldn't say it. Least of all to her mother. She wasn't going to open herself to more rejection. But Giovanni, the son whose needs she'd struggled her whole life to meet—Reyna's heart had space for him. She wrapped his hands in hers. She told him they felt cold, he needed to eat. Feeding dollar bills into the vending machines, she bought Giovanni chips and candy and soda. She was still his mom. If she couldn't recover her mom's love, she could be a better mom to him.

"My baby," Reyna said. She wiped her eyes. "I'm crying because I'm so happy."

Having his mom back in his life, feeling viscerally connected to family, helped Giovanni find his footing. "My strength," he'd started calling her. He plunged into books, schoolwork, the colored pencils he used for sketching. He'd start his day with a cup of instant coffee, boiling the water on an electric hot plate, and turn on the news: Donald Trump's impeachment, George Floyd's gasps, the so-called migrant caravans that fearmongers portrayed as invasions. The outside world looked to Giovanni a lot like a prison of its own, a lesson in vanity and power. Maybe he'd gained an unplanned respite, an immersion course in learning to live with himself.

When the pandemic arrived in 2020, just four months after Reyna's first visit, California's prisons went on "modified" status—canceling programs and limiting movement. Covid preyed on the inmate population, infecting 90,000 incarcerated people across the state and killing 260, including 21 of Giovanni's neighbors. The steady bleat of alarms and sirens unnerved him, but the lockdowns proved a welcome excuse to retreat further. Restricted largely to his cell, distanced from the daily aggravations and pitfalls that made prison an obstacle course, Giovanni found even greater calm and clarity. "During the pandemic was really the one time I felt inner peace," he says. "As messed up as that sounds."

He placed his name on the roster for GED testing, which the prison administered on computer terminals severed from the internet. Giovanni aced the language arts requirement; a few months later, he made it through social studies and science. When Giovanni finally passed the math portion—the subject that most intimidated him—the State Superintendent of Public Instruction and the President of the State Board of Education issued him a high school equivalency certificate. After pissing away nearly a decade in prison, he'd needed only a year to earn it. The milestone came with 180 days of good-conduct credit. "I was like, damn, I'm actually a pretty bright guy," Giovanni says. He mailed the certificate to his mom, who placed it in a frame and hung it on her living room wall.

His GED opened the door to higher education classes at the prison, which brought in instructors from a nearby community college once visiting resumed in 2021. Giovanni took psychology, a three-unit class; the next semester, he took art history, also three units. He'd need sixty for an associate's degree.

"Once you start doing good, it makes you want to do even more," Giovanni says. "I never felt that before. I was always told that nothing I did was good enough."

Because of his achievements in school, Giovanni qualified for new work opportunities. California's Prison Industrial Authority enlists some seven thousand inmates across the state to help run a hundred different kinds of commercial operations, from manufacturing prison clothes and stamping license plates to harvesting fresh eggs and running an optical lab. The pay is meager—ranging from 35¢ to $1 an hour—a form of involuntary servitude that remains enshrined in the state constitution. In 2022, a bill to halt forced labor in the prisons, the "End Slavery in California Act," failed in the legislature. The math made for a tough sell: paying inmates pennies, instead of minimum wage, saves taxpayers $1.5 billion a year.

Giovanni landed in the prison bakery, a shop that produces nearly ten thousand loaves of wheat bread a day for inmates at several Southern California facilities. It meant showing up at four-thirty in the morning, but Giovanni appreciated the training and the responsibility, the chance to contribute something useful to the world. He got certified in safe food handling and industrial safety and health. After thirty days, his supervisor wrote that Giovanni has "potential to grow and become a good worker." He earned about $40 a month—half of which the state withheld, applying it to his court-ordered restitution. Giovanni figured he'd need to pay it someday.

The pandemic also earned Giovanni three federal stimulus checks, a windfall for him and another million-plus inmates that the IRS had tried to prevent. Of the $3,200 Giovanni received, the state once more applied half to his restitution—a circular transaction that again took money from one government agency and shipped it to another. With the state seeking to ease overcrowded conditions and offer more rehabilitative incentives, it accelerated the formula for accruing good-conduct credit. The rate for Giovanni increased from 15 to 33 percent, meaning that for every two days served, he'd get credit for three. Instead of thirty years left on his sentence, he now had twenty.

Not long after his thirty-second birthday, Giovanni allowed himself to consider a relationship, a romance with a pen pal. The idea originated with his newest cellie, a guy from the Coachella Valley area who'd made headlines for a carjacking murder that landed him on death row; he was transferred, and placed with Giovanni, only because the governor imposed a moratorium on all executions. The cellie was involved with a woman from his same desert community, a UPS Store associate who relished his attentive, spiritually uplifting letters. She mentioned that her coworker, a single mom emerging from a breakup, could also use some affirmation in her life, and he agreed to run it by Giovanni.

Michelle was a couple of years younger than Giovanni, spirited and frank, quick with a laugh or a scold. She didn't know much about prison or really want to; she still lived at home with her parents, a nurse and a cemetery foreman, an arrangement that helped care for her four-year-old daughter. The letters Giovanni sent her weren't flowery, or sometimes even legible, but he had sincerity on his side. His words were hopeful and reassuring. He wasn't some dude trying to coax her into bed; he wasn't in a position to even try.

Michelle wrote back, uncertain but curious. She sent a picture. Giovanni told her she was beautiful, which she had a hard time believing, and more importantly, that he saw goodness inside. He knew what it meant to be judged and labeled. "What matters is what's in your heart," he told her.

Giovanni proved easy to talk to: a source of empathy and perspective, wiser than Michelle would have imagined. For better or worse, he'd lived through a lot. Falling for someone in prison seemed dangerous, or at least terribly inconvenient, a long-distance relationship strained by confinement, subjected to eavesdropping and surveillance, and devoid of physical intimacy. It also felt safe. Michelle never had to guess where Giovanni was or what he was up to. He couldn't disappear on her or cheat. If they argued, he'd never raise a hand against her. They faced barriers, but they'd made a connection—one perhaps truer and purer because it didn't depend on the conventions of dating. "I do ask myself sometimes, 'What do I have to offer?'" Giovanni says. "But I love her, and I'm always honest with her."

Still, Michelle didn't feel ready to break the news to her old-school Mexican American parents. So she sneaked around, hiding Giovanni's letters and concealing his calls and inventing excuses to camouflage her visits. A few months into their courtship, Michelle brought her daughter to the prison—a show of faith in the role Giovanni might someday play in their lives. The guards wouldn't let the little girl in. Unbeknownst to Giovanni, he was barred from contact with minors; his crime, no matter how incidentally and unexpectedly, had involved a child. Michelle sobbed. Giovanni felt sick.

They found a way to grow even closer, a workaround as common as it was risky: Giovanni procured a cellphone. Prisons have zero tolerance for mobile devices, which can be used to handle gang business, orchestrate drug deals, and plot escapes. It was hard, though, to take the prohibition seriously— California correctional officials typically confiscated more than ten thousand phones a year. The price for a phone on the inside topped a grand, even two, enough profit baked in that a guard might gamble a $60,000-a-year job to feed the pipeline. At that moment, a former correctional officer at Giovanni's prison was about to be sentenced to three years of federal time for smuggling in drugs and phones.

Giovanni used the cellphone to stay close to his mom, to reintroduce himself to his half sisters, to track down friends lost to the fractures of his childhood. But mostly he called Michelle. The phone was immediate and unregulated, allowing Giovanni to delve deeper into her life, to gain a front-row view to her devotion to her daughter, who talked unabashedly to "Gio" about cartoons and fairy tales. Late at night, curled into his bunk, Giovanni also used the phone to indulge in intimate video calls with Michelle, the best they could do without the marriage certificate they'd need for a conjugal visit. It was like a magic carpet to the outside world, permitting private adventures that Giovanni had been denied for close to fifteen years.

In 2022, acting on an anonymous tip, investigators searched Giovanni's cell. They found an LG phone and photographed its contents. It was his first serious write-up in nearly five years. It cost him seventy-five days of good-conduct credit.

Giovanni felt foolish for having thought he could put one over on the prison authorities, for allowing himself to be so tempted that he'd tried. He wanted to shout that the system had set him up to fail—that he was a human being starved for affection in an institution that was itself complicit in facilitating the market for contraband—but he knew that nobody wanted to hear an excuse. Or even a truthful explanation.

The Truth of Who We Are

The California Department of Corrections and Rehabilitation gave Giovanni a date: May 3, 2023. Sixteen years after his crime, he'd have a chance to show how far he'd come. Giovanni would be invited to stand before a panel of the board of parole hearings and take responsibility for who he once was and what he had done and show how he had grown out of being that person.

The board was supposed to focus on whether a parole candidate would pose an unreasonable risk of danger to society if released, not on the offense that led to the inmate's incarceration. But in determining current dangerousness, the board also had great discretion to explore the candidate's insight into his dangerous past behavior. It wouldn't be enough for Giovanni to express how sorry he was; he'd have to expound on his weaknesses, impulses, triggers, and strategies for never making the same mistake again.

"You can't just say, 'I'm sorry,'" Giovanni says. "They say that sorry is *sorry*. It's a sorry-ass word."

A representative from the district attorney's office, often the prosecutor who handled the original case, traditionally appeared at these hearings. It was a way to keep the offender honest, to ensure he didn't minimize his guilt, but also to put a thumb on the scale against parole. Commissioners usually had correctional or law enforcement backgrounds, which tended to make them sympathetic to prosecutors and reluctant to flout the recommendation of the state. This time, however, would be different. LA had just elected a progressive new district attorney, a former LAPD assistant chief who'd lobbied for Senate Bill 261, and his reformist policies offered Giovanni yet another unexpected break.

As a top LAPD commander, George Gascón had taken charge of the department's training unit in 2000, at the peak of the Rampart scandal, remaking the curriculum to emphasize ethics and civil rights. Now, as perhaps the most controversial DA in the nation, he embraced the principle that "people evolve," and he didn't see how prosecutors—years after winning convictions—had anything of value to say about a parole candidate's current risk. To the dismay of many under his command, he generally barred LA prosecutors from attending hearings and speaking out against parole. It meant the deputy district attorney who'd compelled Giovanni to accept a fifty-one-year sentence probably wouldn't be showing up to say the fraction he'd served was too little.

Gascón reversed another long-standing policy, again inflaming much of his office. No longer would prosecutors notify crime victims about an impending parole hearing or facilitate their appearances. He reasoned that such notifications could be intrusive, retraumatizing survivors or next of kin seeking to move past what likely was the worst moment of their lives. Victims still had a right to be present and catalog the damage the perpetrator had done—they could even invite a prosecutor to speak for them—but they'd have to take the initiative and make their own arrangements. Under those new rules, it was hard to predict whether Francisco would attend Giovanni's hearing, and if he did, what he might say.

On his sourest days, Francisco wallowed in indignation and resentment. He couldn't fathom how any member of the gang that assaulted him could qualify for a second chance. "They have so much evil in their lives—so much evil that the life of a child didn't even matter to them," he says. "For them, no. Not anymore. To change is hard. I would hope that these people someday get a conscience, though really I doubt it."

Francisco couldn't distinguish Giovanni from the rest of 18th Street. It seemed unfair to ask him to try. He'd seen his assailant only once, and only for a few seconds, and then never again. Whatever Giovanni may have done to try to make up for the violence—to surrender, to confess, to testify, to risk retribution from that very same gang—it was all beyond Francisco's view.

But Francisco wasn't always angry. He can be contemplative and prayerful, his struggle to make sense of his ordeal often returning to the divine. The people who did this to him, he says, "they're going to have to pay by not only facing justice but also facing God. He's the ultimate one who is going to judge us, all of us. He is going to decide what is the price each one of us has to pay." If Giovanni were ever to seek Francisco's forgiveness, assuming the carceral system had a mechanism for conveying such a plea, Francisco expects that he'd grant it.

"If I don't forgive, God won't forgive me," Francisco says. "He's going to say, 'How is it that you want me to forgive you if you can't forgive? You've put your pride over your faith—over your love.'"

To prepare Giovanni for the parole hearing, the state appointed him an attorney, a suitability specialist named Karen Fleming. Sharp featured, with a tangle of blond hair, and spry from afternoon gallops on her Icelandic show horse, Fleming was easy to misjudge. She'd spent twenty years as a deputy parole commissioner herself, probing the souls of killers and passing judgment on their rehabilitation. Now in what she thought would be her retirement—an age of yoga and flower design in the hills of Carlsbad—she'd walked away from an unhealthy marriage and gone back to work on the other side of the table, schooling parole candidates on the commissioners' thinking. How she looked at the world was suddenly central to Giovanni's fate.

"I'm not way lefty, you know, a unicorns-and-rainbows kind of lawyer," Fleming says. "I'm not a hug-a-thug kind of gal. I'm real straight. Unabashedly honest. I have looked into the eyes of evil. I have seen people who will never change and should never be let out of prison. I've also watched pure transformation and healing and the real deal. I have seen it. I know what it looks like. I know it's true."

In her experience, men who find their way out of prison have first undergone some kind of awakening, not necessarily religious but undeniably spiritual—a feeling that "they are actually connected to this planet and to other people." Only then does empathy begin to stir, a conscience start to form. "It comes down to the human condition," Fleming says. "Everyone has to unpack their stuff." Some have more to unpack than others: childhood trauma, domestic violence, absent parents, mental illness, substance abuse, learning disabilities, and on and on. "A lot of these guys are late to the party," Fleming says. "It's heartbreaking when I talk to someone and tell them that what happened to them when they were a little guy was not their fault. No one has ever said, 'You know, that is one of the reasons you are the way you are.'"

The pressure cooker of prison, an opportunistic, hypermasculine environment of turf marking and boundary testing, is a hazardous place to do the unpacking: nobody can afford to appear vulnerable. That doesn't make the work any less necessary. "These guys are doing the same thing that most humans have to do if they want a good-quality life," Fleming says. "Unpack our stuff and find out the truth of who we are."

In the final days of 2022, Fleming reviewed Giovanni's prison file. She found it "very, very small"—hundreds of pages rather than thousands—proof that Giovanni had neither a history of serious disciplinary problems nor a record of outstanding achievement. She winced when she saw the write-up for the cellphone; not even a year had passed. "That's not going to begin to cut it," she says. She noted also that he'd been eligible for a 2022 parole hearing but had voluntarily waived it, asking for one more year to focus on his education and develop a post-release plan. That spoke well of Giovanni's self-awareness. If he'd appeared before the board and been shot down, he'd have to wait at least three years for his next chance, maybe as long as five or seven. "My impression," Fleming says, "is that he's waking up and really wants a good life."

Fleming then spoke to Giovanni by video call: "We had the come-to-Jesus talk." If Giovanni was serious about winning over the parole board, he'd need to look deep within, to his darkest place, the recesses in which he'd stashed away the crushing weight of September 15, 2007, and "really get in touch with the harm, the terror he caused." He needed to ask himself not just how he physically destroyed his victims but what he stole from them and their loved ones: Their faith? Their security? Their ability to trust? "We had a conversation about owning his story and going back to who he was and being able to use the right words to adequately describe it," Fleming says. "It's really hard. The burden of committing violent crime and creating victims is huge. Anyone who ever does that has to live with that price."

As a first step, she advised Giovanni to postpone his parole hearing again, by two years this time, until 2025. She also counseled him to stay squeaky-clean for "three years minimum, hopefully five, six years no infractions."

Giovanni groaned at the thought of more delays. His instinct was to go in and face judgment, especially if he was likely to be denied on his first try anyway. Better to get it over with, then aim for the next round. Fleming, this unforeseen ally, was proposing a more excruciating approach, a more purposeful shot. She was challenging him to learn to tell the Giovanni Macedo story in a way that was true and revealing and impossible to deny.

Giovanni listened. He brooded. He had an idea of what he would need to say, all the pain and regret he'd have to unearth. He knew that the hurt he'd caused was immeasurable. But he'd never written a remorse letter, never tried to find the language to express his grief over the young life he'd ended, the other lives he'd shattered. To reflect on his victims the way his new lawyer was asking would require him to fill in blanks with information he didn't have. Giovanni knew next to nothing about Francisco Clemente and Jessica Guzman, even less about Daniela Garcia and Luis Angel Garcia. They were strangers then and abstractions now. He hadn't been invited to hear them testify. He didn't know what they looked like. He'd never even seen a picture of the damage he'd done—of Luis Angel's naked body on the autopsy table. It was shown to a jury, to illustrate the depravity of the Columbia Lil Cycos, but not to Giovanni.

He agreed to wait. He was thirty-four. He wanted to go home, longed to present a better version of himself to the world he'd left as a wounded boy. Someday he'd make the case for his freedom, maybe soon. For now, there was so much to exhume and absorb, so much to put into words.

Author's Note

This is a work of nonfiction: every person who appears in these pages is real. Most are ordinary folks carrying extraordinary burdens. The large majority agreed to share their stories with me, acts of generosity that made this book possible. A smaller number did not volunteer to be named here, either because they declined or couldn't be located, and what I know of them is drawn primarily from publicly available sources, including police reports, court records, and the thousands of pages of transcripts generated by the multiple trials that the events described here produced. Where I've quoted someone I didn't speak to myself, I've identified the source in the notes that follow, and where I interviewed someone in Spanish, I've also included their words as originally spoken. Where people were known by monikers, I stuck to those names. I did so to aid the reader, not to conceal a true identity or impose a villainous one. Only one name is a pseudonym, Reyna Flores, who asked to remain anonymous and who, given the road she's traveled, can use a measure of grace.

Acknowledgments

I moved to MacArthur Park in 2011, shortly after my son's graduation from high school and just before his departure, out of state, to college. Life would be lonelier without him in the house. I hoped that venturing into Los Angeles's feverish core, after several decades of orbiting, would jolt me out of my empty-nester blues.

I leased a loft in the American Cement Building, its facade a mod exoskeleton of concrete X's. My thirteenth-floor unit looked east—at the park, over the lake, across Alvarado Street, and into the world of the Columbia Lil Cycos. The change of scenery worked. I became preoccupied with MacArthur Park's history, its murky waters and precarious fault lines, the sirens and rants and incantations that seeped through my porous wall of half-century-old glass. Several publications invited me to explore the social and economic geography of my new home, including *The American Prospect*, *Los Angeles*, *The California Sunday Magazine*, and *Wildsam*. In the stories I wrote for them, the seeds of this book were sown, and I'm grateful to the editors who encouraged those efforts.

I eventually spotted the kernel of a book in the neighborhood's gang-vendor-police dynamic, but didn't know where to start. Or rather, I did know—newspaper coverage of the Columbia Lil Cycos' 2012 RICO trial had alerted me to the story of Giovanni Macedo—but I dithered over making contact with him, fearing that rejection would end this project before it had begun. I'm indebted to my dear friend and former colleague Héctor Tobar for coaxing me, over margaritas one night, into writing Giovanni a letter. Héctor reassured me: there had to be more to Giovanni than the worst thing he'd ever done.

I received Giovanni's response at the end of 2018. He was surprised that anyone cared enough to hear him out, to consider who he was underneath the label of his crime. He believed that future tragedies might be averted if readers were to learn from his mistakes. I was moved by Giovanni's willingness to open up his life, a gift of trust that came with no conditions or expectations—other than the hope that I, and all of us, would come to see what resides inside his heart. My quest to untangle the threads of his family's immigrant journey took me to Mexico, El Salvador, and Guatemala, where I was received with nothing but kindness. I'm especially grateful to Giovanni's mother and sister, who vouched for me wherever I turned, as well as his half sisters, Ramonita and Ruby, who helped illuminate the life of the biological father they share. And I wouldn't have made it very far without the confidence of Giovanni's lawyers, Richard Lasting and Karen Fleming.

I am thankful to the dozens of others who indulged my requests for their time: former gangsters, the currently incarcerated, prosecutors, defense attorneys, street vending advocates, beat cops, detectives, federal agents, faith leaders, politicos, and the many court clerks and court reporters who facilitated my access to documents theoretically available to anyone but often difficult to locate, transport, and reproduce. A special thanks to Paul Keenan and his wife, Candice, for sharing not just their professional expertise but also their love story, and to David Holmes for treating the characters in this tale with compassion—a quality that encouraged Francisco Clemente and Jessica Guzman to extend me a gracious welcome.

No piece of writing is born immaculate: we all need a community of readers who won't think less of us for being exposed to our imperfections. Three former magazine editors, all trusted friends, took on the task of reading lesser versions of this manuscript. I couldn't be more grateful to Kit Rachlis, Matthew Segal, and Nick Marino for thinking me worthy of their wisdom. I also received invaluable guidance from Michael Mullen and Eric Nazarian, brothers-in-arms who challenged me to dig deeper and think bigger. As part of the process, I retained two fact-checkers: Tom Colligan, an extraordinarily careful reader and thoughtful wordsmith, spent months reviewing these pages for accuracy; Susana Antonia Mullen, my Colombian "sobrina," listened to hours of taped Spanish-language interviews to help capture nuances and refine translations (especially for idioms that lacked obvious English analogues).

I've had the good fortune of being adopted by the Astra House family. My thanks to all the incredibly talented and creative people there who brought *The Rent Collectors* into existence, including Danny Vazquez, who believed in this idea from the start, and editorial director Alessandra Bastagli, who propelled it to the finish line with smarts and sensitivity. In Jay Mandel, I have the best agent an author could ask for.

During the five years I was married to this book, I also married my longtime partner, April Yamashiro. She makes me feel loved, which is the one thing every one of us seeks.

Sources

Part 1

Photo of the MacArthur Park neighborhood used with permission from Forest Casey. His work appears on forestcasey.carbonmade.com.

Chapter 1

"forgotten planet . . . silent uterus" Adolfo Sagastume, *Canto a La Rumorosa* (2013). In the original Spanish: "planeta olvidado . . . útero silente."

"a threat to everyone everywhere" Antonio Villaraigosa, Los Angeles's mayor from 2005 to 2013, was quoted by Alice Walton in "Police Search for Gunman in Infant's Death," *Los Angeles Daily News*, September 18, 2007.

Despite five DUIs Juan Monroy's arrests are documented in Los Angeles Superior Court records.

"take deep slow breaths" Giovanni authorized the release of his medical records to his attorney to aid his defense against murder charges.

"I don't want to be in this world anymore" Giovanni's mother authorized the release of her medical records to his attorney to aid her son's defense against murder charges.

Chapter 2

an urban wonderland Stephen Braun, "Faces of MacArthur Park: Quite Refuge, Place of Fear," *Los Angeles Times*, November 26, 1989.

"as 'twere some open book that God had writ" Eliza Otis, "Fair Westlake," *Los Angeles Times*, September 25, 1898.

"a reminder of the shadows of life" "Suicides at Westlake: Those Who Have Sought Rest Beneath Its Waters," *Los Angeles Herald*, May 18, 1986.

"It's a mistake, and it's a necessity" Tía Dina said: "Es un error, es una necesidad y es una suerte que cuando llega un hijo, lo comprenda."

"When he drank, he was another man" Tía Dina said: "Cuando él estaba alcoholizado era otro hombre, ofensivo muy ofensivo. Él siempre me decía: '¿A ver, qué vas a hacer vos, una prostituta?' Entonces a mamá yo le decía: 'Mira, yo no me voy a dejar que este viejo me insulte.' Entonces, mi mamá decía: ¿Sabes qué, mija? Aprende a callar.'"

"Mauricio's only sin" *Alternativa*, A Publication of the Secretary of Communications of UCA, March 1980, "El único pecado de Mauricio: ser joven y estudiante."

Archbishop Romero United States Conference of Catholic Bishops, "Letter to President Carter on Aid to Military in El Salvador, February 17, 1980." Romero wrote: "I am very worried by the news that the government of the United States is studying a form of abetting the arming of El Salvador by sending military teams and advisors . . . If this information from the newspapers is correct, the contribution of your government, instead of promoting greater justice and peace in

El Salvador, will without doubt sharpen the injustice and repression against the organizations of the people who repeatedly have been struggling to gain respect for their most fundamental human rights."

Chapter 3

It grew by breaking the mold of traditional, multigenerational Mexican American gangs Rich Connell and Robert J. Lopez, "An Inside Look at 18th St.'s Menace," *Los Angeles Times*, November 17, 1996.

"Kind of like a big franchise" The LAPD's Edgar Hernandez made this comment while testifying in United States of America v. Sergio Pantoja, et al., a 2012 federal trial against members of the Columbia Lil Cycos. He also participated in several interviews for this book.

drug capital of the city and **"do a little fire"** Matthew Ormseth, "A Violent Gang, an FBI Informant and the Truth behind One of LA's Deadliest Fires," *Los Angeles Times,* June 9, 2022.

"culture of war" "Rampart Reconsidered: Search for Real Reform Seven Years Later," Blue Ribbon Rampart Review Panel, 2006.

bunker mentality Los Angeles Police Department Board of Inquiry into the Rampart Area Corruption Incident, March 1, 2000.

"a pattern or practice" Tina Daunt, "Consent Decree Gets Federal Judge's OK," *Los Angeles Times,* June 16, 2001.

nouveau riche gangsters Lynn Smith, "New Wealth in Rampart's Red Glare," *Los Angeles Times,* March 18, 2001.

"C'mon, girl, let's go" Oso (Eduardo Hernandez) appears in *Domino* at the twenty-seven-minute mark. In the DVD commentary, director Tony Scott describes what he saw in Oso: "He has confidence and an intelligence and a sense of humor ... When you get guys who live their lives as much on the edge as these boys, it's very hard to duplicate these faces in Hollywood."

"Family and my gang life" Tricky (Sergio Pantoja) testified as a government witness in United States of America v. Sergio Pantoja, et al. This quote is from the public record of his testimony.

"We tried never to bring that into the house" Morena (Ingrid Tercero Flores) testified as a government witness in United States of America v. Sergio Pantoja, et al. This quote is from the public record of her testimony.

"You just had to be bright" Tricky made this comment while testifying in United States of America v. Sergio Pantoja, et al.

Chapter 4

"I only went to elementary school" and **"You have to lose your embarrassment"** The quoted vendors are Francisco Aguirre and Ofelia Ruiz, who were originally interviewed for "The Geography of Getting By," by Jesse Katz, *The American Prospect,* July/August 2012.

"social citizenship" Lorena Muñoz, "Selling Memory and Nostalgia in the Barrio: Mexican and Central American Women (Re)Create Street Vending Spaces in Los Angeles," *Street Vending in the Neoliberal City: A Global Perspective on the Practices and Policies of a Marginalized Economy,* Kristina Graaff and Noa Ha, editors (Berghahn Books, 2015).

"unsightly movable dyspepsia emporiums" "Tamale Politicians to Petition Council," *Los Angeles Times,* February 9, 1903.

"motley array of representatives" "Many Street Vendors in Court," *Los Angeles Times,* August 12, 1906.

"disease-breeding traffic" "John Chinaman Called Menace," *Los Angeles Times,* April 14, 1914.

"the Los Angeles sidewalks are the most misused" "Drive Begun on Peddlers," *Los Angeles Times,* December 17, 1932.

"give our sidewalks back to the people" "Ban on Sidewalk Vending Nears; Questions Remain," *Los Angeles Times,* December 16, 1980.

A ticket forced the vendors to finance their own exclusion Matthew Desmond's *Poverty, by America* (Crown, 2023) makes the case that US economic policies exacerbate the burdens of poor Americans while favoring the affluent.

"who-knows-where" James Rainey, "LA Looks for a Palatable Solution to Street Vending Business," *Los Angeles Times,* December 9, 1993.

"quality of life" "Platform: 'Street Vendor Law Erodes Quality of Life,'" *Los Angeles Times,* June 6, 1994.

"Third World" "Licenses for Street Vendors," *Los Angeles Times,* November 25, 1995.

"a poor image of the City of Los Angeles" "Important Notice: Selling on Streets, Sidewalks, Private Property, Etc.," Office of the City Clerk, Tax and Permit Division, City of Los Angeles, July 1980, contained in the Asociación de Vendedores Ambulantes Records at the Southern California Library.

the LAPD realized early on that public safety would suffer On November 27, 1979, the Los Angeles Police Department issued Special Order 40, which barred officers from initiating police action "with the objective of discovering the alien status of a person."

"the most restrictive street vending ordinances" Alan Citron, "Task Force Formed to Study Legalizing of Street Vendors," *Los Angeles Times,* July 8, 1989.

"a moribund petting zoo" and **"like flowers after the spring thaw"** Gregg Kettles, "Formal Versus Informal Allocation of Land in a Commons: The Case of the MacArthur Park Sidewalk Vendors," *Southern California Interdisciplinary Law Journal,* vol. 49, 2006.

"I wasn't risking it" Baby (former 18th Streeter Edgar Hernandez) made this comment while testifying in United States of America v. Sergio Pantoja, et al. He also participated in several interviews.

Chapter 5

slumlord task force Myrna Oliver, "Apartment Owner Sued in LA Slumlord Crackdown," *Los Angeles Times,* June 4, 1982.

"stronghold" The video has been removed from YouTube, but the government played a copy for the jury in United States of America v. Sergio Pantoja, et al.

a symbolic death and rebirth Alan Meredith Blankstein and Gilbert "Sandy" Sandoval, "In Gangs We Trust: A Close-Up of the New Induction," Reaching Today's Youth, cyc-net.org, July 2004.

"Get up" Giovanni recalled these comments in an interview.

"injurious to the health" and **"standing, sitting, walking"** People of California v. 18th Street et al., 2005 complaint for injunctive relief.

"I always told her, 'Come over here'" Tía Dina said: "A ella siempre le decía, 'Venite para acá, aquí vas a estar más tranquila con tus hijos.' Ella cuando ya se vino aquí, ya era tarde."

"I just saw the need that she had" Juan Monroy said: "Simplemente vi la necesidad que ella tenía. Es que fue así de improviso."

"That's also why I had to distance myself" Juan said: "Por eso fue también que me alejé porque no me gustaba que vieran los pleitos. Porque está jodido ver eso."

Chapter 6

"like their own government" The LAPD's Edgar Hernandez made this statement in a 2005 declaration supporting a gang injunction against the Columbia Lil Cycos.

"We all have rights" Francisco Clemente said: "Todos tenemos derecho. Tenga uno papeles o no tenga papeles. Todos tenemos el derecho de que valga nuestra voz."

"life is very hard—very hard is life" Francisco said: "La vida es muy dura. Es muy dura la vida."

"it was one of two things: work or steal" Francisco said: "una de dos: o trabajas o robas."

"When you start at the bottom" Francisco said: "Cuando tú empiezas, empiezas desde abajo y si no tienes dinero tienes que invertir."

"I don't like being a conformist" Francisco said: "A mí no me gusta ser conformista. Siempre yo he tratado de superarme y tratar de salir más adelante de la conformidad."

"I don't know, I just kept looking at her" Francisco said: "Pues nada, pues la miré y la miré."

"For some reason I like this guy" Jessica Guzman said: "Me gusta ese muchacho por algo."

"like going to Rodeo Drive" Senior lead officer Randall McCain was quoted in "LA Fashion District Scrubs Out Crime with 'Clean and Safe' Team," *California Apparel News*, June 2, 2006.

"I've always been a man who, if I can avoid a problem, I will" Francisco said: "Realmente siempre he sido un hombre que si puedo evitar un problema lo evito."

"Don't stress" Francisco said: "Yo le dije, no, pues no te apures, si quieres llévate tus cositas, vamos, yo te llevo. Allí vas a vender bien tranquila."

"It's not easy being a humble man" Francisco said: "No es fácil ser un hombre humilde y derecho. Créame que cuesta mucho. Especialmente cuando tú quieres portarte bien o quieres hacer las cosas bien, es cuando hay veces te vienen las cosas más pesadas."

"culture of coercion" "CFPB Takes Action against ACE Cash Express for Pushing Payday Borrowers into Cycle of Debt," Consumer Finance Protection Bureau, July 10, 2014.

"quiet encroachment" In *Life as Politics: How Ordinary People Change the Middle East* (Stanford University Press, 2013) Asef Bayat writes: "The nonmovement of the urban dispossessed, which I have termed the 'quiet encroachment of the ordinary,' encapsulates the discreet and prolonged ways in which the poor struggle to survive and to better their lives by quietly impinging on the propertied and powerful, and on society at large." Bayat's work is discussed in *Street Vending in the Neoliberal City: A Global Perspective on the Practices and Policies of a Marginalized Economy*, Kristina Graaff and Noa Ha, editors (Berghahn Books, 2015).

"If we have to pay something to do business" Francisco said: "Pues pienso que es realmente al gobierno que tenemos que entregarle cuentas si es que hacemos negocio o cualquier cosa. No a alguien que no es nadie."

The LAPD had already cited Barrios for illegal vending Los Angeles Superior Court records document the citation of Barrios (Guadalupe Torres Rangel).

"'Hey, what happened with the stuff for the soda?'" Jessica recalled Barrios's words while testifying in State of California v. Luis Silva, et al., the 2008 preliminary hearing that preceded State of California v. Juan Pablo Murillo, et al., a 2010 state trial against members of the Columbia Lil Cycos.

"I did it, I got him hired" Atlas (Juvenal Cardenas Mejia) said: "Sí, le conseguí el trabajo. Cuando él salió no podía ni caminar. No estaba acostumbrado."

"I still remember the scolding" Atlas said: "Todavía me acuerdo la regañada que me dio y me dijo: 'Chamaco del demonio, ¿qué chingados estás haciendo? No seas pendejo, chamaco cabrón. ¡No ves que un animal de esos te puede hasta matar!'"

"I never mistreated anyone" Atlas said: "Yo nunca los maltraté. Ni les decía ninguna grosería. Yo sí que traté de llevarme bien con ellos para que se sintieran a gusto y no intimidados. Y así todos estaban contentos conmigo."

"They'd say to me, 'Right now I don't have any'" Atlas said: "Ellos me decían: 'Ahorita no tengo.' Y yo les decía: 'Bien, no te preocupes. Si viene alguien, dile que ya le distes al Atlas.'"

"I did like watching movies" Atlas said: "Me gustaba mirar las movies y luego me decían: 'Hey, ¿quieres este disco? Es lo más nuevecito.' Y me lo regalaban—por su propia voluntad."

"Many people accept injustice" Francisco said: "Miré muchas personas que sí aceptaban la injusticia. Y hay veces no tiene uno otra opción, pero llega el momento que ya, ya no se puede. Ya es mucho."

Chapter 7

The little homies "can't just stand around" Tricky made this comment while testifying in United States of America v. Sergio Pantoja, et al.

The FBI was listening in The transcript of Tricky and Giovanni's conversation was introduced in United States of America v. Sergio Pantoja, et al.

Chapter 8

"Men and loyal soldiers aren't made or borrowed" The letter from Puppet (Francisco Ruiz Martinez) to the Columbia Lil Cycos was introduced into evidence in United States of America v. Francisco Ruiz Martinez, et al., a 2002 RICO case.

"a clean version of hell" Chris Outcalt, "Murder at the Alcatraz of the Rockies," *The Atavist*, April 2018.

psychosis and suicidal ideation Stuart Grassian, "Psychiatric Effects of Solitary Confinement," *Washington University Journal of Law & Policy*, Volume 22, January 2006.

"Life is what you make of it" Puppet's letter was introduced into evidence in United States of America v. Sergio Pantoja, et al.

"extralegal governance institution" David Skarbek, *The Social Order of the Underworld: How Prison Gangs Govern the American Penal System* (Oxford University Press, 2014).

The Eme couched the maneuver in ethnic pride Robert J. Lopez and Jesse Katz, "Mexican Mafia Tells Gangs to Halt Drive-Bys," *Los Angeles Times*, September 26, 1993.

perforated him with the sharpened tip of a paint-roller handle Chris Blatchford, *The Black Hand: The Bloody Rise and Redemption of "Boxer" Enriquez, a Mexican Mob Killer* (William Morrow, 2008).

"I got involved in his world" Janie Garcia was interviewed by the Reverend Rudy Rubio of Reformed Church of Los Angeles on the "Hood Grace Podcast/Vlog," posted April 9, 2020, on YouTube.

"would have shot it out" Puppet was quoted in the government's trial memorandum submitted by the US attorney's office in the 1996 federal weapon and immigration case against him.

"accountants with guns" versus **"cowboys"** Jim Newton, "A Reconciliation?: Collaboration Yields Many Arrests, Fosters Thaw Between Agents, Officers," *Los Angeles Times*, March 13, 1994.

"piece by piece, brick by brick" Bruce Riordan, an assistant US attorney, delivered the government's opening argument in United States of America v. Francisco Ruiz Martinez, et al.

"Se tiene que fumigar" Puppet's letter was introduced into evidence in United States of America v. Francisco Ruiz Martinez, et al. An excerpt appears in "Feds Aim to Dismantle LA's 18th Street Gang," *All Things Considered,* Mandalit del Barco, June 3, 2008.

"You know how the house has termites?" The audio of this conversation, introduced into evidence in United States of America v. Francisco Ruiz Martinez, et al., appears in "Feds Aim to Dismantle LA's 18th Street Gang," *All Things Considered,* Mandalit del Barco, June 3, 2008.

"When you're in prison, you're literally in the dark" Puppet's attorney, Gerald Scotti, made this comment in his opening argument in United States of America v. Francisco Ruiz Martinez, et al.

Puppet wrote hundreds of letters a year Most of the quoted letters were introduced into evidence in United States of America v. Sergio Pantoja, et al.

Chapter 9

"the cops, they used to go bug people that did illegal vending" Shorty (Jessica Matias) made this statement while testifying in State of California v. Juan Pablo Murillo, et al. She declined several requests for an interview.

"You're not even taking care of us" Shorty recounted her father's words while testifying in State of California v. Juvenal Cardenas Mejia, a 2013 state trial against Atlas.

"He got too big for his britches" Atlas said: "Siempre se les ponía al tú por tú. Él se quiso hacer el héroe."

"The street is for everybody" Francisco said: "La calle es de todos. La calle es para todos los que la caminan."

"Can't you see I'm pregnant?" Francisco recalled Daniela Garcia's words: "¿No miras que yo estoy embarazada? ¿Quieres quitarle el dinero a mi bebé?"

"Everyone pays" Francisco recalled the enforcer's words: "Aquí todos pagan. Si no, quítate y ponemos a otro ahí y de todos modos nos va a pagar."

"Give me fifty bucks, motherfucker" Jessica Guzman recounted these words while testifying in State of California v. Luis Silva, et al.

"I'd like to see who is going to be the first" Francisco said: "Yo nomás quiero mirar quién va a ser el primero que me va a quitar mis cosas. Si tú me las quitas, son tuyas, te las puedes llevar, pero yo créeme que no voy a dejar que te lleves nada, nada porque esto es mío y esto me costó a mí."

"I don't want problems" Francisco said: "Yo no quiero problemas."

"And you, cabrón?" Francisco said: "¿Y tú, cabrón?"

Chapter 10

"My guardian angel" Giovanni made this comment while testifying in United States of America v. Sergio Pantoja, et al.

"commitment to excellence" Face (Juan Pablo Murillo) testified in his own defense in State of California v. Juan Pablo Murillo, et al.

"where I can go, what I can do" and **"I gave him the keys"** Tricky made these statements while testifying in United States of America v. Sergio Pantoja, et al.

"The vendor thing, that ain't my thing" Giovanni made this comment while testifying in State of California v. Juan Pablo Murillo, et al.

"'Hey, you either pay rent or you got to get out of here'" Giovanni made this comment while testifying in United States of America v. Sergio Pantoja, et al.

"He gave confianza" Giovanni made this statement under questioning by Los Angeles Police Department homicide detectives.

"What the fuck is he doing here?" and **"The homie's cool"** Giovanni recounted this dialogue in an interview.

"I didn't want the drama" Giovanni made this statement while testifying in State of California v. Juan Pablo Murillo, et al.

"If you have a problem with somebody" Francisco said: "Si tú tienes un problema con alguien y te peleas y tú le ganas, pues esa persona tiene que respetarte y decirte: 'OK, sabes qué, tú fuistes un buen cabrón, shake my hand.'"

"You need to get the fuck out of here" Tricky recounted this statement while testifying in United States of America v. Sergio Pantoja, et al.

"I will send you to hell" Francisco recounted Tricky's words while testifying in State of California v. Juan Pablo Murillo, et al.

"If the vendor comes back acting stupid" Tricky recounted this statement while testifying in United States of America v. Sergio Pantoja, et al.

"She had to go sell" Jessica said: "Tuvo que salir a vender. Tenía que comprar las cositas de su bebé."

"Get dressed" Giovanni recounted Face's words while testifying in State of California v. Juan Pablo Murillo, et al.

"Don't trip" Giovanni recounted this dialogue under questioning by LAPD homicide detectives.

Chapter 11

"distraction to the people of Los Angeles" Antonio Villaraigosa was quoted by Jill Serjeant in "TV Journalist in Affair with LA Mayor Keeps Job," *Reuters*, August 3, 2007.

"something that had to be done" Giovanni made this statement while testifying in State of California v. Juan Pablo Murillo, et al.

"He was a homie, but he was questionable" Face testified in his own defense in State of California v. Juan Pablo Murillo, et al.

"What the fuck is this for?" Giovanni made a version of this comment under questioning by LAPD homicide detectives, who recounted it in State of California v. Juan Pablo Murillo, et al.

"Didn't I tell you you were gonna do something?"; **"A vendor";** **"You know how it goes"** Giovanni recounted this dialogue in an interview with the Los Angeles County district attorney's office, and it was read into evidence in State of California v. Juan Pablo Murillo, et al.

"Hey, Face" and **"What's up, baby girl?"** Face recounted this dialogue while testifying in his own defense in State of California v. Juan Pablo Murillo, et al.

"I told him to make sure to tell me, let me know who was the guy" Giovanni made this statement while testifying in State of California v. Juvenal Cardenas Mejia.

"We walked in front of him" Giovanni made this statement while testifying in State of California v. Juan Pablo Murillo, et al.

"That's him" Giovanni recounted Atlas's words while testifying in State of California v. Juvenal Cardenas Mejia.

"except the chilango" and **"Don't worry, we're going to fix it"** Former Juice Max employees Evelyn Castillo and Maria Morales testified in State of California v. Juan Pablo Murillo, et al. and State of California v. Juvenal Cardenas Mejia, respectively.

"Debating whether or not to do it" Giovanni made this statement while testifying in State of California v. Juan Pablo Murillo, et al.

"To make sure he was dead"; "Tunnel vision"; "I didn't want to get distracted" Giovanni made these statements while testifying in State of California v. Juan Pablo Murillo, et al.

"Let's go, fool!" Giovanni recalled this statement while testifying in State of California v. Juan Pablo Murillo, et al.

"a lethal absence of hope" Gregory Boyle, *Tattoos on the Heart: The Power of Boundless Compassion* (Free Press, 2010).

"You fucked up" Giovanni recounted Tricky's words while testifying in State of California v. Juan Pablo Murillo, et al.

Chapter 12

"We were all there like crazy people" Jessica said: "Estábamos todos ahí como locos pidiendo una ambulancia. La ambulancia tardó como horas, para nosotros eran horas."

"It was very ugly" Jessica said: "Fue muy feo. Muy, muy feo."

"life-threatening at that point" Cameron Nouri testified about Francisco's injuries in State of California v. Juan Pablo Murillo, et al.

"It was quite, quite, quite hard" Francisco said: "Eso sí fue bastante, bastante, bastante duro. Yo, la verdad, pensé que ya no iba a subsistir."

"I saw what is life" Francisco said: "Yo miré lo que es la vida y la muerte. Créanme que yo pasé muchas cosas. No sé si era por la droga que te ponían en el hospital o qué era, pero yo miré muchas cosas que la verdad es duro de entender."

"You have to accept" Francisco said: "Hay que aceptar que existe el bien y existe el mal. Y si tú haces mal, mal vas a pagar. Es más mejor hacer las cosas lo más mejor que puedas y arreglar ahorita lo que tú puedas arreglar porque cuando te mueras ya no vas a poder hacer nada. Dios va a llegar y te va a decir, a ver, tú ¿qué hiciste? ¿Te portaste mal? ¿Hiciste mal con esta persona? ¿Al contrario, fuiste un hombre soberbio?"

"My baby!" and **"Look at him, look how he is!"** Jessica described Daniela's response to the shooting: "¡Mi bebé! ¡Mira a mi bebé, cómo está!" Daniela could not be located, and neither Jessica nor Francisco knew how to reach her.

"She went crazy" Shorty made this comment while testifying in State of California v. Juan Pablo Murillo, et al.

"Well, this is what they're saying" Tricky recounted this dialogue while testifying in United States of America v. Sergio Pantoja, et al.

"Don't worry about it" and **"I'll try to fix it"** Giovanni recounted this dialogue while testifying in State of California v. Juan Pablo Murillo, et al.

"The cold-blooded murder" Antonio Villaraigosa was quoted in "Police Search for Gunman in Infant's Death," by Alice Walton, *Los Angeles Daily News*, September 18, 2007; **"in terrible pain"**

Villaraigosa was quoted in "3 Gunmen Are Sought in Baby's Death," by Ari B. Bloomekatz, *Los Angeles Times*, September 18, 2007.

"Rockwood had passed by and shot" Tricky made this comment while testifying in United States of America v. Sergio Pantoja, et al.

"to take the attention away"; "there was going to be a change in the money situation"; "I was given the blessing from Puppet" Tricky made these comments while testifying in United States of America v. Sergio Pantoja, et al.

Part 2

Photo of La Rumorosa used with permission from Guillermo Buelna. His work appears on flickr.com/ photos/buelna.

Chapter 13

a "showboat" or a "holler guy" "Athlete of the Week: Is He a Guard? Is He a Forward? He's Westlake's Paul Keenan," *Los Angeles Times*, December 31, 1986.

"a bird on the wire" Paul Keenan recounted the content of Tricky's calls while testifying in United States of America v. Sergio Pantoja, et al.

"In good-type words" Tricky recounted this comment while testifying in United States of America v. Sergio Pantoja, et al.

Chapter 14

"You see anything happen tonight?"; "You should know, you were there" Shorty recounted this dialogue while testifying in State of California v. Juan Pablo Murillo, et al.

"If I would not have gone back, people would be saying that I knew what happened" Shorty made this comment while testifying in State of California v. Juan Pablo Murillo, et al.

"I know you know what happened"; "I don't know nothing"; "If you snitch" Shorty recounted this dialogue with Grumpy (Cipriano Estrada) while testifying in State of California v. Luis Silva, et al.

"I know you were there" Shorty recounted this dialogue with Raven (Stefani Brizuela) while testifying in State of California v. Juan Pablo Murillo, et al.

"I don't know what you're talking about" Shorty recounted this dialogue while testifying in State of California v. Luis Silva, et al.

"I know you know something" Shorty recounted this dialogue while testifying in State of California v. Juan Pablo Murillo, et al.

"You better not go snitch to your padrino Hernandez" Shorty recounted this dialogue while testifying in State of California v. Juvenal Cardenas Mejia.

"I was scared and shocked" Shorty made this comment while testifying in United States of America v. Sergio Pantoja, et al.

"I told them I wasn't there that day" and **"I lied"** Shorty made these comments while testifying in State of California v. Juan Pablo Murillo, et al.

"We've found the suspect" Villaraigosa was quoted as saying "Hemos encontrado al sospechoso" in "Detienen a un sospechoso por asesinato de un bebé," by Jorge Luis Macías, *La Opinión*, September 19, 2007.

"My message is, go home and take care of yourself" Thich Nhat Hanh was quoted in "Peace Activist Brings a Message of Hope," by Ari B. Bloomekatz, *Los Angeles Times*, September 30, 2007.

"There's somebody who wants to talk to you" and **"Why'd you do it?"** Clever (Luis Silva) recounted these exchanges in an interview.

"not consistent with basic human values" US district court judge Dean D. Pregerson was quoted in "Judge Orders Creation of Central Jail Reform Panel," by Megan Garvey, *Los Angeles Times*, June 20, 2006.

"haunt me for the rest of my life" Baby made this comment while testifying in State of California v. Juvenal Cardenas Mejia.

"Tell me what happened or I'll throw you off the roof" and **"I guarantee you, your brother wasn't there"** Baby recounted this dialogue while testifying in State of California v. Juvenal Cardenas Mejia.

"The truth is" Atlas said: "La verdad que yo no sabía ni cómo se llamaba. Pero no me creyó."

"I just told him that, you know, my brother" and **"taken out"** Baby recounted this dialogue while testifying in United States of America v. Sergio Pantoja, et al.

"I needed to find him before, you know" Baby made this comment while testifying in United States of America v. Sergio Pantoja, et al.

Chapter 15

"For the way he dresses up, looks like a gang member" Daniela's description is contained in an LAPD investigative report filed in State of California v. Juan Pablo Murillo, et al.

"It was my fault" David Holmes recounted this dialogue in an interview.

Chapter 16

"Where are we going?"; "Mexico"; "Nah, that can't happen" Giovanni recounted Face's words in an interview.

"dropping a dime on us" Giovanni recounted this dialogue while testifying in State of California v. Juan Pablo Murillo, et al.

"needed to keep low-pro" Midget (Flor Aquino) recounted these comments while testifying in United States of America v. Sergio Pantoja, et al. She also participated in an interview.

"We used to hang around together and party" Midget made this comment while testifying in United States of America v. Sergio Pantoja, et al.

"You did what?" and **"Hell, no"** Giovanni recounted Face's words in an interview.

"just in case we didn't make it back" and **"I'm going to be out"** Midget made these comments while testifying in United States of America v. Sergio Pantoja, et al.

"There's been a change of plans" Midget recounted Face's words while testifying in State of California v. Juan Pablo Murillo, et al.

"He said we were going to drop Rusty off" Midget recounted this comment while testifying in United States of America v. Sergio Pantoja, et al.

Chapter 17

"I didn't go and tell my wife" and **"I mean, that's my wife"** Tricky made these comments while testifying in United States of America v. Sergio Pantoja, et al.

"It's easier to kill them in Mexico" and **"Making him feel comfortable"** Tricky made these comments while testifying in United States of America v. Sergio Pantoja, et al.

"One of the main reasons why he sponsored me" and **"That's what I was being groomed for"** Tricky made these comments while testifying in United States of America v. Sergio Pantoja, et al.

"a very fierce, super fierce woman" Teresa Macedo said: "Mi mamá era bien brava, bravísima. Nosotros lo que queríamos era amor y cariño, no golpes y la vida nos dio muchos golpes."

"He was just out there trying to make his little living" Teresa Macedo said: "Nomás andaba ahí trabajando pues haciendo su luchita. Estaba bien porque no andaba robando. Ya si la gente se dejaba chingar, eso era otra cosa. Él así era, bueno pa' los negocios chuecos."

"When he left, he said he was going to better himself" Roberto Macedo said: "Cuando se fue de aquí, él dijo que se iba para superarse, para darle una buena vida a mi mamá. Más, algo que no sucedío, pues porque nunca le mandó nada. Yo no sabía que si existía or no existía, la verdad."

"He was a gambler, my brother" Teresa Macedo said: "Era jugador mi hermano. Pa' jugar tiene que tener inteligencia. Le iba bien porque creo que no trabajaba."

"running around, trying to figure out how to cure him" Teresa Macedo said: "andaban buscando cómo curarlo. Andaban creo que hasta con hechiceros."

"She came back for Giovanni and left" Teresa Macedo said: "Ella se vino nomás por Giovanni y se fue. El niño no se quería ir. Como la dejó de ver un rato. En el aeropuerto, cuando fuimos a dejarlo, lloraba y yo decía: 'Pues no, que vaya con su mamá, pobrecito.'"

"They said they were going to go look for the address" Midget made this comment while testifying in United States of America v. Sergio Pantoja, et al.

"Knowing stuff that you are not supposed to gets you in trouble" Midget made this comment while testifying in State of California v. Juan Pablo Murillo, et al.

"I told him that if he was a US citizen" Midget made this comment while testifying in United States of America v. Sergio Pantoja, et al.

"Face just kind of like kidnapped me" Midget recalled Giovanni's comment while testifying in United States of America v. Sergio Pantoja, et al.

"This is the homeboy Ranger"; "Mucho gusto"; "The way I figured it"; "Fuck it" Tricky recounted this dialogue while testifying in United States of America v. Sergio Pantoja, et al.

"So basically, that cleaned my hands" and **"That happened to be my wife's birthday"** Tricky made these comments while testifying in United States of America v. Sergio Pantoja, et al.

"He just told him that he couldn't use the phone"; "He was pretty quiet"; "he better drink up" Midget made these comments while testifying in United States of America v. Sergio Pantoja, et al.

"He kept on bugging Face" Midget made this comment while testifying in State of California v. Juan Pablo Murillo, et al.

"Well, I'll show you" Giovanni recounted this comment while testifying in United States of America v. Sergio Pantoja, et al.

"He was pretty pumped up"; "He was already pumped up"; "He insisted" Midget made these comments while testifying in State of California v. Juan Pablo Murillo, et al.

"They told me that they weren't going to drop him off nowhere" Midget made this comment while testifying in United States of America v. Sergio Pantoja, et al.

"I knew that if anything happened to him" Midget made this comment while testifying in State of California v. Juan Pablo Murillo, et al.

Chapter 18

"They got the wrong person inside jail" Shorty made this comment while testifying in State of California v. Juvenal Cardenas Mejia.

"just get it over with" Shorty made this comment while testifying in State of California v. Juan Pablo Murillo, et al.

wasn't the shooter Jorge Luis Macías, "LAPD tras la pista del asesino del bebé en LA: El detenido 'no fue el gatillero,' afirma la policía," *La Opinión*, September 26, 2007.

"the kind of stuff you imagine" Civil rights attorney (now Superior Court judge) Ron Kaye was quoted in "Newly Public Videos Show 2008 LA Jail Beatings," by Dina Demetrius, KCET.org, October 23, 2017.

$55 million "Report and Recommendations of the Special Counsel to Sheriff Civilian Oversight Commission Regarding Deputy Gangs and Deputy Cliques in the Los Angeles County Sheriff's Department," February 2023.

"skinny" Jessica said: "delgado, delgado, delgado, bien delgadito."

"It hurts me so much" Francisco said: "A mí sí me dolió mucho porque pobre niño, él no tenía la culpa de nada."

"dress him in his little clothes" Jessica said: "También incluso acompañé a su mamá a vestirlo en su ropita ahí donde ya lo tenían todo frío y congelado."

"bad guys" Francisco said: "los malos . . . La sonsacaron y ella cayó."

"so that she can fix her problems" Francisco said: "que ella arregle sus problemas y nosotros vamos a arreglar los nuestros."

"She opted for a bad path" Francisco said: "Ella optó por agarrar un mal camino. No quiero que tú, como su amiga, al rato vaya, oh, mira esto, lo otro, ni que no sabes qué, mejor aquí la mochamos."

Security caught Daniela shoplifting The arrest of Daniela Garcia is documented in Los Angeles Superior Court records, as are the penalties that were imposed and the treatment options she was offered.

Chapter 19

descansos A. J. Bermudez, "A Few Notes on the Past (and Possible Future) of Public Mourning," *Literary Hub*, May 23, 2022.

"At Campo Alaska" Text used with the permission of José Javier Villarreal, the author of a related book of poetry, *Campo Alaska* (Almadía, 2012). In the original Spanish, it reads: "En Campo Alaska están los que ya no están, los que no llegaron, los que iban a llegar, los que se fueron, los que no son visibles, lo que fue, lo que no fue, lo que pudo ser y sus fantasías. Es como si todos estuvieran vivos y muertos. Así es la realidad, el todo."

"So I moved to the front" Giovanni made this comment while testifying in State of California v. Juvenal Cardenas Mejia.

"I felt weird" Giovanni made this comment while testifying in State of California v. Juan Pablo Murillo, et al.

"Die, motherfucker" Midget recalled Ranger's words while testifying in State of California v. Juan Pablo Murillo, et al.

"You're a good homie" Midget recalled Face's words while testifying in State of California v. Juan Pablo Murillo, et al.

"I kind of like was froze"; "I had been going to nursing school"; "I told them that I felt a pulse"; "So I just put him down"; "I didn't want to look" Midget made these comments while testifying in State of California v. Juan Pablo Murillo, et al.

"I was, like, maybe somebody found him" and **"They just told me that it can't be"** Midget made these comments while testifying in United States of America v. Sergio Pantoja, et al.

"any discrepancies" and **"That kind of seemed not normal"** Charles Gipson, a US Customs and Border Patrol agent, testified in United States of America v. Sergio Pantoja, et al.

"I had took one for the team"; "You want me to mention your name?"; "I don't want nobody to know" Midget recalled this exchange while testifying in State of California v. Juan Pablo Murillo, et al.

Chapter 20

"doing something else"; "Ain't nobody doing no dope slanging for free, dog"; "Tell him that when I get there"; "They looking for the shooters"; "the little kid"; "Pizza Loca"; "Federal Bureau of Investigation, can _I_ help _you_?" Transcripts of Face's calls were admitted as exhibits in State of California v. Juan Pablo Murillo, et al.

Chapter 21

An outlandish disaster Rebecca Solnit's _A Paradise Built in Hell: The Extraordinary Communities That Arise in Disaster_ (Viking, 2009) examines the ways that "disaster liberates us," upending routines and shattering social norms.

"What the fuck is going on?" and **"It's all bad"** Giovanni recounted this dialogue in an interview.

"He was saying, 'Send for me'" Juan Monroy said: "Él me decía que yo lo mandara para acá: 'Mándame para acá. Mándame pa' Guatemala.'"

"Turn yourself in" Juan recounted this dialogue with Giovanni: "Entrégate, mijo. Quiero que te entregues. Es bien para ti. Es que yo no cometí nada. Si no lo hiciste, no lo hiciste."

Chapter 22

"Daddy, what's going on?"; "I mean, that's a game changer"; "Why?" Tricky recounted this exchange while testifying in United States of America v. Sergio Pantoja, et al.

"I went from being a gangster to being a rat" Tricky made this comment while testifying in United States of America v. Sergio Pantoja, et al.

"Habla con los juras" Tricky's letter to Morena was admitted into evidence in United States of America v. Sergio Pantoja, et al.

"I mean, I'm scared" Tricky made this comment while testifying in United States of America v. Sergio Pantoja, et al.

"who is being the rat" David Holmes testified about the jailhouse conversations in State of California v. Juan Pablo Murillo, et al.

"cripple our company" Declaration of Swift CEO Sam Rovit in Swift & Co. v. Immigration and Customs Enforcement Division of the Department of Homeland Security, December 5, 2006.

"ironic twist" Defendants' Memorandum in Opposition to Plaintiff's Motion for Preliminary Injunction, Swift & Co. v. Immigration and Customs Enforcement Division of the Department of Homeland Security, December 4, 2006.

"I just started working towards, like, a change" Giovanni made this comment while testifying in State of California v. Juan Pablo Murillo, et al.

Chapter 23

"I'm going to send my boy to practice" Tricky recounted this statement while testifying in United States of America v. Sergio Pantoja, et al.

"What interested me was the fine line the character must constantly walk" Josef Adalian, "Lopez Going Gangbusters," *Variety*, November 16, 2006.

"machismo ran in our blood" Isaac Guillen, *State Raised: From the Halls of CYA to the Halls of UC Berkeley* (independently published, 2021). Isaac also participated in several brief interviews.

"they didn't care that I was tatted up" Isaac Guillen, *State Raised: From the Halls of CYA to the Halls of UC Berkeley* (independently published, 2021).

"He was excited about ideas" Victoria Kim, "A Hard Fall for Lawyer Who Struggled to Escape Gang Life," *Los Angeles Times*, June 5, 2012.

a **"very sharp" public defender** Isaac Guillen, *State Raised: From the Halls of CYA to the Halls of UC Berkeley* (independently published, 2021).

"Mafia friendly" Chris Blatchford, *The Black Hand: The Bloody Rise and Redemption of "Boxer" Enriquez, a Mexican Mob Killer* (William Morrow, 2008).

" 'he's cool, he's not undercover' " Isaac made this statement while testifying in United States of America v. Sergio Pantoja, et al.

" 'I saved your life' " Isaac recounted this incident while testifying in United States of America v. Sergio Pantoja, et al.

"He keeps a running tally" and **"so it's not just one document"** Isaac made these statements while testifying in United States of America v. Sergio Pantoja, et al.

"being nice"; "it looks promising crap"; "I want to be set for life"; "I really hope she gets right"; "I will find another hyna"; " 'Cuz she ain't all that" These excerpts from Puppet's letters were introduced into evidence in United States of America v. Sergio Pantoja, et al.

"To restrict attorney access" Supermax investigator Joe Guadian testified in United States of America v. Sergio Pantoja, et al.

"We need to be real on all issues" Puppet's letter was admitted into evidence in United States of America v. Sergio Pantoja, et al.

Chapter 24

"I heard he's dead" The LAPD's Edgar Hernandez recounted Shorty's comment in an interview.

"Hey, where's your sister at?"; "She's been looking for you"; "Not hard enough"; "They tried to kill Rusty" Edgar Hernandez testified about speaking to Mayra's sister in State of California v. Juan Pablo Murillo, et al. He recounted this dialogue in an interview.

"Hey, big dog" and **"Who's this?"** Edgar Hernandez recounted this dialogue in an interview.

"You can't come out here doing anything stupid" and **"Yes, sir"** David Holmes recounted this dialogue in an interview.

Part 3

Photo of the Clara Shortridge Foltz Criminal Justice Center used with permission from Miguel Rodriguez. A gallery of his downtown Los Angeles images appears on silent-observers.com.

Chapter 25

"Your job's cool, huh" Giovanni's interrogation was recorded and produced in discovery in State of California v. Juan Pablo Murillo, et al.

Chapter 26

to resolve a DUI charge Midget's DUI case is documented in Los Angeles Superior Court records.

"We tried cleaning it" and **"I told him that wasn't going to be enough"** Midget made these comments while testifying in United States of America v. Sergio Pantoja, et al.

"that's the way he was going to start dressing" Midget made these comments while testifying in United States of America v. Sergio Pantoja, et al.

"I didn't know who he was"; "I told them that I didn't know who was the other guy"; "If I had to go to jail or had to leave" Midget made these comments while testifying in State of California v. Juan Pablo Murillo, et al.

"nobody from the hood knew" Midget made this comment while testifying in United States of America v. Sergio Pantoja, et al.

Chapter 27

"most corrupt policeman in the city of Los Angeles in its history" Edward Humes, "Is Bill Leasure the Most Corrupt Cop in LA?" *Los Angeles Times,* October 27, 1991.

"crying spells" Israel Macedo was interviewed by a social worker in 2008 to help with Giovanni's defense.

"Why are you telling me this?" Juan Monroy said: "¿Y por qué me dices eso. Si no eres de migración? Aquí nos ayudamos uno al otro."

"Reentry of a Removed Alien" Juan's immigration case is documented in New Mexico federal court records.

Chapter 28

"What I used to do for a living" Shorty made this comment while testifying in State of California v. Juan Pablo Murillo, et al.

The LAPD booked Shorty's parents The arrests of Andres and Juana Matias are documented in Los Angeles Superior Court records, as are their respective vending citations.

"long trip" Shorty made this comment while testifying in United States of America v. Sergio Pantoja, et al.

"Money comes and money goes" Shorty made this comment while testifying in State of California v. Juan Pablo Murillo, et al.

Chapter 29

"My life" Francisco said: "Mi vida, para mí, ya estaba perdida. Más que nada, ya estaba muerto."

"an angel" Francisco said: "un angelito que apenas Dios lo había mandado aquí a la vida."

"Excuse me" Francisco said: "Discúlpeme pero el corazón es muy sensible y hay veces te dobla más los sentimientos que lo que tú eres cabrón en la calle."

"I know what it is" Francisco said: "Yo sé lo que es vivir sin papá."

"They're wherever" Francisco said: "Ellos están dondequiera, en todos los estados, en todos los países. En todos lados están esas personas, no te puedes esconder."

"Why did they do this" Francisco said: "¿Por qué me hicieron esto si es que son muy hombres? Porque no son hombres o supuestamente ellos se creen muy chingones, pero a la mera hora no son eso. Son hombres cobardes."

"He is the only one" Francisco said: "Él es el único que me la va a poder quitar, nadie más. Nadie, ni ellos, así pasen balazos, cuchilladas, lo que sea. Si Dios no quiere que me muera, no me voy a morir."

"a small room" Jessica said: "un cuarto bien chiquito, chiquito, chiquito el cuartito."

"The accident definitely brought us closer" Francisco said: "Sí, eso ya nos hizo que definitivamente ya nos uniéramos, especialmente que yo sabía que ella ya estaba embarazada. Cuando ya me pasó esto, yo le dije a ella que ya no quería que se fuera."

"I don't know, but I see myself as if I were dead" Francisco said: "No sé, me miro como si yo ya estuviera muerto y pasando como aquí como un vivo, es como si estuvieras vivo mirando donde tú ya hubieras quedado muerto. Es algo, algo increíble."

"Fine" Jessica gave this response while testifying in State of California v. Luis Silva, et al.

"Sometimes I just have some pain" Francisco gave this response while testifying in State of California v. Luis Silva, et al.

"Are you OK, Francisco?" Geanene Yriarte, a deputy district attorney, questioned Francisco in State of California v. Luis Silva, et al.

"I feel somewhat confused"; "The scar, is that something"; "this one looked more like the person" Francisco made these comments while testifying in State of California v. Luis Silva, et al.

"overwhelmed by all the evidence" Clever was represented by Michael V. White in State of California v. Luis Silva, et al.

"This is an individual who obviously knew" Geanene Yriarte made this comment while arguing against dismissal in State of California v. Luis Silva, et al.

"You know what, Mami?" Francisco said: "¿Sabes qué, mami? Por ti, Dios me tiene aquí. Créeme porque si no hubiera sido por ti, yo pienso que tal vez no lo hubiera hecho, pero él quiso que yo me quedara para que yo te mirara en tu vida y te ayudará a salir adelante. Por ti, me dejó vivir."

Chapter 30

When they filed for bankruptcy The Guillens' chapter 11 filing is documented in US Bankruptcy Court records.

"I wasn't worried about the indictment"; "Hey, the feds work like that"; "I thought, 'Yeah, OK'" Isaac made these comments while testifying in United States of America v. Sergio Pantoja, et al.

"I read it actually a couple of times"; "It told me, this dude don't even care about you"; "Game over" Isaac made these comments while testifying in United States of America v. Sergio Pantoja, et al.

Chapter 31

"The past is the past" Lil Primo (David Gonzalez) said: "El pasado ya pasó. Aprendí a vivir sin rencores."

"Yes, ma'am" and **"Yes, sir"** Giovanni testified in State of California v. Juan Pablo Murillo, et al.

"That's not new for you" Barrios's lawyer, William Jacobson, questioned Giovanni in State of California v. Juan Pablo Murillo, et al.

"Now, this shooting of this vendor" and **"You were saying whatever"** Face's attorney, Gary Maestas, questioned Giovanni in State of California v. Juan Pablo Murillo, et al.

"Because you wanted the gang more" James Cooper, the attorney for Big Guy (Yovanni Velasquez), questioned Giovanni in State of California v. Juan Pablo Murillo, et al.

"wanted to tag along" Face narrated events while testifying in his own defense in State of California v. Juan Pablo Murillo, et al.

"the instigator, the controller" Los Angeles Superior Court judge Larry Paul Fidler made these comments at Face's sentencing at the conclusion of State of California v. Juan Pablo Murillo, et al.

"I'm an innocent man" Face made these comments at his sentencing.

"some real—people might say—strong language" Judge Fidler made these comments at Giovanni's sentencing at the conclusion of State of California v. Juan Pablo Murillo, et al.

Chapter 32

"I'm a worker" Francisco said: "Yo soy un trabajador."

"Look at my fingers" Francisco said: "Mira mis dedos."

"Do you have records?" and **"How'd you do that if you don't have papers?"** Francisco recounted this dialogue as: "¿Tiene comprobantes?" and "¿Cómo le hizo si no tiene papeles?"

"Well, here, if there's a will, there's a way" Francisco said: "Pues, aquí el querer es poder. Estamos en un lugar donde hay posibilidad. Lo único que pasa es que la gente no quiere, o tienen miedo, o no tienen la inteligencia de decir, 'Yo puedo, yo puedo, todos podemos.'"

"It's not about having papers" Francisco said: "No es que tú tengas papeles. Es tu mentalidad."

"the last gasp of white America in California" The quote, attributed to Art Torres, appears in Patrick J. McDonnell, "Brash Evangelist," Los Angeles Times, July 15, 2001.

"I know there are some people out there hollering" "President Bush Discusses Comprehensive Immigration Reform in Glynco, Georgia," georgewbush-whitehouse.archives.gov.

"Without papers" Francisco said: "Sin papeles, es como que vives nada más la mitad aquí y la otra mitad tienes un pie allá."

"much heavier" Francisco said: "Esto ya es más pesado."

"How is it possible" Francisco said: "¿Cómo es posible que la policía me iba a tratar a mí así? ¿Cómo es posible que la policía se preocupe por uno?"

"The truth is" Francisco said: "La verdad, lo quiero mucho como amigo. Yo hasta pido a Dios por él. Él tiene un trabajo muy peligroso y uno no sabe cuándo te puede tocar."

"I did everything" and **"My life changed a lot"** Francisco said: "Hice todo, el test del driving y la computadora, y como en tres días ya tenía yo la licencia" and "Mi vida cambió mucho. Luego, empecé a arreglar todo."

"David taught me a lesson" Francisco said: "David me dio una lección."

Chapter 33

"something that concerns me"; "it does seem unfair"; "part of the problem of going to trial"
Judge Pregerson was speaking at Oso's 2015 sentencing at the conclusion of United States of America v. Sergio Pantoja, et al.

"day to day, week to week" and **"might as well be the AT&T of criminal enterprises"** Kevin Lally, an assistant US attorney, made these comments in United States of America v. Sergio Pantoja, et al.

"That's why I don't want them to catch you" and **"Never mind"** The recording of the call between Ranger (Javier Perez) and his nephew was introduced into evidence in United States of America v. Sergio Pantoja, et al.

"there was a resemblance" Tiburcio Aguilar recalled Ranger's words while testifying in United States of America v. Sergio Pantoja, et al. Aguilar also participated in an interview.

"Do you have any concern for your safety" and **"Is there any doubt in your mind"** Nili Moghaddam, an assistant US attorney, questioned Giovanni in United States of America v. Sergio Pantoja, et al.

"Because I'm telling" Giovanni made these comments while testifying in United States of America v. Sergio Pantoja, et al.

"You mentioned that you met a man named Ranger" and **"How is it that you remember"** Ranger's lawyer, Lawrence Jay Litman, questioned Giovanni in United States of America v. Sergio Pantoja, et al.

"I know it's him" and **"You don't forget the face"** Giovanni testified in United States of America v. Sergio Pantoja, et al.

"literally enjoyed wine, women, and song" Lawrence Jay Litman filed objections to the government's presentencing report for Ranger in United States of America v. Sergio Pantoja, et al.

"I wish I could tell you stuff" and **"I don't want to be remembered like that"** A recording of Oso's interview with the FBI was admitted into evidence in United States of America v. Sergio Pantoja, et al.

"a completely amoral sociopath" Anthony Solis, the lawyer for Leonidas "Druggy" Iraheta, who stood trial with his twin brother, Vladimir "Jokes" Iraheta, made this comment in United States of America v. Sergio Pantoja, et al.

"Those are the rogues" Oso's lawyer, Michael R. Belter, argued in United States of America v. Sergio Pantoja, et al.

Chapter 34

"death fence" Mike Davis, "Hell Factories in the Fields," *The Nation*, February 20, 1995.

"Do I know you?" Giovanni recounted this dialogue in an interview.

Chapter 35

"You know, it never occurred to me" Atlas said: "Pues la verdad, nunca me pasó por la mente agarrar papeles falsos ni usar nombre falso. No estaba escondido."

"I was aware" Atlas said: "Estaba consciente, consciente de que había pasado algo feo."

"Because I didn't kill anybody" Atlas said: "Yo no maté a nadie, por eso yo lo tomé muy a la ligera."

"Extortion, yes" Atlas said: "La extorsión, sí, lo reconozco. Pero yo nunca agarré armas. Si voy a pagar, que sea por algo que yo hice."

"I'm no one" Atlas made this statement in an interview with LAPD homicide detectives, who summarized his comments in a 2012 police report.

"started to become upset" Victor Avila made this comment while questioning Francisco in State of California v. Juvenal Cardenas Mejia.

"should leave that place" and **"looking at us"** Francisco made these comments while testifying in State of California v. Juvenal Cardenas Mejia.

"something was going to happen to a vendor" Baby made these comments while testifying in State of California v. Juvenal Cardenas Mejia.

"pointed out at the vendor that didn't pay" and **"They said, 'That's the vendor there'"** Shorty made these comments while testifying in State of California v. Juvenal Cardenas Mejia.

"Atlas was the one" Giovanni made this comment while testifying in State of California v. Juvenal Cardenas Mejia.

"anything to the effect of 'Don't do this'?" Victor Avila questioned Giovanni in State of California v. Juvenal Cardenas Mejia.

"I mean, everybody knew" Giovanni made this comment while testifying in State of California v. Juvenal Cardenas Mejia.

Part 4

Nighttime photo of Calipatria State Prison used with permission from Stephen Tourlentes. His series on detention facilities after dark is featured in "Of Lengths and Measures," prison-insider.com.

Chapter 36

"a dumping ground" and **"When Mexico sends its people"** Katie Reilly, "Here Are All the Times Donald Trump Insulted Mexico," *Time*, August 31, 2016.

"beautiful wall" "Trump Wants to Build 30-Foot-High Wall at Mexican Border," cnbc.com, March 19, 2017.

"deportation force" Tom LoBianco, "Donald Trump Promises 'Deportation Force' to Remove 11 Million," cnn.com, November 12, 2015.

"We have at least eleven million people" Aaron Blake, "Donald Trump's Slow-Motion Flip-Flop on Illegal Immigration," *Washington Post*, August 23, 2016.

"recent talks about changes to our nation's immigration policy" Letter to the Los Angeles city council re: "Sidewalk Vending Policy," Joe Buscaino and Curren D. Price, Jr., November 22, 2016.

"will lift this shroud of fear" Jenna Chandler, "Los Angeles City Council Votes to Regulate, Legalize Street Vendors," la.curbed.com, November 28, 2018.

Chapter 37

"Hurt people hurt" Scott Budnick was originally interviewed for "Outside Man," by Jesse Katz, *The California Sunday Magazine*, March 2015.

"People who commit offenses before their capacities are fully formed" Newt Gingrich, "A Second Chance for Young Offenders," *HuffPost*, April 13, 2015.

Israel had been arrested Israel's case is documented in Los Angeles Superior Court records.

Chapter 38

Reyna was arrested Los Angeles Superior Court records contain the details of Reyna's misdemeanor conviction (under her legal name).

"I told her, 'Look, mi amor'" Tío Chepe said: "Le dije: 'Mire mi amor, hacé algo para bien tuyo y para bien de ellos también. Te voy a dar cinco palabras que son claves, para que las agarres como vos querrás, como una oración, como un mantra. Pero no tenés idea, lo misteriosamente poderosas que esas frases son para la paz y la tranquilidad de uno.'"

"Oof, how difficult it is" Chepe said: "¡Uf, qué difícil es liberar a alguien que te ha hecho más daño! Pero al liberarla a ella te estás liberando vos."

Chapter 39

"people evolve" Frank Stolze, "'People Evolve': Why DA Gascón Reversed Decades of Parole Policy to Support Release in Most Cases," LAist.com, May 6, 2021.

"They have so much evil in their lives" Francisco said: "Ellos tienen mucha maldad en su vida, mucha maldad al no haberles importado la vida de un niño. Pues ellos, ya no, ya no. Para que cambien está duro. Ojalá que estas personas tengan algún día conciencia, aunque yo realmente lo dudo."

"they're going to have to pay" Francisco said: "ellos van a tener que pagar todo esto que hacen, no nomás con la justicia, sino con Dios. Él va a decidir cuál es el pago de cada uno."

"If I don't forgive" Francisco said: "Si yo no perdono, Dios no me va a perdonar. Él te va a decir, '¿Cómo quieres que te perdone si tú nunca perdonaste? Pudo más tu orgullo que tu fe y tu amor.'"

Photo by Eric Nazarian

Jesse Katz is a former *Los Angeles Times* and *Los Angeles* magazine writer whose honors include the James Beard Foundation's M. F. K. Fisher Distinguished Writing Award, PEN Center USA's Literary Journalism Award, a National Magazine Award nomination, and two shared Pulitzer Prizes. His writing has appeared in the anthologies *Best American Magazine Writing*, *Best American Crime Writing*, and *Best American Sports Writing*. As a volunteer with InsideOUT Writers, he has mentored incarcerated teenagers at Central Juvenile Hall and the former California Youth Authority. His first book, *The Opposite Field*, was set in LA's immigrant suburbs.